GLOBAL PERSPECTIVES

A Handbook for Understanding Global Issues

Ann Kelleher
Laura Klein

Pacific Lutheran University

Prentice Hall
Upper Saddle River, New Jersey 07458

Library of Congress Cataloging-in-Publication Data
KELLEHER, ANN.
    Global perspectives: a handbook for understanding global issues /
by ANN KELLEHER and LAURA KLEIN.
        p.   cm.
    Includes bibliographical references and index.
    ISBN 0-13-852393-2 (paper)
    1. International relations.   2. Social history—20th century.
3. Economic history—20th century.   4. World politics—1945–
I. Klein, Laura F. (Laura Frances), [date]. II. Title.
JZ1242.K45   1999
909.82'5—dc21   98-27903

Editorial director: *Charlyce Jones Owen*
Editor in chief: *Nancy Roberts*
Senior Acquisitions editor: *Beth Gillett*
Associate editor: *Nicole Conforti*
Production editor: *Edie Riker*
Cover director: *Jayne Conte*
Cover design: *Kiwi Design*
Buyer: *Bob Anderson*
Marketing manager: *Christoper DeJohn*

This book was set in 10/12 Times Roman by East End Publishing Services and was printed and bound by Courier Companies, Inc. The cover was printed by Phoenix Color Corp..

Printed in the United States of America

10   9   8   7   6   5   4   3   2   1

ISBN 0-13-852393-2

Prentice-Hall International (UK) Limited, *London*
Prentice-Hall of Australia Pty. Limited, *Sydney*
Prentice-Hall Canada Inc., *Toronto*
Prentice-Hall Hispanoamericana, S.A., *Mexico*
Prentice-Hall of India Private Limited, *New Delhi*
Prentice-Hall of Japan, Inc., *Tokyo*
Simon & Schuster Asia Pte. Ltd., *Singapore*
Editora Prentice-Hall do Brasil, Ltda., *Rio de Janeiro*

Contents

4 *Economic Development*   *53*

5 *Perspectives on Economic Development*   *85*

Preface

A NOTE TO READERS

Global Perspectives: A Handbook for Understanding International Issues has been designed to help readers answer important questions about the contemporary world:

- Why do the thousands of cultural groups in the world have such different solutions to human problems while human beings have so many needs in common?
- Why are a billion people on the planet poor and malnourished?
- What makes it so difficult to take action to solve the atmospheric problem of global warming?
- Why do some political conflicts result in war?

These and other questions are being asked about problems facing the world at the turn of the twenty-first century. Issues arise from trends of cultural diversity, economic interdependence and dependence, deterioration of the natural environment, and political conflict. These general, long-term issues become specific through events in the news.

Making sense of international news is not an easy task. Yet informed citizens in a participatory democracy must make an effort to take on that task. This often means working at becoming self-educated about global issues, a process that is made more difficult by the one-sided polemics of the many and often conflicting interest groups. For those beginning to learn about international events, the mass media does not always help much. In many cases, television, radio, newspapers, and news magazines have neither the time nor space to provide the needed background information, historical context, or varying perspectives. Thus, events are reported as distinct or as isolated from one another. They seem to erupt suddenly, presenting major problems. A civil war, an environmental disaster, or an economic crisis, for instance, produces major controversies over what actions should be taken. How can a person learn enough to be able to analyze a wide range of world problems?

Concepts   This book provides a beginning process for thinking about the world's long-term trends, and about how they are reflected in specific situations. It assumes explanations for human behavior are possible—that events do not just happen. Each chapter introduces concepts for sorting out what is going on in the world. Learning to think conceptually means using ideas and generalizations that link events to each other and provide explanations for why they occur. For example, this book defines and applies such words as *culture, ethnic group, power, interests, capital, industrialization, development, ecosystem, carrying capacity,* and *balance of power.*

Perspectives   Applying concepts remains only the first step. An informed citizenry must know not only why events happen, but also why people often disagree intensely over how to interpret and respond to those events. The answer lies in perspectives; that is, in a set of interrelated principles, world views, and values that people use to determine what actions should be taken. There are several perspectives about any given issue that can be used to diagnose an issue and reach solutions.

Understanding that different people use different perspectives to arrive at their varying opinions can help explain why issues of debate seem to take on a life of their own. The problems these issues produce seem insoluble. Discussions over an endangered species or a US foreign policy toward China, for instance, can become full-blown disagreements with no apparent resolution. People involved in an argument or debate apply their own perspectives, sometime unconsciously. Implying more than just different points of view that can be debated pragmatically, perspectives are value-based beliefs about what is right or wrong. Learning about alternative perspectives will enable readers to understand why fierce debates and conflicts can break out. Therefore, understanding world events involves knowing what perspectives are being applied.

Interrelatedness   Finally, it is important to realize that even people who choose not to engage in policy debates as conscientious citizens still inhabit the planet. The decisions people make in their daily lives become part of the worldwide consumption network. Choices about what to buy and how much water to use, for example, affect people not only locally but in other countries as well. The world is becoming increasing interconnected through its cultural, linguistic, economic, ecological, technological, and political systems. What people do is part of these systems. Educated people should be aware of the short- and long-term consequences of their lifestyle choices.

In short, by the end of this book, readers will be able to:

• Explain the historical development of trends affecting today's world.
• Link current events with general problems and long-term trends.

- Define basic concepts needed to explain the reasons for trends and specific events.
- Apply several alternative perspectives to analyses of world events.
- Evaluate the feasibility and effects of a variety of coping strategies and solutions.

A NOTE TO INSTRUCTORS

This book has been created from a need we felt for a handbook to use in our own classes: as such, it has been written with the instructor, as well as the student reader, in mind. The book's chapters build on each other to cumulatively offer a comprehensive overview of the contemporary world and its issues: Chapter 1 introduces basic information on the historical trends shaping the modern world.

Chapters 2 through 9 of the book are written as related pairs. The first chapter of each pair provides the data and important concepts for understanding the issue under consideration—from ethnicity and economic development to ecological sustainability and political conflict. Each of these chapters also includes a case study. The second chapter of the pair discusses several perspectives for analyzing the issues being examined before moving on to an analysis of the case study introduced in the proceeding chapter. The perspectives have been chosen to complement each other, while at the same time reflecting the real ways in which people think. In addition, politically or socially charged terms that can limit readers' thinking on any perspective have been avoided in favor of more broadly descriptive labels. Each perspective, therefore, is described fairly and in a way that encourages readers' understanding of how well-meaning and educated people can disagree.

Instructors will use this handbook in different ways, drawing on their own expertise to add examples and bring in new topics. It is important to encourage students to discover that the events they read about in newspapers and discuss in class can be best understood by applying the perspectives to their analyses. A seemingly endless list of issues can be used in lectures and for research projects—immigration, developing world debt, US–Japanese trade relations, Latinos in the United States, and Chinese development strategies are a few examples. In our classes, monographs on cases drawn from throughout the world are assigned, as are books on such recent events as the successful programs of Kerela, India, the results of conflict on Guatemalan peasants, and the fight for the Ecuadorian rainforest by oil companies and indigenous peoples. The potential list of useful cases is arguably indefinite.

As a handbook, *Global Perspectives* offers a structure for analysis rather than in-depth explanations or data for all issues. Other readings, videos, maps, personal slides, speakers, computer programs, and pedagogical devices will enrich the use of the book. In addition, novels, autobiographies, and films can be particularly helpful in sparking students' interest and involvement in the subject matter. The issues and approaches that *Global Perspectives* offers allow students to look critically at the world around them and begin to see the patterns and understand the trends. All people have a responsibility, particularly at the beginning of the new millennium, to understand global issues.

ACKNOWLEDGMENTS

We would like to thank the many people who have helped make this book possible. It is a result of years of teaching and learning from the Global Perspectives course we have team-taught since 1980. Well over a thousand students have taken the course and many have helped us clarify our ideas through their thoughtful questions, challenges, and opinions. Through the years other instructors have also joined the course and made their contributions. We want to thank Drs. Mordachi Rozanski, Gregory Guldin, Elizabeth Brusco, Veeda Gargano-Ray, and December Green, who have taught sections of the course and contributed to the development of the book's concepts and examples. We also need to express our gratitude for the support of Pacific Lutheran University, which allowed us to design and team-teach the interdisciplinary course.

Many colleagues and friends have reviewed drafts of the manuscript and provided useful feedback including H. Lowell Ashman, Lenoir-Rhyne College and Phil Kelly, Emporia State University. Drs. Sheri Tonn, David Vinje, Norris Peterson, and James L. Taulbee, and Ms. Elizabeth Sullivan, have especially given of their time and expertise. The assistants at the university's Division of Social Sciences spent many hours on the manuscript. We thank Peggy Jobe, Sharon Raddatz, and Linda Nichols for their hard work and good humor. We also want to thank our colleagues and friends at Pacific Lutheran University for their support, and the faculty of the anthropology and political science departments for their patience. Finally, we are indebted to our good friends and families, whose support was vital to the successful completion of this endeavor.

Introduction to the Modern World

The past is prologue.

—*William Shakespeare*

Every man takes the limits of his own field of vision for the limits of the world.

—*Arthur Schopenhauer*

This brief chapter sets the stage for those that follow. Since the focus of this book is the contemporary world, it is necessary to review briefly the major perceptions of reality and themes of history that have created modern life. All people have local knowledge of what the world is and how it functions. This is necessary for daily life. To understand the complexity of the modern world, however, individuals have to recognize that their view of the world is both limited and historically created. People living under different circumstances have different, but no less certain, understandings of the nature of the world, and their understanding, like all others, differs from the perceptions of their ancestors. This chapter outlines some basic issues and events that define the modern world.

PERCEPTIONS OF THE WORLD

Earth is home to all humanity and, as such, might be expected to be universally understood in a common way, but it is not. Differences about the nature of Earth are more apparent than the similarities. Some authors have described the world as small, while others write that it is vast. In fact, people experience both. In daily living, the scale can be as small as one-on-one encounters. Through travel and learning, the scope of interaction can increase to planetary proportions. The world is "us," but it is populated by a variety of people. The world seems constant, but it is always changing. Given these contradictions, people inevitably explain what goes on in the world very differently. Seeking such explanations becomes more difficult because we are a part of what we want to understand. Even the maps used to image the world are distinct from one another. To some, topographical features comprise the world; to others, the world is made up of political units or states; and to still others, the world consists of the different peoples inhabiting it. All three characteristics, and others, together define the world as we know it.

The Physical World

The map used by those who see the world as the physical planet Earth reflects a topography that has no boundaries or place names. It is a unified reality divided only by natural features. It emphasizes mountains, deserts, rivers, oceans, and lakes. No purposeful human creations show on this map. In this context, human differences and constructions seem insignificant and transient. This does not mean, however, that geographical realities are unchanging or protected from human agency. The physical maps drawn of Earth's distant past are different from those of the present. Some of these differences are evolutionary. Volcanoes have developed, erupted, and created islands and mountains. Rivers have moved and glaciers advanced and retreated. Even the continents themselves have broken apart or moved together over time. Other changes, the ones caused by humans, are more revolutionary in nature. Deserts have grown in size, rivers have been dammed, forests have been cut, and lakes and oceans have been polluted.

The Political World

People who see the world politically place an overlay on the physical map. Their map boasts a series of lines that differentiate the states of the world. This representation predominates on the walls of many American classrooms. It implies that the significant differences among people and places are political. South America is divided into Ecuador, Colombia, Brazil, and so on, rather than by the Andes Mountains and the Amazon River. Like the topographical map, the political one changes over time, but the rate of change is far more rapid. A political map of the world ten years old is terribly out of date. New states have been created from the division of old ones; others have been produced from the end of colonial relationships. The political map of the world a thousand, or even five hundred, years ago would show vast areas unclaimed by states. Unlike the topographical map, the political one is made and changed solely by human agency.

The Ethnic World

Cultural maps of the world have, until recently, been found mainly in the offices and classrooms of anthropologists. These maps divide the world into *culture areas* or portions of the world where the people within the boundaries are more culturally alike than those outside the lines. These are collections of related cultures, whose people share similar beliefs, customs, languages, and skills. On these maps, South America is divided into Amazonian Indians, highland Quechua and Aymara (Inca), and urban Mestizos, among others. These maps no longer are considered esoteric due to the growing awareness of the role ethnicity plays in world affairs. These maps, too, are rapidly changing. The cultural map of five hundred to a thousand years ago would include the Incan peoples and indigenous Amazonians but Mestizos did not yet exist. Immigrants from Europe and Africa would soon appear and create new cultures in the region. Migrations from region to region have created significant population shifts throughout human history. Humans have moved and adapted to new environments and new cultures. These maps change, like political maps, through human actions.

Each map is a valid image of reality but none is complete. The world is a complex interaction of physical, political, and cultural elements. When change occurs in one sphere, changes in the others often follow. At any point in history, these elements intersect to form a reality. It is no wonder that people living at that time believe that their world must be both permanent and proper.

EMERGENCE OF THE MODERN WORLD

It follows that the world as we know it is a historical way station on a very long road. Particular events that occurred in specific places over hundreds of years have lead to the present situation and will influence the future. Things could have occurred differently, but they did not. It is important to look to the past to understand how the modern world came to be. By doing so, it will appear that the modern state system that seems so obvious and permanent is, in fact, recent and changeable. The division of the world into state-controlled areas is relatively new and strongly influenced by a historically dictated European colonial model. History is not uniformly moving in one direction, however, and over time states have divided into noncentralized, often ethnically defined units just as such units have centralized into states. History suggests that continued changes in the world system are to be expected.

The World in 1350

It is hard for modern people to consider a past when their states did not exist or existed on the periphery of global events. As historians look deeply into the past, all states disappear. In order to understand the modern world, it is necessary to understand what came before it, to look briefly at the world before the contemporary system was developed. Even in this brief review, it should become clear that the world system of the past was as complex and volatile as the present one and that its history challenges common assumptions about the stability of social and political systems. Further, because the world as we know it has changed dramatically within only several hundred years, it is reasonable to expect equally dramatic changes in the future.

This review has as its starting point the mid-fourteenth century. At this time, continents that were often pictured as uncivilized by Europeans in later centuries, were indeed the centers of civilizations. Every continent had seemingly stable, stratified, and economically sophisticated trading societies with elaborate art and architecture during these years. Soon, however, European exploration and colonialization would begin, creating the new power centers that continue to define the current world system. Even today, people who are descended from the great civilizations of this earlier time continue to remember their historical antecedents, with pride, as highly developed at a time when European society was seemingly more primitive.

In 1350, elaborate civilizations with classical arts and monumental architecture could be found throughout the world. By this time, China had been for centuries an elaborate state with sophisticated forms of education, art, economy, and social organization. Since 1279, the Yuan Dynasty had been established by the Mongol conquest. By 1350, revolts had begun that would lead to the Ming Dynasty in 1368. Chinese scientists had already developed nautical knowledge and ship-building technologies that were unknown in Europe. In the Americas, a number of civilizations thrived. Among the best known are the Mayans in the Yucatan of Mexico, whose elaborate cities with pyramids and temples were regional centers of religion and trade. The Aztecs, who the Spanish conquerors would first meet, had just built their capital at Tenochtitlan, in present-day Mexico City. South Americans had similar cultures to those in the north with one major civilization coalescing in the mid-fourteenth century. The culture of the Incas was just developing and their empire would grow to control all its neighbors. Incan building expertise was unsurpassed in the world at the time. Another kingdom, called Chimor, however, was expanding to contest Incan power. Chan Chan, the great city of the region, continued to thrive.

International trade was important for many of the civilizations of the time. Africa was home to a number of complex societies in 1350. In the north, for example, the city of Timbuktu was a center for trade and learning within the Mali Empire. As a university center it ranked among the finest in the world. Its trade depended on the gold and salt it exchanged for goods made from leather, cotton, iron, and copper from trading partners in the region. To the south the walled city of Great Zimbabwe, in what is currently the country of the same name, was an advanced trade center with goods from the Middle East and Asia passing through its markets. In Southeast Asia, Islam spread and a number of trade cities became prominent. One, the Malacca state on the Malay Peninsula, was on its way to dominating the important East-West trade routes. In the still isolated Americas, trade routes ran for thousands of miles. Mexican trade traveled far to the north, as Mexican artifacts and architectural styles found in archaeological sites in the southeastern United States and along the Mississippi River have documented. The people, now known as Mississippians, had a complex class system and long-range trade that extended far south. They built cities with elaborate architecture, including large earthen pyramids, long before Europeans reached the New World.

This was also a time of international political expansion. By 1350, Islam was on the rise. The Ottoman Empire, which would grow to conquer most of the Middle East, northern Africa, and southeast Europe, was expanding rapidly. In India, Turkish raiders were overtaking the existing principalities in the north. In Africa, the Songhai Empire was expanding and soon would annex Timbuktu. To the east, Ethiopia was a flourishing Christian empire. Throughout the Americas, the Incas, Aztecs, and their rivals vied for political and economic control of their agricultural neighbors.

In Europe, the fourteenth century was a period of near-constant political and social turmoil. French and English monarchs, who headed the most politically organized societies, began the so-called Hundred Year's War (1337–1453), which was actually a series of intermittent battles, peasant uprisings, and revolts by regional princes. For most Europeans, the fourteenth century was a time of poverty. The Black Death (now known as the bubonic plague), which reached Europe in 1347, killed millions of people and lowered the average life expectancy in England from thirty-four to seventeen years at the height of the disease (Tannenbaum 1965:37–38). Also during this time, technologies from distant lands, such as gunpowder and the compass from China, spread to Europe. If the fourteenth century was not the pinnacle of European civilization, the fifteenth century would be a new beginning. Europe would emerge a century later, with the centralized political systems and technological innovations in transportation and weapons of war to begin centuries of exploration and dominance.

European Expansion (1400–1900)

Exploration   Europeans still did not know much about the world's other civilizations by the end of the fifteenth century, but they did know about some of the riches that came from Asia. The spices of "the Indies," used for food preservation and medicines, were traded to Europe at high prices. Europeans wanted a direct route to Asia that would eliminate the Ottoman Empire and other middlemen and, therefore, cut costs. With improvements in sailing ships and navigation devices, Europeans were ready to move out of Europe to trade on their own terms.

The Portuguese and Spanish were the masters of early exploration. Prince Henry the Navigator (1394–1460) of Portugal, who established a school for navigators, led his country's push to exploration. In 1445, Portuguese crews discovered that slaves and gold were available in coastal Africa. By 1498, Vasco de Gama reached India, and Portugal claimed the sea route to Asia. Lisbon replaced Venice as the city for Far Eastern trade, but it soon was challenged by Dutch cities. Spain looked for a western route to the Indies. Funded by Queen Isabella of Castile, Christopher Columbus reached the Caribbean in voyages between 1492 and 1502. The Indies seemed at hand in 1513, when Balboa first saw the Pacific Ocean. Yet, it remained for Ferdinand Magellan to sail from Spain, around South America, and to the Philippines in 1519.

For the most part, this early era of exploration was economically motivated, and many trade ports were established. Settlement and conquest were in the futures of Asia and Africa, but many people in the Americas suffered. Spain used the Caribbean for farming and mining and its local people as forced laborers. This practice, combined with several epidemics, led to their near-total extinction. On the mainland, Spain's goals, often termed "Gold, God, and Glory," also led to disaster. By 1521, Hernando Cortés had conquered the civilizations of Mexico. In the name of religion, all books and artifacts considered "pagan" were destroyed. Beautiful items made of gold or silver were melted down for their metal value. By 1536, the Incan civilization had suffered a similar colonial experience at the hands of Francisco Pizarro and Diego de Almargo.

France and England had less success than the Spanish and Portuguese in the early period of exploration. Their agents searched for a northern route west to Asia, the so-called Northwest Passage. Failing that, the French and English made conflicting claims on North America that they would settle by war. The people on this continent had no gold and silver artifacts. Their riches remained to be exploited through settlement by farmers and trappers.

Colonialization   Europe changed dramatically during the first two centuries of exploration. The Reformation wars, economic growth, and technological advances changed the face of the continent. Spain faded into relative obscurity as a European power but kept its extensive American possessions. Similarly, Portugal, held on to the Asian colonies and Brazil but became a small power in Europe. France and especially England and the Netherlands thrived with resources from their colonies and the growth of their commercial classes.

In the Americas by the eighteenth century, the Caribbean plantation system was in full operation with African slaves providing the labor. British colonies on the East Coast of North America were growing, as was the French settlement of Quebec. The French claimed a vast amount of land, but much of it was populated by Native Americans who traded with French trappers. English settlers, many with African slaves, however, populated the British colonies. Native people there had been decimated by epidemics brought by the settlers, and the survivors were pushed off of their farmlands.

By the nineteenth century, the situation in North America had again undergone dramatic change. A peace in 1763 sealed Britain's defeat of France in North America and left the French with only their islands in the Caribbean. In 1776, however, the Europeans in the thirteen colonies began their successful bid for independence, and only Canada and some Caribbean islands remained for Great Britain. At nearly the same time, the India Act brought India into the British colonial fold.

The late nineteenth and early twentieth centuries were marked by imperialism, when European states completed their conquest of virtually all the world. The Industrial Revolution provided both the means and the cause for increased expansion. Industrializing Europeans needed raw materials and new markets. Also, as nationalism grew stronger, national pride was built in part by colonial success. A paternalistic missionary zeal played a role as well. The perceived needs to bring Christianity to pagans and civilization to people considered "inferior" were often used to rationalize colonial enterprises.

While European states achieved colonial hegemony over most countries in Asia and forced open trade with Japan and China, the subjugation of Africa tells the story of direct colonialism. Before the 1880s, Europe's interest in sub-Saharan Africa focused largely on the slave trade. This had allowed the colonies in the Americas to thrive and earned prosperity for many Europeans and Americans. Attitudes about slavery changed, however, and it was now considered morally reprehensible. Virtually all contact with tropical Africa was on the coast. Despite five hundred years of exploiting the resources of Africa, Europeans knew practically nothing about its interior lands or people.

With the British occupation of Egypt in 1882, the European division of Africa and direct rule over its peoples had begun. At the Berlin Conference in 1884–1885, representatives of the interested states convened to divide the continent. The public rationales for the conference included bringing an end to the slave trade and ensuring free navigation and trade in the Congo River basin. European explorers were moving inland, and King Leopold II of the Belgians had established the Congo Free State in the center of the continent controlling trade on the Congo River. Delegates at the Berlin Conference affirmed Leopold's claim to the Independent State of the Congo and shortly afterward he began ruling it as a personal possession. It was later deeded to Belgium, in 1908. Other European states were given smaller colonies in central and western Africa.

Shortly after the conference, East Africa was similarly divided up. In the south, the British took control of South Africa in 1902, after fighting the long and bloody Boer War with the white settlers since 1899. By the end of the first decade of the twentieth century, virtually all parts of tropical Africa had been claimed by France, Great Britain, Italy, Spain, Portugal, Belgium, or Germany. The division of the continent had been accomplished by European states in their own interest, with no consideration given to the claims of the native people. By the First World War, few places on Earth remained without the stamp of a European state on them. Those few peoples who maintained their independence were often tied economically or militarily to Europe. Culturally, Christian missions had spread throughout the world and converted millions to their faith and an admiration of European culture. For a time at least, Europeans had succeeded in gaining control of the world.

DEFINITION OF THE MODERN STATE

Europeans used their version of the state to achieve worldwide dominance. Its highly centralized organizational structure was capable of concentrating large-scale human and material resources over very long periods. During the colonial era, the European state spread worldwide and became the primary institution for people to interact internationally. Since states have been, and many people think still are, the most powerful decision makers affecting international events, learning about current world issues begins with analyzing the nature of the modern state. Four primary characteristics define a state:, *territory, government,* a *loyal population,* and the *recognition of other states.*

Territory This element of a state may seem obvious at first, but the notion of a precise border existing between independent political units is a relatively recent one. Many empires did not control land so much as populations, often leaving their boundaries inexact because they did not matter very much. As long as subject peoples paid their taxes, fought when conscripted, and did not rebel against the ruling elite, they were allowed to keep their cultural identity and regulate the activities of their daily life, such as education, religion, property inheritance, and ownership. Resources were considered more important than the direct control of individuals or specific pieces of land. Empires usually did not consider territory a symbol of their power or prestige, and therefore, as something worth fighting over. The importance of territory, became much more prevalent as the modern state developed in Europe, a place where many peoples and separate political jurisdictions existed in a confined space.

Government   All persons living on the territory of a modern state relate to the government directly. Before the modern state, empires and feudal systems considered most of their subject peoples as existing in groups whose leaders spoke for them and saw to it that the rules the government imposed were obeyed. Those in political power were far away, often physically as well as perceptually. The governments of modern states, in contrast, consider their people as citizens and indivisible parts of the whole population.

Government is defined as the one institution in a society that has the legitimate claim to exercising decisive authority over its population. It requires payments and regulates certain categories of behavior. It can even deny liberty and, in extreme cases, life if a person violates specified laws. Governments have a virtual monopoly on force and the right to make and enforce laws, which everyone must obey. Thus, governments are highly centralized, powerful institutions. The key to their effectiveness lies in the word *legitimacy*. A government achieves legitimacy when its people believe that it is justified, that its laws ought to be obeyed, and that its rule conforms to commonly accepted political values. Such political values have changed over the centuries. A currently prevailing one accepts a government as legitimate if it represents the will of its population as expressed through elections. A former idea causing consent to governmental authority was the idea of a God-given hereditary monarchy. If major segments of a population begin to consider the government as illegitimate, it is forced to rule solely on the basis of its monopoly of force. Inevitably, this type of government becomes oppressive and authoritarian. The situation can become dangerous if people avoid compliance or initiate rebellion. In either case, a government only relying on force has less ability to make enforceable decisions than one that is perceived as legitimate by its people. Legitimacy, therefore, is needed for effective rule.

A Loyal Population   Citizens generally identify with the modern state, at least to some extent. Their feeling of loyalty, called *patriotism*, is distinguished from *nationalism*, which is an individual's identity with an ethnic group based on several shared characteristics, such as language, history, and religion. Empires did not always expect or demand to be the primary focus of identity and loyalty for most of the peoples they ruled. These attitudes were required only of members of the governing elite. The modern state that evolved in Europe, however in its most developed form, fused nationalism and patriotism, at least as ideals. Each state was assumed to have one dominant cultural group, hence the designation *nation-state*, which was the term used for decades. The "nation" part has been dropped in recent years because virtually every state in the world today includes more than one cultural group.

Distinguishing between cultural nationalism and state patriotism helps clarify one of the most significant causes of current conflicts. The clash of identity between the two occurs because, generally, one cultural group controls the government, society's most powerful institution. This creates a situation whereby the dominant group, either consciously or unconsciously, discriminates against other groups. In the 1990s, for example, over forty countries have cultural groups wanting some form of political representation separate from their existing governments, including the Scottish Nationalist Party in the United Kingdom and the French-speaking Quebeçois Party in Canada.

Recognition of Other States   The recognition of other states can become significant when a government changes hands by way of revolution. If most countries of the world fail to recognize the new government as legitimate, economic and political difficulties can result. North Korea provides a case in point.

States thus become weaker when one or more of the four characteristics of a state are questionable. Government leaders strive to make policies that attempt to strengthen their control over territory, legitimate rule, instill their patriotism, and gain respect from other states.

TRENDS OF THE POST WORLD WAR II WORLD

Events in today's world occur in the context of the modern international system. Therefore, adequately explaining the causes of, and responses to, international issues depends on knowing how the current international system functions. That system is defined as the organizations and processes that people use to interact across state borders. The modern state is the most powerful institution in the international system and it has a major impact on many others, such as the United Nations, by setting their policies. States have changed in their relationships with each other and with international organizations during the decades since World War II (1939–1946). The war altered how the world works. The international organizations and trends comprising the current international system were either established after the war or transformed because of it. Four of the most significant general trends since World War II include US leadership, the Soviet challenge, the end of colonialism, and the world's increasing interconnections.

These four trends continue to provide the context for world events, although each has undergone substantial change. The United States is still the world's most powerful state, but it operates in an increasingly complex international environment and needs positive economic and political relations with other states to retain its leadership. Other actors in the international system, states in the developing world, other industrial states, Russia as successor to the Soviet Union, and international organizations have different interpretations of current world issues. In order to understand at least some of the reasons for their varying points of view and their roles in international events, it is necessary to review the trends in the international system since World War II.

US Leadership

The United States emerged from World War II as a hegemony—a dominant world power. It was the only great power that had not been physically and psychologically devastated by the war. Its economy and confidence were at an all-time high. Internationally, the United States used its preponderance of power to establish the international system's institutions and rules. These organizations can be divided into two categories: economic institutions, such as the World Bank, and political institutions, such as the United Nations. The general principles underlying these organizations are derived from the US diagnosis of World War II's fundamental causes. The United States believed its prescriptions would be the best antidotes for a war-prone world.

According to the thinking of US policy makers, as well as many others around the world, the most devastating war in human history had primarily two underlying causes, one economic and the other political. The Great Depression of the 1930s hit only Germany harder than the United States. Each state's setting higher tariffs to protect its own economy only made the downturn worse for all states and ensured the Depression's spread worldwide. In fact, the highest tariff in US history was passed in 1932. Each state reacted with some degree of political change, but the changes in Germany proved to have devastating consequences. Hitler's Nazi Party, a particularly degenerate and racist version of fascism, came to power in Germany in 1933. Its hypernationalism extolled the state as the ultimate good, demanded absolute obedience to the government and its dictator, and predicted that the "master race" of Germans would control the world by eliminating "inferior" peoples. To the fascists, war benefited society since it destroyed the weak. Virtually every analysis of the causes of World War II cited Nazi policy at the top of the list.

The United States and its allies were convinced that following the war, the international system had to be structured so as to foster worldwide economic prosperity, and to identify, plus weaken, potentially aggressor states. Economically, expanding international trade through open markets was essential to each state's prosperity, which, in turn, provided the conditions for stability and peace. Politically, the sobering experience of World War II convinced the world's great powers that international security required mutual effort: Leading states had to adopt internationalist policies and work together in responding to aggressors before they grew into major threats to the peace.

Three institutions were established in the 1940s to organize the international economy. Called *international governmental organizations (IGOs)* because states comprise the membership, together they were designed to stabilize the international economy and ensure economic growth. The International Bank for Reconstruction and Development, called the *World Bank*, offered economic aid in the form of loans to countries whose projects were approved. This IGO was originally planned to assist in European recovery, but recipient countries changed over the years as former colonies achieved independence in the 1950s and 1960s. Loans for economic development rather than rebuilding became the World Bank's task, a much more massive undertaking. Whereas Europe already had the prerequisites for healthy industrial economies, the newly independent states did not.

The *International Monetary Fund (IMF)* provides member states with loans to restore international confidence in a country's currency if its value plummets. Like the World Bank, the IMF first helped Europe but, over time, its loans shifted primarily to newly independent, less industrialized countries. Both the World Bank and the

IMF have weighted voting, which means that those countries paying the majority of the institutions' annual assessments have the majority of the votes. Thus the contributors, not the borrowers, control policy making and the terms of the loans tend to reflect those of commercial international banks.

The General Agreement on Tariffs and Trade (GATT), the forerunner of the present-day *World Trade Organization (WTO),* was assigned the task of lowering tariffs and other barriers to trade. The mechanism devised to achieve increased trade through lower tariffs is called *most-favored nation status.* In practice, this consisted of an agreement between two states to lower their tariffs with each other to match the lowest that each charged any trading partner in a specific product category, such as clothing or automobiles. Over time, as more and more states granted most-favored nation status to each other, tariffs around the world were reduced substantially.

As the worldwide political IGO, the *United Nations* began in 1945 with the adoption of the UN Charter. Initially, its main task was tackling threats to security; however, because the founding states understood peace to be linked to economic factors, several specialized agencies were created to address related issues, such as the Food and Agricultural Organization. The two main UN bodies—the *General Assembly* and the *Security Council*—have different roles. The General Assembly provides a forum in which each member state has one vote and there is no weighted voting. The UN Charter gives the Security Council the key role in responding to threats to world peace. Some Council members have more power than others. Of the fifteen member states in the Security Council, five have permanent seats and the other ten are elected to two-year terms by the General Assembly. The United States, the United Kingdom, France, Russia, and China are permanent members, chosen because they were the winners in World War II. Each of these five members has a veto over any resolution passed by the Security Council.

The United States has thus used its leadership to establish international institutions capable of coordinating economic and political relations among the world's countries. This has proven farsighted for reasons US policy makers did not realize at the time; namely, that one state's dominance would not continue for long and that a common framework had to be in place for debating and dealing with the world's problems. The next three post–World War II trends challenged US leadership and redefined major global issues.

The Soviet Challenge

Within only months after the end of World War II, differences between the United States and the Soviet Union began to surface. For example, the states argued over what factions should come to power in Eastern European countries. By the late 1940s, the differences had crystallized into a superpower rivalry. Another geographically large, resource-rich state with a sizable multiethnic population and major military power was challenging the United States for world leadership. Two characteristics combined to make the adversarial relationship more intense and the consequences of war more threatening than earlier competition, such as that between France and Great Britain in the 1700s. First, the US versus Soviet rivalry introduced a new and devastating military threat—nuclear weapons. Second, the struggle was explained in terms of deep ideological divisions that gave form and focus to policy making. People used these *ideologies* or sets of interrelated ideas, to give meaning to events and to legitimize political institutions.

Probably because of the threat of nuclear war, the post–World War II superpower competition proved to be unlike other historical periods of intense state rivalries. No war was fought between the two main antagonists directly, which is why the term cold war was used. Wars relevant to the rivalry occurred often, but they have been called proxy wars because the parties involved were clients of the superpowers. During the Vietnam War, for example, North Vietnam's weapons were supplied mainly by the Soviet Union. The US rejoinder came as it supported the insurgents in Afghanistan who were fighting the Soviet Union. The antagonists divided Europe into two rival military alliances. The North Atlantic Treaty Organization (NATO), organized by the United States, faced off against the Soviet Union's Warsaw Pact.

With elaborate networks of alliances and aid recipients, the foreign policies of both states became fixated on each other. Both the Soviet Union and the United States interpreted everything that happened in the world in terms of their rivalry. International relations analysts have defined this period as *bipolar* because the world had two main centers of power. The enemies confronted each other for over forty years, until the Soviet Union dissolved in the 1990s because of decisions made by its own people. Its member republics became independent states without a war, a rare event historically.

Russia, the republic that controlled the now-defunct Soviet Union, inherited its permanent seat in the Security Council and its status as one of the world's leading states. Yet, Russia does not command the Soviet Union's economic, military, or ideological power. The fact that it cannot act as a counterweight to the United States has fundamentally changed world politics. The United States is freer to act in international conflicts when it chooses to become involved. The US and (to a large extent) European economic and political system has become the prevailing world standard.

The End of Colonialism

From World War II on, a steady stream of newly independent states took their places in the United Nations. The number of UN members grew particularly in the 1960s, when decolonialization spread to most of Africa. Fifty states had founded the United Nations in 1945, and by 1955 UN membership had grown to seventy-five. These numbers increased to 117 members by 1965, 141 by 1975, 157 by 1985, and 185 by 1995. With a large majority in the General Assembly, the states in Africa and Asia, often supported by those in Latin America, began asserting their priorities, especially their need for economic development.

The newly independent states did not see the world as bipolar but as *multipolar;* that is, as comprised of many power centers. The terms *First World, Second World,* and *Third World* were coined in part to reflect their disagreement with the prevailing bipolar perception of the international system. The First World represented the already industrialized states in the West with their free-market economies and multiparty politics. The Second World reflected the Soviet Union and its Eastern allies with their one-party systems and government-controlled economies. The Third World referred to the rest of the world's states with their lower levels of industrialization, higher levels of poverty, and vulnerability to actions taken by the more powerful countries.

Leaders in Third World states thought that by coordinating their policies they could become another power center. Their first attempt to do so occurred as early as 1955, at a conference in Bandung, Indonesia. The attending countries initiated the Nonaligned Movement (NAM) to differentiate themselves from the United States and its allies, and the Soviet Union and its allies. Subsequently, Third World states followed this political initiative with a coalition designed to bring their economic plight to the world's attention. This network, called the Group of 77, grew to include 130 states by the 1990s. It established the UN Conference on Trade and Development (UNCTAD) as an organization focused solely on Third World issues.

It was not until 1973 that less industrialized states scored some success in negotiations with the First World. The Organization of Petroleum Exporting Countries (OPEC) used an embargo of oil to triple the price paid for a barrel of crude oil. In the heady atmosphere this produced, Third World states passed a series of resolutions in the General Assembly reflecting their interests, such as recommending more foreign aid. None of the resolutions were implemented, and by the early 1980s OPEC's negotiating position had been undermined by the world's oil glut. Yet during the 1970s, Third World countries had managed to focus attention on the different set of problems they faced and to redirect some World Bank and IMF resources. The less industrialized states became more than just places where the Soviet Union and the United States could play their bipolar game by proxy.

Increasing Interconnections

As the numbers of states and IGOs have increased, so too have *nongovernmental organizations (NGOs)*. These private agencies link people across international borders in a wide variety of ways, such as by occupation, religion, personal interest, and issue activism. A sample listing of NGOs would include professional groups, such as the International Skeletal Society with pathologists and orthopedists as members, the Catholic Church and the World Council of Churches, Rotary International, Amnesty International, Care International, and the International Red Cross. In addition, the number of businesses with overseas affiliates has exploded over the years. Currently, about three hundred IGOs and five thousand NGOs channel international contacts among governments, groups, and individuals.

The proliferation of organizations has greatly contributed to the complexity of the international system. No longer are most international interactions bilateral ones in which states deal one-on-one with each other. More and more states, even the most powerful ones, engage in multilateral diplomacy within the framework of IGOs as an established way to address issues. Common positions are negotiated, resolutions are passed, and actions are taken in cooperation with other states. Also, whether using bilateral or multilateral relations, states are no longer the primary channels for international interaction. People have created ever-expanding networks of NGOs and businesses, each with its own priorities, policies, and communication links.

The explosive expansion of international activity in the decades since World War II continues today. It is a necessary reaction to the ever-accelerating globalization of issues, institutions, and interaction processes, whether economic, ecological, linguistic, social, philosophical, or political. The pace of technological innovation shows no sign of abating and, together with population growth, continues to shrink the psychological and actual space among people of the world. The increased speed of communication and transportation can be applied peacefully, as in email, or during war, as with missiles, for example. International decision-making networks aim to foster the former and forestall the latter. The international scope, importance, and complexity of issues facing the planet's peoples demand cooperative and coordinated responses. No longer can one state or even a small group of states manage, much less negotiate, solutions to the world's problems.

This introductory chapter has provided an overview of the major historical trends affecting today's world, both long-term trends, and those since World War II. It has elaborated a definition of the dominant institution in the international system, the state, and noted other organizations that people use in responding to current events and issues. The rest of this book describes and analyzes problems arising from four general, world issues: cultural diversity, economic interdependence and dependence, deterioration of the natural environment, and political conflict. Human beings, therefore, are presented in four contexts: cultural, economic, biological, and political. As a reminder that the four issues apply to the lives of real people, each of the relevant chapters begins with an introduction to specific persons directly affected by one or more of these issues.

TERMS AND CONCEPTS

bilateral international interactions

bipolarity

culture areas

General Assembly

ideologies

international governmental organization
    (IGO)

International Monetary Fund (IMF)

international system

legitimacy

most-favored nation status

multilateral international interactions

multipolarity

nationalism

nongovernmental organization (NGO)

patriotism

Security Council

state

United Nations

World Bank

World Trade Organization (WTO)

DISCUSSION QUESTIONS

1. Who ruled your local area in 1350? What were the most important historical events since then?
2. How does this history differ from the one you learned previously? What elements are consistent?
3. Compare the ethnic, physical, and political maps of North America. What does each tell you about your region?
4. What post World War II events served to limit the power of the United States?
5. What attitudes might the former Soviet Union and the Third World have had toward the international economic system of IGOs?

RESEARCH PROJECTS

1. Collect ten different maps of one continent. Be sure that the maps represent different time periods and types of maps. Use the maps to explore the history of the continent and the perspective of the map makers.
2. Review the history of one cultural group from Africa, South America, or Asia. Who has held power over these people in the last five hundred years? What changes have occurred and what have they meant to the people involved?
3. Find out the overseas connections of businesses and private organizations in your area.
4. Choose a state and read about its history since World War II. What was its position in the bipolar conflict between the United States and the Soviet Union?
5. Talk to your grandparents or other people you know about their impressions of the cold war era. Record and compare their responses. Is there any pattern?

INTERNET RESOURCES

United Nations Homepage: *http://www.un.org*. A good source of information on the member states and the current projects of the United Nations and its affiliated organizations.

2

Ethnicity and Global Diversity

The first step to understanding global issues is reviewing the diversity of the world's peoples. It is this diversity that often makes it difficult to resolve common world problems. An examination of the differences, or perceived differences, between people is essential to understanding the world situation. While defining these differences, cultural identity is a significant underlying factor that is often overlooked by analysts who use states as their main (or only) frame of reference. Cultures, ethnic groups, genders, and class play a role in the decisions that individuals make about their lives. The decisions that governments make are equally influenced by these and other concerns. Therefore, in order to fully understand international debates it is important to know which identities within a state are privileged and which are discriminated against.

All people, both leaders and followers, within any political system are informed not only by their state imperatives, but also by their different values and views of reality. Thus, the well-educated leader of one country can diametrically disagree with the equally well-educated leader of another country, and neither will yield to the other's understanding. Bitter disputes, many of which may lead to war, may be based on claims to land or resources that seem insignificant to outsiders. Many will die to preserve their country's rights to seemingly trivial places or things. When contemporary people of European descent study their history they look at the children's crusades, the Inquisition, and witchcraft trials with utter bewilderment. Time has so changed European traditions that the past has become a different, and somewhat distasteful, culture to modern Europeans.

It is clear that cultural beliefs are very powerful. Some people will fight to the death to maintain them, while others will deeply disagree with these same beliefs and be unable to support them. This is the reality of the world today, as it has been throughout human history. To create a peaceful and cooperative world, people must come to understand the differences that exist between cultures and respect the depth of those differences. People may not like one another but, if they are going to work together, they must agree to disagree on what they cannot resolve and find solutions to their conflicts, which must be resolved or violence will result.

This chapter introduces significant ethnic changes and cultural distinctions in the contemporary world in order to begin to explain why people value various economic, political, and environmental issues differently. It rejects the assumptions of the Victorian theory of Social Darwinism, which still echo in some arenas. The assumptions that the most technologically advanced societies are chosen by nature to rule the world and that less complex societies are doomed to extinction are now repudiated. Different societies adapt to different environments and succeed or fail in those contexts.

The case study involving the Inuit of Nunavut, presented at the end of this chapter, illustrates many of the concepts introduced in the chapter and provides a case for further analysis. It is an important case because it presents the contemporary effort of one state, Canada, to deal with the ethnic variation within its boundaries without resorting to force or state disintegration. The development of a new territory with an ethnically defined legislature can offer, if successful, a new model for other states with similar ethnic enclaves.

CULTURE: THE DEFINITION OF HUMANITY

In 1990 a group of American college professors, who taught a variety of international courses, traveled to Thailand in order to learn more about the people of that country. They found themselves sitting in a rural village asking questions of the residents. The group leader asked the townspeople if they had any questions for the Americans. The first question came from a soft-spoken woman who asked: "Did you plant your rice fields before you left home?" None of these urban American professionals knew how to answer the question.

The incident in Thailand demonstrates the existence of two contrasting truths of humanity. The first is that all humans share a common heritage: a *human culture* that allows us to understand the basic needs and capabilities that all people share. The second is that different groups of people have developed their own ways of dealing with these human problems in their own environments: *specific cultures* that the members of particular societies share. Americans and Thais both understand the need for people to provide sufficient nutritious food for their families, but the way they obtain that food is radically different. "How can these people leave their fields in the summer?" the Thai woman wonders. The Americans recognize the importance of this question but ponder, "How do we explain that we talk and write in the winter and earn enough to pay for a year's food?" Each is capable of understanding the other, but the explanations are not simple because they are embedded in complex cultural systems. Each needs to translate the questions and answers for the other, not only in linguistic terms but in cultural ones as well.

Culture

As the vignette implies, culture is central to understanding human life on the planet. That is why the first concern must be to define culture, a term that has so many different meanings. Natural scientists see a culture in a Petrie dish. Some artists find culture in opera and classic literature, but not in rap or comic books. In this book, the term *culture* is used as defined by cultural anthropologists. Traditionally, anthropologists begin by quoting the first academic definition, offered by Edward Tylor in 1871. According to Tylor (1871:1), culture is "that complex whole which includes knowledge, belief, art, morals, law, custom, and any other capabilities and habits acquired by man [*sic*] as a member of society." The strength and utility of this historical definition rest in the fact that cultures are indeed complex, patterned, and learned.

Children learn the culture shared by the adults in their world. There is nothing biologically innate in culture. The Thai child learns how to grow rice and other related social traditions, from eating habits to religion to gender rules. Reared in another culture, the same child might adopt very different traditions and might never eat rice. The culture that children learn involves a complex mix of skills, beliefs, and facts that allow them to function successfully as adults in their respective societies.

As cultural traits are developed, they are integrated so that they support one another. The term *holism* is used to mean that all traits of a culture influence all others. Therefore, the religious beliefs of a culture complement the economic system, and the political system is supported by the kinship system. In traditional Inuit culture, for example, the importance of hunting and gathering in the economic system is reinforced by the political focus on consensus and dispute resolution, the centrality of nuclear families, and the importance of animal spirits in religion. A change in any one element would change all the others.

While culture shapes human society, it is located in the minds of individuals and encompasses every aspect of life. Culture, therefore, consists of patterns of belief and guidelines for behavior learned by individuals as they become full members of a society. Individuals can learn a second culture, but usually not to the same level of completeness as the one they learned in childhood.

Cultural Change

One of the most common observations made about the modern world is that it changes constantly. Most people laud some changes, from new medical breakthroughs to improved technology for special effects in films, as progress. Other changes, such as social shifts in family composition or immigration patterns, are publicly condemned as destructive of morality. At the same time, the seemingly exotic areas of the world are presented as unchanging realities. This perception is not true. In fact, change is inherent in all human cultures. Since culture is the adaptation of society to environment, changes in environment, both physical and social, always trigger changes in cultures. Cultural change, then, is necessary for continued human survival. Logically, there are two categories of cultural change: *internal* and *external.*

Internal Change   Internal cultural changes are those that are created by people within a society that is changing. In the end these changes can be seen as evolutionary, but in the short term, they appear as *inventions*. Important inventions are new ideas or techniques that are constructed from the mass of collected knowledge and are adopted as valuable by members of the society. Successful innovations are those which are seen as useful or desirable within the contexts of their specific culture. Internal changes are negotiated by the members of a society and ultimately sustain the flavor of the culture itself. This is not necessarily true, however, of changes from external sources.

External Change   External changes are those that are invented or promoted in one culture and introduced, from the outside, to another culture. In the most benign fashion, these changes are voluntary. Innovations from one cultural area of the world are seen as desirable and other cultures clamor to adopt them. These innovations can be trivial—such as new music styles from the Caribbean, new fruits from the tropics, or new soft-drink flavors from Europe—or important—such as new drug therapies from France or new computer technology from the United States. Exposed to new cultural traits through everyday living, individuals adapt those that fit their lives and tastes.

More broad-based and philosophical innovations can also be adapted voluntarily. The recent adoption of the capitalist model by former communist countries is a clear example. After decades of foreign pressure to overthrow communist regimes, the changes came from within. Trade agreements between countries that are ideologically divergent, such as the United States and China, also demonstrate the ability of vastly different cultures to integrate their respective practices voluntarily. Such agreements represent the victory of economic needs over political dogma. Many external changes, then, are the result of the open and welcomed diffusion of desired ideas and material goods.

Some external changes, however, are not welcomed and are *involuntary*. Within the historic context of colonialism, it is easy to find cases of nations with superior military technology that forced their ideas and methods on colonized nations. Often these changes were defined by the stronger state as being "for the good" of the colonizing nation. The spread of Christianity and British social customs in the colonies of Great Britain during the nineteenth century illustrates this well. While there is clearly no evil in the practice of Christianity or the playing of cricket, the fact is that these specific practices were impressed by the colonizer without respect for the culture of the colonized people. The traditional religions and rituals were often outlawed in the colonized nation and any practitioners were punished. Those who adopted British customs, in contrast, were rewarded with employment and material goods. Some who adopted the new traditions also adapted them into their own culture. Today one can find variations of Christianity around the world. In Mexico, saints are reminiscent of older gods and in New Guinea variations of cricket include war and sex dances.

Other social practices and restrictions were mandated as well. In the nineteenth century, several African nations allotted political offices to women. In the state of Buganda, for example, the women of the royal family had courts with judicial roles. Under the British, who ironically were then headed by Queen Victoria, the offices of the women were eliminated while those of the men were maintained. At the same time, the military and punishment for capital crimes were placed in the hands of the British governor so that Europeans controlled all forms of physical force. The male leaders were allowed to remain in office but their powers were substantially truncated. Such imposed changes instilled dependency on the colonial states.

Culture and Economic Adaptations

At first, it might appear that the variations among societies and cultures are so vast that any attempt at generalization would be fruitless. It is possible, however, to group cultures into four categories that describe the cultural and economic bases of most societies: *gathering* and *hunting, agriculturalism, pastoralism*, and the *state*.

These categories can be called evolutionary in the sense that they proceed from simple to complex technology but not in the sense of Social Darwinism. The categorization does not assume the moral superiority of more complex stages nor does it argue that contemporary cultures in the simpler stages are backward or ancestral to their more complex contemporaries.

Gatherers and Hunters   There are few self-reliant groups of gatherers and hunters left in the world today. Small enclaves can be found in the arctic, the deserts, and the tropics, but even these exist encapsulated within a modern state. In the past, however, independent foragers thrived across the globe. This was the original way of life for all humanity. The economic base of this simplest form of human society is the gathering of wild plants and hunting of wild animals for food. Economics within this system takes the form of *generalized reciprocity*. People in bands share with one another. They give without the expectation of equal or immediate return. All benefit from the successes of any one individual. People only go hungry if no one is able to find food. Once the plants and animals of one area are depleted, the people are forced to move their camps to a new place. The only goods they can own are those they can carry. This means that bands need large areas of land and individuals own little wealth.

The social implications of this economic system are profound and repudiate some of the assumptions held by citizens of state societies. Social classes do not exist in such societies since all individuals own roughly the same material goods and perform the same tasks according to their age and gender. There are no designated leaders in bands and, while some individuals may be more admired or liked than others, group decisions are made by consensus and all people are given a say. Competition within and between bands is minimal. In short, gatherers and hunters lead generally egalitarian lives in small groups in which cooperation is the essential ideal.

Agriculturalists   One of the most important innovations in the history of humanity was the domestication of various staple plants. Once established, dependence on domesticated plants allowed populations to grow well beyond the capabilities of foraging societies. Additionally, farmers can settle in permanent towns where they can own, work, and defend their fields. Outside of the family, generalized reciprocity gives way to balanced reciprocity where equal return is expected for each gift. Differences in wealth develop between those families with good lands that have access to more food and better trade goods and those that do not. Permanent homes allow for the collection and storage of material goods.

Members of agricultural societies, or tribes, own personal possessions and some are wealthier and more prestigious than others. Raiding between groups is common in this type of society because of political issues as well as the fact that people have things worth stealing. Poorer clans and communities become dependent on the generosity of richer ones in times of need. This dependency often leads to differences in status and prestige. Equality is not an ideal in most tribes. Social rank becomes an issue and some people are born into a better life than others. There is still some flexibility, however. While tribes, unlike bands, recognize leaders in their groups, tribal leaders are rarely permanent and there is no office of chief in simple agricultural societies. Outstanding individuals in war or peace are recognized and followed.

Pastoralists   Whereas agriculturalists depend on domesticated plants, pastoralists depend on domesticated animals. Some pastoralists, including the Nuer, Dinka, and other people of eastern Africa, are farmers as well, but they consider farming secondary in status to herding cattle. Others, such as the hill tribes of Afghanistan, the Sami of northern Europe, and the Bedouins of the Middle East, have traditionally depended almost entirely on their herds for food. In these tribes, nomadic movement is the norm. Herds, generally owned by clans, are moved over hundreds of miles to graze on ever-new fields. These groups, unlike bands, however, have the use of animals to help with transportation and heavy work. Horses, camels, and in the case of the Sami, reindeer, allow for a far different trek from that of the bands. Domesticated animals also provide security not found with hunting. Barring catastrophic accidents, a relatively stable food source can be relied on to feed a relatively large population.

Like the agricultural tribes, differences in wealth among pastoralists are clear and dictate differences in status. Ownership of large herds and the rights to rich grazing areas confer high status on members of the clan. Prestige as well as power are important issues here. Wealthy individuals wield both influence within their family groups and power in their relations with others. Raiding is common in these societies. Herds are more easily stolen and maintained than fields and the heroics of warriors on horseback belong to the romance of human history.

State Organization   The development of primitive state organization over five thousand years ago was a major turning point in human history, as was the creation of the modern state much later. In this system, political organization takes precedence over economic organization as a defining feature. Most *primitive states*, like most tribes, are dependent on agriculture as the major source of food. A major difference, however, is that states employ economic specialization and market exchange to an extent well beyond that of any other stage of social organization. Among clans one would find farmers growing a variety of foods for their own needs with some surplus for trade; among states one is more apt to find individual farmers growing crops for the market. Additionally, bilateral nuclear families, rather than clans, become the primary kin groups. Among other things, this means that the support of a wide array of kin is gone. Individual families become far more vulnerable than ever before.

The primary legal identity of an individual in a state is based on political or geographic designation. Rather than say "I am the son of Zarn" or "I am a member of the Dingo clan," people in states announce that they are "from Sydney" or "a Canadian." Their rights, privileges, and obligations stem more directly from their citizenship than from their personal relationships.

This does not mean that all people in a state are equal within the system. One of the hallmarks of the state is a class system. Certain groups of people are considered inherently better and more privileged than others. Individuals who are born into urban families that are close to the centers of power are likely to hold important offices as adults. Individuals born into peasant families are fated to be peasants. Specializations of many kinds based on education, status, gender, age, and many other factors are common in states.

The core criterion of a state is a centralized political organization. Leadership becomes defined by offices that must be filled. Laws and courts, which decide disputes, are formalized and dictate the behavior of citizens. All this must be paid for and the participants must be fed and this is made possible through taxation. Police and military forces support the order and power of the leaders.

Warfare is common in state systems. Competition for land and scarce resources between states can become fierce. Expanding populations demand new sources of food, minerals, and land. Before the expansion of modern states throughout the world, primitive states could expeditiously overrun less powerful tribes. In more recent times, similarly powerful states face off with far more deadly results.

Industrialism changes the productive focus of the state system from the farm to the factory. The goods produced by urban workers and the mechanism to create those goods owned by the elite define the wealth of a society. The difference in financial and social status differential between the urban rich and poor mirrors that previously found in the urban elite-peasant relationship.

Cultures, Subcultures, and Other Classifications

People speak about American culture, French culture, Bantu culture, Kurdish culture, and the like with a general understanding that the people in each of those cultures differ in distinctive ways from the others. More important, perhaps, is that all Americans (here meaning from the United States) identify as Americans and clearly recognize that they are *not* French, Bantu, or Kurds. At the same time, not all Americans are identical and each has additional distinctive social identities. Some Americans are upper-class males of African heritage who use Spanish as a mother tongue, while others are middle-class Navajo women who speak Diné as well as English. The United States, of course, is a state that prides itself on the wide diversity of its citizens. Still, even more culturally homogeneous nations such as Japan and Saudi Arabia see significance in certain human variations.

Ethnic Groups   Literally, *ethnic group* means "culture" or "cultural group," but commonly the term is used to specify cultural groups that are minorities in a larger, heterogeneous nation. Ethnic groups include *indigenous people*, those who first lived on this land and no longer control it, but also include later migrants to the country. Apache and Tlingit, then, are ethnic groups in the United States but so are the Amish, Cuban Americans, and Cajuns. Individuals descended from each ethnicity are American citizens and fully invested in the country. Some have left the traditions of their ancestors so far behind that they no longer identify with the group at all. Most, however, recognize a common identity with others of similar descent and share traits from language to marriage customs to food that are important to them.

For the most part, as many American towns can demonstrate, a mixture of ethnic groups enriches a community. New Orleans, New York, and Santa Fe are very different cities due, in large part, to the peculiar mixture of prominent ethnic groups that each city boasts. Internationally, the national cultures of Latin American states enjoy a dynamism based on the blending of native, African, and European cultural elements. The variety of foods, language, celebrations, and ideas broadens the lives of everyone who lives there.

Unfortunately, this ideal synthesis is not always the reality of multicultural states. In some cases, ethnic identities take priority over the state identity and ethnic rivalries erupt. Antagonism toward, or isolation from, citizens of different heritage ensues. Sometimes this dissension springs from events that occurred long in the past and/or far from the current site. For example, tales of the Armenian Massacre or the Irish potato famine remain important issues in American Armenian and Irish ethnic communities. Often differences in religion (Jews in Nazi Germany, Muslims in contemporary Europe, and B'hais in Iran), in language (Spanish speakers in the U.S. Southwest and French speakers in Canada), or in physical appearance (African Americans and Asians in West Africa) are used to characterize the value or nature of the individuals within those groups.

In some cases, as the preceding examples suggest, the differences between ethnic groups can cause minor social discord, threaten the integrity of the state, and even lead to genocide—the extinction of an entire ethnic group. The relative powers of those who hate and those who are hated anticipate the results. In areas where the power is not overwhelmingly one-sided and where there is no overriding authority restricting it, long-term ethnic antagonisms, such as those in Eastern Europe and parts of Africa, can result in civil wars with extensive bloodshed.

Indigenous People   One category of ethnic groups, *indigenous peoples,* has become conspicuous in headlines. For the first time, guidelines for the treatment of First Nations issues are actively being discussed in the international arena. News stories report that rock stars appear at concerts with Native Amazonian people demanding their rights and health professionals plead their case in hopes of gaining indigenous knowledge of tropical drugs and treatments. Indigenous peoples represent the last groups of colonized people from the era of European colonization who remain under the control of foreign societies. The United Nations declared the 1990s as the "Decade of Indigenous Peoples."

Indigenous cultures, or *First Nations*, are those traditional societies that have been enveloped by a nation-state with a distinctively different cultural base. They are the original people of an area who have lost political control over their ancestral lands and do not fully recognize the moral authority of the state government to dominate them. The best recognized indigenous cultures include the Native Americans of both North and South America, the aboriginal people of Australia, the Sami of Scandinavia, the San (Bushmen) of the Kalahari, the Ainu of Japan, and Native Hawaiians. They differ from most other ethnic groups by maintaining a prior claim to the land controlled by the state. They differ from other colonized peoples because the colonizers have settled in large numbers and, after generations, have stayed. The colonizers will not return to their native land because they now define this land as their home.

"Races"   *Race*, the category of human diversity that would be mentioned first by many people, is probably the one most poorly understood. Americans will assert that there are four human races color-coded as white, black, red, and yellow or by geographic heritage as European, African, American, and Asian. Upon reflection, others might include people from Australians to Hispanics.

Few Americans realize that they echo the scientific classification of race that has been widely discounted by the anthropologists and biologists who study human diversity. At this point in human development, all people from Aachen to Zimbabwe belong to the same race: *Homo sapiens sapiens*. The only other possible race of modern humans, *Homo sapiens neanderthalensis*, became extinct some thirty thousand years ago. The physical variations seen in people around the world are minor, and scientifically they do not have the depth of true racial differences seen in other animals. One of the reasons for this is that animals that develop races have had geographically isolated populations that have reproduced within these isolated groups. Over time, adaptations to particular environments became dominant in specific populations and not in others. Over even more time unique species could have developed. The history of *Homo sapiens* is, however, such that there have never been these types of truly isolated populations. Asia, Africa, and Europe formed an extenuated, but common gene pool with no barriers to breeding at their borders. The Americas and the Pacific have been populated in biologically recent times and did not have time to form new races before they were reintroduced to the Old World.

It is obvious that people are physically different and that groups of people can look different from others. The scientific reticence at using categories like race is not based on any denial of human physical diversity, but quite the opposite, the recognition of the complexity of that diversity. The popularly held racial classifications emphasize a few physical traits, largely skin tone, hair color and texture, and nose shape. They tend to ignore the more biologically significant traits such as blood types and genetic markers. Many American children would argue that dark skin (high melanin) means Africa and, indeed, dark skin is often found in parts of sub-Saharan Africa. Not all people of African heritage have dark skin (see the San or Pygmies as examples) and many people among those with the darkest skin tone come from Australia or Melanesia, far from the so-called "Dark Continent." Aboriginal Australians are not Africans, but many of the former have darker skin than many of the latter.

Most specialists in human physical variation today look at clines, and not *biological races*. *Clines* are the frequencies of particular genetic traits in different parts of the world. The percentages of blood types in different regions are examined, as are the frequencies of particular diseases. Traits like propensity to diseases are emphasized, rather than hair, skin, or eye color because the former makes a difference to human welfare and potential while the latter group of traits should not.

However, in spite of the biological reality, many societies do classify people in categories that are based on perceived physical differences. What most people do not realize is that the classification of these so-called *social races* differs around the world and over time. The US Census questionnaire has changed racial categories several times and today strays from the color-code classification by adding Hispanics to the list. Other countries recognize a different collection of races. Brazilians are said to recognize forty different races. Under apartheid in South Africa, white, black, Asian, and colored were the primary categories. A person with a mother of European heritage and a father descended from sub-Saharan Africans would be called "colored" there. If he moved to the United States, he would be called "black."

If race is such a difficult concept to concretize, how does it retain such power in the modern world? One answer may be found in a brief review of the history of racial categories. Americans now speak of the Hispanic race, although it would be difficult to define what is physically distinct about Hispanics. This is because the category, in fact, depends on language and culture, not biology.

A century ago similar races existed in America; for example, the Irish race and the Jewish race. Popular and academic literature of the time used these races as givens. Caricature of simian-looking Irish and hook-nosed sinister Jews portrayed these types. There is no Irish or Jewish race today (outside of the philosophies of extreme hate groups) because these were social categories of a particular time when a majority of Euro-Americans who held cultural prejudices against these groups wished to distance themselves from them. To label a group as a different kind of human using scientific jargon allows others to discriminate against them in a manner that social differences could not justify. Better education or equal opportunity, the argument often goes, would not make them the equals of the superior race because their inferiority is inbred and not easily modified. This argument allowed many groups to justify slavery while at the same time claiming to value the human soul or spirit. In many societies around the world, those ethnic groups most despised by the majority are categorized as inferior races.

Genders *Sex* might appear to be a physical universal without the difficulties of the term *race*. As mammals, the breeding strategy of *Homo sapiens* is based on the sexual reproduction of males and females. It would, therefore, appear that male and female should be unified categories. But purists would note that normal frequencies of hermaphroditism, variety in sexual preferences, and genetic varieties beyond XX and XY are found in all populations and, therefore, that an exclusive male-female dichotomy is not the full biological story. For the most part, however, categorizing men and women as different physically is basic biology. However, the extension of beliefs about male-female differences beyond the primary sexual ones is open to disagreement. In fact, the dispute over the biological reach of sex is widely interpreted in ways compatible with cultural beliefs. Societies that believe that women are incapable of particular types of work outside of the home, for example, assert that they are biologically incapable of doing such work without harm. It was this type of explanation in the United States of the mid-nineteenth century that lead Sojourner Truth, a former slave, to assert in a now-famous speech for women's rights that she had done all the hard physical jobs and, as she put it, "ain't I a woman."

Gender, distinct from sex, is the term used in the social sciences, as a cultural definition. Different societies define the proper roles and the assumed capabilities of men and women differently. In some societies, there are more than two genders. In India the Hijra form is a third gender category that anthropologist Serena Nanda (1990) asserts is "neither man nor woman." Real Hijras either are natural hermaphrodites or undergo surgery to remove external sex organs. Their ideal role in society is to be followers of the goddess Maia, and they are called upon to dance at weddings and childbirth celebrations in order to bring the blessing of fertility. Less ideally for the Hijras, many are employed as prostitutes in the cities. In Native America, the Navajo recognize *nadles* as a third gender of people who have the blessings of both males and females and who often have special supernatural abilities. The classification of berdache (Williams 1986), or more properly "those of two spirits," in other Native American groups is also recognized as a (normal) third gender. While the vast majority of people around the world are labeled as man or woman, additional categories are recognized in some cultures.

A more obvious variation can be found by looking at the definitions of man and of woman in different societies. Most Americans would identify a fully veiled woman as a Muslim from the Middle East and a figure in a football uniform as an American male. Similarly, they would assume a person identified as a Roman Catholic priest is a man and one identified as a hula dancer is a woman. However, these visual intercultural assumptions are often more complex. In the nineteenth-century plains of North America, a farmer was clearly defined as a male by the Euro-American settlers. Equally clearly, the Native American residents defined a farmer as a female. In each culture the role of farmer was sex-linked but in opposite ways. Each found the gendered concepts of the other absurd and even distasteful. This became an issue, and one little understood by the US government when it attempted to "civilize" the Plains Indians by making them farmers. The resistance to farming by native men in this area was taken as a sign of laziness and backwardness. At the same time, no effort was made to help native women develop their farms because nondomestic work by women was not taken seriously within the equally cultures-bound gender expectations of Euro-Americans. Over time, such differences in gender expectations in North America have often led to the disenfranchisement of native women in economics and politics (Klein and Ackerman 1995).

Only recently have the issues of women's rights as intrinsic to human rights been genuinely argued in the United Nations and other international bodies. The widespread impact of varying rights being granted to men and women in different states had often been ignored in discussions of global issues. However, overwhelming data demonstrate that women and children are more often found in poverty than men throughout the globe and this mandates new research and calls for new programs.

Some cultural issues, such as the so-called female circumcision in some African and Asian societies, have become international disputes. In this tradition girls have some of their sexual organs surgically removed or altered in a coming-of-age ceremony. As a result they are recognized as women and are ready for respectable marriage. Many from other parts of the world are appalled by this practice and call it genital mutilation. The United States has granted an African woman, who fled her county to avoid the procedure, refugee status based on the argument that if she were returned to her country she would be forced to undergo the operation. Most argue that these operations often endanger the health of the women, while others point out that the procedure permanently destroys the women's pleasure in sexual relations. Both contend that good health and sexual pleasure are basic human rights, which are being denied.

Diplomats and many citizens from countries that practice female circumcision argue that others are meddling in an important family and gender tradition that is private. They assert that outsiders are ethnocentrically judging them. They assert that surgeries that are more hygienic should be the solution to health problems and point to a parallel to male circumcision as performed in the West. Moreover, they argue that moral behavior and female submission are important in their states and that the surgery supports proper female behavior.

Clearly, there are very different interpretations of human rights and gender status at work here. The issues have become more complex because of immigration. The movement of people who demand the surgery to western countries have made the issues important in many states which had never needed to address them before. Countries like the United States and France now have laws banning the genital operations. Immigrants are forced to either adapt to the customs of their new countries or seek, often dangerous, illegal surgeries. As all countries become increasingly heterogeneous, conflicting concepts of gender and individual rights can only generate more controversy between and within countries.

Classes   A final global category, and one that has no biological base but great human consequence, is social hierarchy or *class*. National and international decision makers are drawn from the upper classes and reflect upper-class understandings and goals. While as noted, bands and tribal societies maintained relative social equality, states by their definition do not. With the dominance of the state form come almost global-class strata. Poverty tied to powerlessness and great wealth tied to great power prove true not only when dealing between states, but within them as well.

Stratification is a difficult concept for Americans because it conflicts with the deeply held ideal of human equality and the fictive identification of the United States as a classless society. Even so, class is an element of American society and the ideal of equality is taught to children as equal opportunity rather than equal results. Therefore, there can be rich and poor, powerful and powerless, as long as all people have the right to reach the high positions. Every child, or boy it was said until recently, can grow up to be the president. The fact that this is not, and has never been, true is a painful cultural contradiction that many Americans would like to change.

Most states do not recognize all their citizens to be equal. In fact, people are valued, paid, and respected according to the social status they hold. Some obtain their status by birth. Royalty and the wealthy elite, for the most part, are born into families that already have royal titles or wealth to pass on. This type of position is often called an *ascribed status*. The opposite, an *achieved status*, is one that is earned by the actions of an individual. For example, in England, Queen Elizabeth II holds an ascribed status while the prime minister has earned an achieved status. The next monarch of England is expected to be the son of the reigning queen, while the next prime minister almost certainly will not be a child of the current one. Some societies are more fluid with respect to social movement than others, and an individual, not born in it, can become part of the wealthy elite by earning vast amounts of wealth and socially learning the correct behavior of the group. Some nonroyals may even marry into the royal family and earn the title of princess or prince. For the most part, however, most citizens of states change little from the status or class of their parents.

One of the problems in the contemporary world is the pervasiveness of the underclass, which is linked to ethnic background. In many countries, minority ethnic groups deprived of opportunities to rise in the social system have remained subservient, dependent, and poor through centuries. While slavery as an institution has been internationally prohibited, servitude remains. The roles of Indonesian servants in Saudi Arabia, Gypsies (Romi) in Europe, and Koreans in Japan all, in different ways, reflect an ethnic group stratification.

Reactions to Diversity

Human diversity is a reality of everyday life and, while it is increasing in most societies, it has been an issue throughout history. This history has not been a uniformly peaceful one, however. Many countries have celebrated human diversity, but in others it has been the reason for legal discrimination, war, human slavery, and even genocide. The following concepts can help explain why.

The most common reaction to cultural diversity is *ethnocentrism*, which involves judging the customs of another culture according to the one's own standards. This can be as simple as judging other's food preferences, declaring, for example, that eating dog or rancid whale skin is disgusting and that eating pig or "spoiled" cow milk (that is, sour cream) is natural. On a more serious level, members of one religion might declare the practices of another immoral or illegal. These cultural differences being condemned need not be very different than those followed by the critics. In fact, seemingly minor differences are often more severely condemned than extreme ones. For example, in largely Christian jurisdictions, laws exist against snake handling in the religious services of minority Christian denominations in parts of the southeastern United States. At the same time, the use of poisonous snakes in some Native American religious ceremonies in the Southwest are protected by law. Ethnocentrism, then, appears throughout societies at different levels of cultural diversity.

Ethnocentrism is difficult to combat because there is a positive reality that helps cause the negative outcome. Universally, children are reared to appreciate and adapt the culture of their parents. As they learn, they are enculturated so that they can function as full members of their society. They learn that their religion is true, their customs are good, and their political system is just. The child, who does not learn this, does not fit in. It should be of little surprise, then, that when they are adults these individuals see other religions as false, other customs as inappropriate, and other political systems as unjust. In a homogeneous setting, this would cause little trouble but in a heterogeneous world, it creates problems when groups interact.

Cultural relativity is the term used to describe a form of solution to this problem. Cultural relativity suggests that the actions of people within each culture should be evaluated according to the rules of that culture. The person who eats a dog in Vietnam, then, is evaluated differently than an American who might do the same in the United States. A concern often voiced is that cultural relativity taken to its logical extreme would allow for moral anarchy. Would the murders of thousands, or millions, as has occurred in even recent history be acceptable because the nation that allowed these deaths deemed them appropriate? From the perspective of most religious and ethnic systems the answer would surely be no. Politically, the United Nations asserts that there are universal human rights that supersede any national values.

The balance between ethnocentrism and cultural relativity is a delicate one. Patriotism, putting the well-being of one's state before one's own, is an admirable trait but it is a form of identity that gives priority to the state. Is nationalism good if one's government causes deaths or denies freedom to other peoples? However, accepting people as different but still as human, is far more difficult than popular slogans suggest. Where extreme ethnocentrism exists, it may be impossible to understand people from other cultures and hence to deal with them successfully in business or diplomacy. Extreme cultural relativism makes it impossible to raise issues of human rights violations or environmental ruin beyond the boundary of one's own culture.

Racism and *sexism* further hinder world cooperation, within countries and worldwide. When individuals judge other individuals based on perceived biological differences, it tends to distort their understanding of the world. Africa became "the Dark Continent" in European minds and Africans became defined as a different and inferior type of people. As "inferior" people, they were perceived as needing the benefits of European civilization and consequently colonialism. The slavery of Africans was justified by this assertion of innate difference. Likewise, differential immigration laws, which encourage and discourage migration throughout the world, are often based on racist assumptions.

Similarly, sexism allows people to use their perceptions of appropriate gender behavior to judge other nations. The images of veiled and draped Islamic women are used by other societies as evidence of the "backwardness" of some Arab countries without understanding the meaning of Purdah or female seclusion. At the other extreme, women who traditionally wear little clothing (such as those in the Pacific Islands) and those who wear sexually alluring clothing (Latin or Caribbean women during Carnival), are used as evidence of the "backwardness" of those cultures. Even the presence of women in high political office is used by some to indicate the weakness of such a "henpecked" country. At the same time, countries with few women in high political office are taunted as medieval. Concerns over human rights, as noted earlier, are confused by sexism.

Governmental responses to human diversity within domestic borders have historically taken many forms—from acceptance to forced conformity to reservations to genocide. Recently, governments have seen a need to deal with the increasing diversity in new ways that conform to international standards of human rights. In many states, the treatment of indigenous peoples has become the test case. Because indigenous peoples have historically been treated brutally and now are among the most powerless people in contemporary states, their treatment can be seen as proof of a country's commitment to human rights and its openness in dealing with human diversity.

CASE STUDY

NUNAVUT: A NEW TERRITORY FOR AN INDIGENOUS NATION

The case chosen for discussion in this section is that of Canada's evolving policies toward one group of indigenous people—the Inuit of the land called Nunavut. While any one of hundreds of other cases could have been used, this one is particularly compelling. Canada is now experimenting with a form of semiautonomy for ethnic minorities which, if successful, will create a form of governance that allows for indigenous peoples to live their own ways of life while at the same time remain a vital part of the larger state. Nunavut may prove a model for future agreements around the world.

The Inuit of Nunavut are an indigenous people who developed a gathering and hunting type of culture in the Arctic, one of the most environmentally challenging areas of the world. They have maintained many of their traditions but have felt threatened by contemporary Canadian and territorial governmental policies. In a very short time they have demanded and received Canadian approval for, and aid in, establishing a new Inuit controlled and designed territory: Nunavut. The Canadian government and the Inuit of Nunavut have embarked on a bold experiment in cooperative cultural living that many countries are watching carefully.

The Inuit of Nunavut

Most Americans are familiar with the name *Eskimo* and have a popularized image of people living in igloos, hunting arctic animals, using dog sleds, and rubbing noses. Any greeting-card store will sell pictures of darling, round-faced, smiling children wearing fur ruffs and clutching husky puppies. What most Americans do not realize is that the Inuit, meaning "people" in their native language, as most are called today, are modern First Nation people, no more or less adorable than others, and that those who live in the eastern part of the Northwest Territories are about to become the masters of a new Canadian territory: Nunavut, meaning "Our Land."

The Inuit are one of a few cultures that spread over three continents and who are citizens in four states. They live in Asia (Russia), North America (United States and Canada), and Europe (Greenland, a part of Denmark). This discussion focuses on the Canadian Inuit of Nunavut, but it is important to note that while cultural variations exist regionally, there is a remarkable consistency of language, cultural skills, and values throughout gathering-and-hunting adaptations in Arctic environments.

Gathering-and-Hunting Cultures The adaptation to arctic life is one of the wonders of human history. The arctic is a dry, cold area with little permanent vegetation and extreme seasonal shifts in the amount of daylight. Summers are light, bountiful, and short. Individuals not enculturated in an Inuit society simply could not exist there. The Inuit, however, had invented tools and skills that made them the masters of this environment. They also focused on the mammals of the region as their major economic resources, making hunting, rather than the seasonal gathering of vegetation, central to their survival.

Coastal resources, including species of seals, whales, and walrus, and inland sources of caribou were augmented by fish, polar bears, and musk oxen. Season and local environment dictated the focus of the hunt. Special tools for these hunts included kayaks, harpoons, stone oil lamps, dog sleds, and intricately designed parkas and snowhouses in winter. The hunting group, usually composed of family members in difficult times, was dependent on the skill of the men, the hunters, and the abundance of natural resources. Too often families perished in severe seasons. Traditions, including female infanticide, were used to restrict populations in the worst areas (Balikci 1984:424; Dumas 1984:392).

As is common in gathering-and-hunting bands, the nuclear family was the central unit, but here, extended families played a large role in daily life as well. The husband-wife bond was vital for survival with the men and women each having critical tasks that must be done to live. Unmarried adults were rare and were reduced to a dependent position with married relatives. Related nuclear families lived close together with the elders and especially skillful hunters playing prestigious roles. Unlike most bands, social rule dictated some inequality in that women were in some ways subordinate to men and the younger subordinate to the older, but exceptions always existed. Food was shared, but it was more restricted by kinship relationships or partnerships than pure generalized reciprocity would suggest (Wenzel 1995).

In another departure from the band model, the Inuit displayed far more interpersonal conflict than those in more favorable environments. Like in other bands, Inuit religion was individualistic and emphasized deities connected with the environment. All individuals had souls within them that were considered essential to their well-being. The shamans were religious specialists who were called for help in times of illness or other distress. Their connection to supernatural spirits brought them secular power as well, since they could use their powers for good or evil.

Judging by the values of many Canadians of other ethnicities, there was a dark side to early Inuit culture. Murder and suicide were realities in Inuit society just like our own. The perceived real threat of starvation sometimes led to cannibalism and infanticide. Work was hard and not always interesting. The menace of the environment and the potential threat of the shamans loom dark compared to the equally ethnocentric popular image of the cute Eskimos.

While the hardship of the region would not be denied, it is clear that many Inuit loved the Arctic and prided themselves in the accomplishment of living successfully there. They were part of the land physically and spiritually and knew the value of human cooperation. Canadians of European and Inuit heritages might agree on the details of the traditional Arctic lifestyle but disagree wildly on their evaluation of its worth.

Changes   The development of Inuit culture was largely internal until quite recently. Areas where traditional cultural life was the norm continued to exist into the mid-twentieth century. Surely internal changes in the forms of technical and social inventions by the Inuit over the centuries allowed for their unsurpassed adaptation to the Arctic. While it is not known when Inuit ancestors first reached the Arctic, it is clear that small physical changes developed that were conducive to life there as well. The shape of facial features and the short, broad-chested body type common among the Inuit are well adapted to protecting the internal organs from extreme cold.

The Inuit's contact with other cultures predated their very early introduction to Europeans. In fact, the discarded term *Eskimo* is said to have derived from the denunciation of an unfriendly Indian nation to the south. They were part of the first known meeting of Europeans and North Americans when the Vikings came to the far north. Despite this early introduction, major external changes and the beginnings of adaptation to Western ways have come late. The early interactions with foreign whalers and explorers were infrequent but produced new trade goods, especially metals, which were eagerly and voluntarily adopted as improvements to the traditional tool chest. On the negative side, however, these contacts brought new diseases.

More intense external changes in most areas did not occur until the fur trading era of the early twentieth century. A debt-driven relationship with fur companies developed in many areas. The fur companies were soon joined by the Royal Canadian Mounted Police with Canadian law and missions preaching a Christian message. Both launched campaigns against community disorder, traditional religion, and especially the Inuit religious practitioners. As communities adapted to the new economy and lost the skills of the old, the 1930s Depression came and wiped out the call for furs. Many of the people who had adapted the new ways suffered greatly in comparison to those in the hinterland who had not changed. Many of the more acculturated migrated to larger, more southern communities and became dependent, while others starved.

The Second World War brought military bases to the Arctic, and with them came previously unknown wealth. New technologies, especially airplanes, brought access to the North into the realm of the common people and allowed trade to expand dramatically. Similarly, snowmobiles replaced dogs but increased the need for cash to pay for fuel. Wage labor became available and new health facilities were built introducing Western medicine for the first time. Unfortunately, this close meeting with a new population also brought new diseases causing epidemics for the Inuit who had no immunity to them.

After the war, the Canadian government heightened its civilian presence with monetary allowances, health care, and compulsory schools. That these all led to dependency was clear, but what was not as obvious was the particular problem of schooling. Canada viewed the compulsory schools as services to allow Inuit children to join in the opportunities that all Canadians were to enjoy. But racism meant that even individuals well educated in Euro-Canadian scholarship were not offered employment equal to others. In some places, this was far more extreme for men than women. Women acculturated at a more rapid rate than men, and were accorded higher status in Canadian society. This caused a deep gender schism in some communities (McElroy 1976).

Even if education had allowed immediate access to a Canadian middle-class existence, there would still have been deeply rooted problems. First, the blanket assumption that this new way of life was better was ethnocentric in that it aimed to destroy Inuit culture. Education was in English with a southern Canadian-based curriculum. Traditional Inuit skills were either denigrated or ignored. Children spending their hours in these classes lost the opportunity to learn the extremely technical skills needed to survive in the traditional way. Second, the regulation requiring children to attend schools in permanent communities for much of the year placed their parents in a quandary. They had to move into these towns or leave their children with others for months each year. Most chose to keep their families together in towns and the adults took whatever employment existed there. Art provided an income to many. A lasting problem is that town jobs generally do not provide the satisfaction or prestige, at least for men, that a traditional lifestyle does (McElroy 1976; Graburn and Lee 1990). One result of this is that problems connected with alcohol abuse grew rapidly among the Inuit. There was an approximately a 30 percent increase in alcohol-related problems from the 1960s to early 1980s (Vallee, Smith and Cooper 1984:674).

Inuit Nationalism   One of the unexpected outcomes of the Canadian education was the emergence of a group of young, educated Inuit who used the system to demand their rights as First Nation people within Canada. It was only in 1960 that the native people of the Northwest Territories were given the right to vote in Canadian elections. In just a decade, the Committee for Original Peoples Entitlement (COPE) was established to assert the land and political interests of Inuit and other northern First Nations. The next year an action group, the Inuit Tapirisat of Canada (ITC), was formed to pursue the land claims and political rights of the Inuit in particular. During the 1970s they developed a plan for a separate territory to be carved out of the Northwest Territories, north of the treeline. This largely Inuit-populated territory was to be called Nunavut and was to be developed in the future into a fully Inuit-controlled province. Not all Inuit are enfranchised within Nunavut, however. Inuit in Quebec, Labrador, and western Northwest Territories are not included. Initially, the government strongly opposed this plan, which treats the Inuit people as a nation, rather than as individual Canadian citizens. A 1982 plebiscite of all voters in the Northwest Territories determined that 58 percent supported it. This strong support from many non-Inuit helped further the cause in Ottawa, the Canadian capital.

External forces also intervened. The strategic and mineral value of this region is important to Canada. When, in 1985, the United States sent a ship, *The Polar Sea*, through Arctic waters without asking for Canadian permission, it was seen as an initial act in a potential claim over "uninhabited land." This challenge to Canadian sovereignty over these waters has been answered in part by recognizing the claims of the Inuit who have a long-standing international recognition to residence in the area. Nunavut as a populated and organized territory of Canada is an unassailable assertion of possession.

For the Inuit, like many Canadian First Nations, a growing awareness of the lack of aboriginal rights in the Canadian constitution pushed them to action. Additionally, the fact that the unique cultural rights of French speakers in Quebec were being taken more seriously than the First Nation claims, worried many First Nation leaders and forced them to action.

The Territory of Nunavut   On April 1, 1999, Canada will begin a new chapter in its relationship with its indigenous people. On that day the Northwest Territories will be split into two territories and the territory of Nunavut, with Iqaluit as its governmental capital, will be officially established. Nunavut, at 770,000 square miles, will be one-fifth the size of Canada, larger than any other territory or province within that state. In this vast land will live a population of less than 27,000 people, about 80 percent of them Inuit (Nunavut Implementation Commission 1995). At the same time, the Inuit Federation will become "the largest private landholder in North America" (Dickason 1992:416), owning outright 18 percent of Nunavut.

The Nunavut Implementation Commission has been formed to determine the final government organization. This government will have the same powers as those in other territories. Clearly, all citizens of Nunavut—Inuit and non-Inuit—will be equally eligible for office, but the vast majority of the population are Inuit and the working language of the government is slated to be Inuktituit. Given a relatively clean slate, the commission is investigating a variety of ideas that would create a government form compatible with Inuit ideals. Suggestions for legislatures with male and female seats for each region and residency rules to protect the territory from southern intrusion are being discussed.

Only the Inuit are recognized in the land-claim settlement administered by the Tungavik Federation of Nunavut. In this settlement, they own 353,610 square kilometers (136,530 square miles). They also have claim to the subsurface mineral rights on 36,257 square kilometers of that land. The remaining 82 percent of the land remains Crown land. The Inuit also have the right to hunt and fish on Crown land and to receive a percentage of mineral development that might occur there. In addition, they claim half of the seats on territorial management boards, with the federal representatives holding the other half. The federal government will pay the Inuit $1.15 billion over fourteen years. The major concession from the Inuit of this territory, and it is a deeply controversial one, is that they give up all future claims to land and water in Canada.

Analysis

The development of Nunavut changes the nature of Canada itself. Nunavut has a cultural and linguistic identity that is rivaled only by the French Province of Quebec. In this, it affirms the multicultural nature of Canada. The Inuit, who have been seen as a racial group and treated with racism and ethnocentrism through most of Canadian history, are now addressed as equals. The road from gathering and hunting has been rapid.

Nunavut addresses cultural diversity in a new way by giving local power while retaining national unity and sovereignty. The growth of Nunavut can follow the road of internal and external *voluntary change* at the same time. The Inuit nation can be recognized while patriotism for Canada remains secure. It is a territory that recognizes the rights of all Canadians, but privileges those whose language and culture fit the north. For example, the concept of gender equality in political power is seen as important and is being addressed in the development of a territorial government. Nunavut is a huge social, political, and economic experiment for Canada that will serve as an example, either good or bad, for the treatment of less powerful ethnic groups internationally.

TERMS AND CONCEPTS

agriculturalism

class

clines

cultural relativity

culture (human and specific)

ethnic group

ethnocentrism

external changes

gathering and hunting

gender

generalized reciprocity

holism

indigenous peoples/First Nations

industrialism

internal changes

invention

involuntary changes

pastoralism

primitive states

race (biological)

race (social)

racism

sex

sexism

status

voluntary changes

DISCUSSION QUESTIONS

1. What are the limits to cultural relativism? When do cultural practices become international human rights abuses?
2. What North American laws or customs might citizens from other parts of the world find morally or ethically unacceptable?
3. What are the racial categories in your community? How are they used?
4. How do concepts so basic to American values, such as human equality, become problematic in the international arena?
5. Are there any indigenous nations in your state? If so, discuss their history and contemporary situation. What are their rights and privileges as indigenous peoples?

RESEARCH PROJECTS

1. Nunavut is an unusual, but not unique, example of a modern society due to its low population and remote location. Review the situation of indigenous peoples in Australia, Greenland, Siberia, or northern Scandinavia. What is the legal situation in the area? How does it differ from Nunavut?
2. Investigate a controversial issue, such as female genital mutilation (female circumcision) or capital punishment, from the point of view of a culture that supports it and from the point of view of a culture that rejects it.
3. Choose a major international story in the news and investigate the cultural background of the countries or ethnic groups involved. Does this change your understanding of the situation?
4. How does the US Census define the ethnic/racial categories of Americans? How has this changed in the last four Census periods? What does this tell you about America and the categories of people?
5. What customs and traditions have immigrants from other countries brought to your community? Have they historically been welcomed? Has their situation changed over time?

INTERNET RESOURCES

American Anthropological Association: *http://www.ameranthassn.org* A good source for information on the association's activities that includes links to a wide choice of related cultural sites.

Anthropology in the News: *http://www.tamu.edu/anthropology/news.html* Maintained by the Department of Anthropology at Texas A&M University, this site provides information on cultural issues that are currently in the news.

Indigenous People: International Decade 1995-2004: *http:www.un.org/ecosocdev/geninfo/indigens/dpi1608c.htm* Part of the larger UN page, this site offers information on the reasons for and activities related to the UN "International Decade."

3

Perspectives on Ethnicity and Global Diversity

Nunavut is an outdated idea, one of the last applications
of the postwar ideal of national self-determination.

—Gurston Dacks 1986
(quoted in Purich 1992:79)

Nunavut is not just an important achievement for Inuit. It
will be an important inspiration for other Aboriginals in
other parts of the world.

—John Amagoalik 1993
(quoted in Pelly 1993:29)

Reasonable people can look at the same situation and come to very different conclusions. They can use the same data and interview the same people. They can use
the same standards of reason and be of equal intelligence. Still they may come to
different, perhaps opposite, opinions and be absolutely convinced that those who
disagree with them are wrong. Such informed yet conflicting opinions are based
on the fact that people deeply hold different sets of complex, value-laden ideas
about the nature of the world and the human condition: the way that things are
supposed to be.

People use these fundamental notions to interpret all new situations that arise.
Academics talk about paradigms and theoretical interpretations and scholars are
taught to be aware of their influence on the construction of new theories. This same
situation is true of all interpreters, but most people are unaware of the force of paradigms on their opinions of world events. Since ethnicity, class, religion, and region
influence the learning of values and manners of thinking, it is not surprising that
similar people hold similar perspectives.

In this book, we call these differing sets of interpretive ideas *alternative perspectives,* and we will examine the most prominent among them for each major issue discussed in Chapters 3–9: cultural diversity, economic development, ecology, and peace and war. The task is *not* to judge the perspectives in terms of which ones are "right" or "wrong," but to see how and why sensible people approach the issues differently. In this chapter on cultural diversity, we explore three alternative perspectives: *global unity, state primacy*, and *cultural pluralism.*

GLOBAL UNITY

Individuals and groups who believe in the concept of *global unity* assert, as the term suggests, that the division of the world into specific political or economic entities is outmoded. They see the contemporary world as one in which all peoples are joined in complex interactions and where all economies are tied to a true *world* market. It is just as easy to purchase a Coca-Cola in South Africa as it is in Hong Kong or Chicago. Americans wear clothes made in Mexico and India, while Mexicans and Indians watch American television programs. Development projects in Brazil and Indonesia affect the world's climate. Inventions and disasters in one part of the world are quickly felt in others. In these circumstances, according to those who believe in global unity, the only logical course is to encourage the further political integration of the world's people.

The question is *how* to further unification along. One response is that it is already happening, as the preceding examples suggest. Other examples include cultures that are becoming universally understood. They are the leaders who set the standards in global affairs. More isolated cultures are less significant and the individuals who identify with them must change or continue to be insignificant. An extreme goal of such a policy would be a world governed by "superior" cultures and populated by people who culturally resemble their most successful inhabitants.

Emphases on external, and often involuntary, change and industrial states are fundamental to this perspective. Societies, or ethnicities, based on a gathering-and-hunting, tribal, or primitive state organization are outdated. Efforts focused on improving the lot of such people without changing their lifestyle to fit into the world system could be deleterious to them.

By viewing isolated cultures through the global unity perspective as evolutionary anachronisms, one can consider any encouragement of their continuation as going against historical logic and condemning individuals to primitive and hard lives. Inherently this belief is a modern version of Social Darwinism, which was influential on American and European thought a century ago. Social Darwinism evoked the concept of "the survival of the fittest" and applied it to cultural evolution. Those cultures that were more complex had proven themselves the fittest. This logic was used to justify colonialism by arguing that the colonial powers were bringing civilization to the less fortunate. Now it has evolved to assert that the contemporary world powers are best suited to lead all peoples toward a successful world civilization.

Assimilation

One common view held by advocates of global unity is that the more backward cultures will disappear when individuals recognize the benefits of a more advanced culture. This belief has formed the social policies of many colonial states. Called *assimilation,* it holds that, over time, people will ultimately give up the customs of an inferior culture to become members of a superior one.

Many social policies are built on the awareness that the road to assimilation is dependent on education, especially of a culture's youth. But those who do not support assimilationist policies are particularly opposed to this aspect of them. Many indigenous people complain that the national education policies of the dominant culture constitute a form of *ethnocide.* The aboriginal people of Australia, for example, have been very vocal on this issue. Thousands of aboriginal children were removed from their families at very early ages and sent to boarding schools where they were punished for speaking their own languages or practicing their own religions. The curriculum was created for Anglo-Australians and based on the understandings of European heritage. When the "educated" aboriginal children returned home, they were strangers to their families and their cultures.

Interestingly, there is a liberal idea at the core of the assimilationist agenda: It assumes that "primitive" people are capable of being educated and of becoming a part of the modern world. Their backwardness is viewed as being based on their limited knowledge, rather than on an innate limitation. This basic idea has existed throughout much of the history of the United States, not only in its Native American policy, but in immigration theory as well. The ideal of the American "melting pot," even if it is not a reality, is assimilationist in nature. It promotes an image of the United States as welcoming people from all nations, though immigrants are expected give up their previous ways in order to become Americans. Thus, while, new cultures flavor the melting pot, at the core it remains American. The contemporary political debate over the possibility of mandating English as an official US language can be seen as a confrontation over assimilation.

Acculturation

Conceptually related to assimilation, *acculturation* holds that individuals will modify their cultural upbringing in order to adapt to a new culture. They will not give up their original culture entirely, but they will adjust it to fit the new circumstances. Assuming the desirability of a global culture, it follows that people wish to take on many of the superior traits they find in people of other cultures. While education plays a role in acculturation, it need not be forced and it need not replace the original culture completely. The idea is that minority groups, First Nations, and non-industrial nations should be "allowed" to learn the political and economic systems of the successful states and the ideals that support them. Family organizations, art, religion, dress, and other cultural elements that do not (in theory) impede modernization need not change for acculturation to succeed.

Acculturation to the material traits of a popular culture can be ubiquitous, as the international recognition of Coca-Cola and McDonald's demonstrates. The spread of Christianity, Buddhism, and Islam throughout the world through mission-ization, for example, is more comprehensive. However, acculturation does not aim to create an absolute copy of a cultural model. McDonald's in Israel serves kosher hamburgers, and significant variations in Islamic and Christian practices exist in different areas of the world. Therefore, new ideas are accepted but in a way that make sense with the existing ideas.

Syncretism

Syncretism refers to the mixing of cultural ideas from different sources in order to create a new reality. The religions of rural Latin America, which merge the identities of traditional local gods with those of Roman Catholic saints, are an example. The processionals in celebration of saint days in Mayan towns echo the ancient religious practices as much as the Christian ones.

However, syncretism is not always acceptable to those who champion acculturation in its other forms. Pope John Paul II has preached vehemently against modifications of the teachings of the Catholic Church while supporting the use of local languages in church services. Those who believe in acculturation in the service of the centrality of superior cultures require that the key items of the superior culture be accepted. To the pope, of course, that essential item is the religious understanding of the Catholic Church.

Subjugation

Subjugation is an extreme authoritarian approach to unifying cultures that is rarely advocated today. It proposes that people of superior groups should control the lives of people of inferior ones. Policies of subjugation reject an active, or at least internally originated, role for members of the weaker society. As justification, it assumes that the individuals of inferior societies are themselves inferior. Racism can flourish in this atmosphere. Social practices such as nineteenth-century American slavery and twentieth-century genocide in Nazi Germany, Rwanda, and Burundi were justified by practitioners using themes of racial superiority and policies of subjugation.

Paternalism

Those advocating any of the solutions suggested for assuring the unification of world cultures often run into accusations of *paternalism,* which literally means "acting as a father." More broadly, it means taking a superior position over others and trying to control their actions. It is done "for their own good" because the superior figure "knows better." The protected individuals or groups are treated like children. Outlawing the handling of snakes in the rituals of the Holiness churches of the American Southeast can be viewed as an example of paternalism. The larger society, which does not accept this biblical interpretation of snakes handling, dictates that those who do recognize snake handling as an important religious act are wrong, and endangering themselves, and must be stopped for their own protection. Paternalism, itself, is not illegal, but it is rarely welcomed by those treated as inferior.

STATE PRIMACY

While the *state primacy* perspective of the world does not define the superiority of types of systems, it does privilege a specific type of political organization: The state is viewed as the most important unit for both national and international interaction. According to those who hold this perspective, the primary political identity for all groups and individuals should be as citizens of the state of their birth or adoption. The state primacy perspective does not argue for universal similarity in cultures or centralized power between states. In fact, it gives states a tremendous amount of autonomy in deciding the nature of their own realms. Its vision of the ideal world, then, includes many different states, each of which determines the ethnic policies of its residents.

National identity that is the same as state identity is not as common as many Americans would assume. The concepts *nation* and *state* are quite different. A nation is made up of a group of people who identify themselves as a unified and unique culture. A state, in contrast, is a complex political structure that may include citizens from a variety of nations. When the Navajo in the United States, the Cree in Canada, or the Yanamamo in Brazil call themselves "nations," they use the term in its proper form. In fact, most indigenous peoples are, as the term *First Nations* suggests, real nations. Koreans, for example, control the ethnically homogeneous states of the Republic of Korea and the Democratic People's Republic of Korea. The nation of Korea is larger than the two states, however, and people who identify as Koreans live around the world. Koreans who are citizens of either Korean state are governed by the laws of their own state and other Koreans are not. In some states, such as the United States, many Koreans are full American citizens who maintain a Korean identity; in others, such as Japan, Koreans are identified as "not Japanese."

Can people be members of more than one nation or fit into two or more cultures? The philosophy of the modern state relies on the belief that people can indeed do both. Is the American citizen of Korean heritage part of the American nation? If the answer were no, then the United States would be a state without a nationality, which clearly is not the case. Americans, as a national group, share values that throughout the world are recognized as defining the American personality. At the center of these values is the admiration of the strong individual. Children are taught to be independent. They honor their families but are reared to leave them and set up independent homes and lives as adults. Material gain and competitive success gained through fair play are parents' goals for their children.

American popular culture ennobles heroes in films, particularly the action hero who single-handedly overcomes evil and reestablishes good. This hero sets his or her own rules and does not slavishly follow a society's dictates. Cooperation stands in the background and appears only when the marginalized police, family, or sidekicks do menial tasks to allow the hero to perform the important work. All glory goes to the individual.

Even in political issues, the politician who plays the hero role by exuding confidence, being glib, and offering simple solutions in election campaigns is seen as more potent and electable than a thoughtful politician who attempts to explain real complexities. The core political values of "life, liberty, and the pursuit of happiness" are defined in terms of the individual, and it has been individual rights that many thousands of Americans from hundreds of ethnicities have died.

Within the reality of this common culture, American nationality is also defined as a mixture of other cultures, each of which has added its own character to the whole. Even if it is not a true melting pot, America has been described as a mosaic of different color tiles or a lumpy stew with multiple ingredients. While the United States is one of a few states that defines itself as multiethnic, many other states in the modern world are also multiethnic in composition, if not in ideal.

Patriotism

From the state primacy perspective there is no inherent evil in the multiethnic state as long as the state identity takes priority over ethnic identities. Patriotism, the placing of one's primary loyalty in the state, is the real key. As long as individuals function first as Brazilians, Indonesians, or Russians, especially in issues of state interest, the interests of state primacy prevail. During World War II, for example, Native Americans volunteered for military service in the United States at a far greater rate than other Americans. Their loyalties to their own First Nations did not inhibit their American patriotism. In fact, the United States benefited in many ways from their cultural skills. The history of the Navajo "code talkers" of that war illustrates this brilliantly. Navajo soldiers were assigned to communications and sent classified messages to one another in the Navajo (Dene) language. German code breakers were never able to decipher these communications because they were not true codes and the Germans did not recognize them as a language. These Navajo soldiers thus performed unique patriotic duties as citizens of the United States.

While advocates of the state primacy point of view would likely accept and applaud examples like that of the Navajo code talkers, they maintain a deep distrust of the power of ethnicity, viewing it as weakening patriotism and creating rifts in the state system. Numerous cases can be cited to support this concern: Recent civil wars based on ethnicity have been fought in countries from Bosnia to Liberia; ethnic violence, such as terrorist incidents of the Tamil of Sri Lanka or the Irish Republican Army, and political crises, such as the threat of the Quebeçois to break up Canada, have redefined their states. These and other situations threaten the primacy of a state.

State Power

The solutions to these problems lie with the states themselves, according to this perspective. The state has the right, and perhaps the duty, to defend itself from internal and external threats. Issues concerning the distribution of rights and privileges between types of people within the state must be decided within the state. Given the nature of the state, the power to decide such issues resides in an elite group with control of governmental offices. The fact that the elite group is often composed of individuals from similar ethnic background is sometimes considered unfortunate, but it is considered unimportant compared to the need for state security. It is also asserted that the situation is best understood from the local perspective and that outsiders cannot understand the real circumstances.

Critique from the Global Unity Perspective

Advocates of global unity reject the state primacy perspective on two grounds: first, because states are artificial constructs based on historical accident rather than natural groupings; and second, because most world problems are global in scope rather than confined to the local interests of states. Cooperation is thus negotiated rather than mandated in this perspective.

A particularly troublesome issue that reappears around much of the world is the position of minority groups that straddle around state boundaries. In the state primacy perspective, the state contends that the interests of ethnic minorities are secondary in importance to those of the state. Members of the same ethnicity in other states are seen as different people with different citizenship. The Inuit, as noted earlier, live in a contiguous circumpolar land that covers four states. They have a national identity as Inuit and national identities as Russian, American, Canadian, and Danish. In the latter identities, they have clear administrative rights and privileges, but in the former, they do not. General Inuit issues have been championed by newly formed circumpolar and First Nation organizations. The fact that international agencies including the United Nations welcome these new cultural organizations with observer status, and that international meetings are covered with extensive press coverage, are seen by state nationalist proponents as threats to the important primacy of the state system.

Global unity advocates see a daunting problem when state nationalists put their faith in the rectitude of nation-states. They do not always seem worthy. There is no mechanism, in this view, to deal with states that harm groups of people living at their borders. There are no established ways of dealing with human rights issues in states that do not abide by international standards. If a state defines the slavery, murder, or active discrimination of a particular group as acceptable, can outsiders legitimately provide help to the victims?

The recent case of *apartheid* in South Africa provides a clear example. Here, a numerical majority in the state, the original inhabitants were legally defined as inferior and had all aspects of their lives severely circumscribed. Near-universal condemnation (supplemented by boycotts) was directed at South Africa; however, because of the nature of the state system, direct action was not immediately effective. If state primacy was absolute, even the boycotts were inappropriate. Many nations, including China and the former Soviet Union made just such assertions when other nations condemned their internal actions. The example of South Africa can be used to justify the stand of state primacy as well. It was largely the internal changes made by South Africans themselves that overthrew the internationally despised practice of apartheid.

CULTURAL PLURALISM

Whereas the advocates of global unity prioritize a united world and those of state primacy prioritize the state, the advocates of *cultural pluralism* prioritize the autonomous rights of individual cultures, regardless of their power. In this view, nations, cultures, ethnic groups, and indigenous peoples are the units of interest.

Proponents argue that people identify with these groups and, if one believes in human equality, then these groups too must be equal. All recognize, of course, that such equality does not exist in political or economic terms. Rather than seeing ethnic pluralism as a validation of evolutionary failure (as followers of Social Darwinism do), cultural pluralists see this as the result of a particular people's history, which is set in a world of institutionalized inequality. They argue that the privileging of some cultures over others should not give the system ethical authority.

Tolerance

Cultural pluralism mandates *tolerance* of cultural differences without ethnocentric judgment. The fact that people are different is acceptable. People whose cultures are similar are no better or worse than those whose cultures are very different. All cultures must be granted respect and their people, human rights. To tolerate some custom or belief is not necessarily to like it or adopt it. A Jew can tolerate the practice of Christianity in the community without converting to that faith and vice versa. People of any faith can believe in the superiority of their own religion, but they can also tolerate others believing differently. A more difficult question might be raised when the basic values of the religions are inherently in conflict. Can a Christian tolerate the practice of Satanism in the community? In the United States, the legal answer is still yes but the emotional response of individuals in such a situation is often a strong no.

One question of tolerance, of course, is at what point it stops. As with the argument about cultural relativism, tolerance of the intolerable cannot be moral. Two areas of contention inevitably arise for advocates of cultural pluralism. One issue arises frequently when the rights of one culture are seen as limiting the rights of another. When the Hopi and Navajo in the United States, or Jews, Arabs, and Christians in Jerusalem claim religious rights over the same lands, what is the culturally diverse solution? Outsiders might believe that a compromise that dictates sharing would be fair, but the participants in the dispute might violently disagree and complain that the presence of the others corrupts the sacred area.

A similar dilemma is faced when the rights of one culture inadvertently harm others. Many simple agricultural cultures practice slash-and-burn agriculture. They burn the remnants of last year's fields in order to fertilize them for the next crops. Mayan farmers in Yucatan do this yearly. This process creates a great deal of smoke for several weeks. More recent residents of the area, including those who run the tourist areas of the Yucatan, feel the fires are deleterious to their health and economic way of life. Globally, some environmentalists find the mass of slash-and-burn fires harmful, causing smoke in the atmosphere and adding to deforestation throughout the planet. The Mayans, and others, find this economic system crucial to their survival in their cultures. Still others find it detrimental beyond the confines of Mayan lands. Where does tolerance lie?

The other issue is equally difficult. People ask if there are moral truths that transcend tolerance. In fact, few ideals beyond the highly abstract value of human life appear in all cultures and, even this, is interpreted in different ways. Morality is an aspect of cultural learning. Therefore, any definition of what should be universal morality is inherently ethnocentric since it is based on the author's cultural truths. However, to reject the idea of universal standards of morality is to accept anything as proper as long as it is done in other societies that approve of it. It would be a rejection of the idea of human rights. Neither stance in the extreme is reasonable. Fortunately, for advocates of the cultural pluralism perspective, most cases do not exist at the extremes.

Diversity Within States Individuals who hold a cultural pluralism perspective tend to advocate the acceptance of diversity both within states and between states. In the former they come into conflict with advocates of both other perspectives. Those interpreting the world through the lens of global unity hold that the superior cultures of any state and the world should dictate to, and change, inferior cultures. Those viewing the world through the state primacy perspective, in contrast, hold that diversity within a state is the business of that state. The view of cultural diversity on this issue is that states must accommodate the cultural differences within their borders. State autonomy is not sacrosanct when human lives are at stake. Mistreatment of ethnic minorities is a human rights issue and must be addressed in the domestic and the international arenas. Actions such as boycotts, trade sanctions, and invasions are acceptable in order to protect cultural groups. The use of UN peacekeeping forces in Somalia and Bosnia are acceptable breaches of state sovereignty because of the severity of the situation on innocent inhabitants. The lack of international action to protect the victims of the Holocaust in Nazi Germany is often cited as an international shame that must never be repeated. This extreme object lesson energizes international campaigns against a variety of concerns from female circumcision to rainforest destruction.

Advocates of cultural diversity perspectives strongly support the rights of indigenous peoples to establish legal rights including autonomy, self-governance over their own affairs, and even semi-sovereignty. They advocate for new forms of organizations that vary radically from the historic reservations or homelands that have been assigned to indigenous people in the Americas, Australia, and Africa. In reservations, the power of administration was held strongly in the hands of individuals appointed by and accountable to the dominant state and, in some cases, the movement of the residents was restricted outside of the reserve. The new vision of homelands, however, clearly challenges the sovereignty of the state itself by allowing internal power to those with distinct national identities. Advocates claim, however, that this form of recognition of indigenous status actually strengthens the state by negating the threat of internal discord.

Diversity Between States Diversity between states is also celebrated by the cultural pluralism perspective. The fact that different states have different cultures allows for a richer variety of opportunities for all people. The opposite—a world assimilated into one culture—would be dull and relatively colorless, given the loss of the vast spectrum of arts, languages, dress, and architecture. Even scientific discovery, long assumed to reside solely in Western education, is enlivened with local knowledge drawn from traditional cultures. Searches for "new" animals in Asia and drugs from "new" plants in the Amazon are led, in part, by holders of indigenous knowledge who have long known of these animals and plants. In fact, a new legal question of ethnic intellectual property rights, or the right to this knowledge, has arisen since these discoveries have led to large industrial profits for those far from the site. Protection of such diversity of knowledge can be vital for the solution of future global problems. All states, then, should be encouraged to support fully all the cultures within their borders. International agencies should provide money for this purpose if the state is too poor to do so itself. Further communication between states that broadens knowledge of these cultures also should be encouraged.

Relationships between states need to accommodate the cultural differences that might arise. Acknowledgment of differences and similarities is encouraged. Problems that arise from clashing differences must be mediated or resolved. Gender differences, for example, can create embarrassing problems. When Salote, the queen of Tonga, arrived for the coronation of Queen Elizabeth II in 1953, she was featured in newspapers around the world. Not only was she the sole female-ruling monarch attending as part of the commonwealth royalty, she was also physically quite imposing. The six foot, three-inch queen did not seem comfortable in the fashion shows and luncheons that other queens attended. As a woman, however, she was not fully welcomed at the political meetings that were otherwise male affairs. She simply did not fit the English gender expectations of the 1950s. The ideal of acceptance of cultural differences between states can conflict with internal cultural beliefs.

Those who hold a cultural pluralism position to its extreme often are opposed to the state as an institution. Since the nature of the state is inherently hierarchical, they argue, if equality is a goal, the state, itself, is part of the problem. The natural unit of human society, they might continue, is the culture, not the state. Therefore, a world made up of smaller, autonomous cultures might be the next logical stage of human evolution. This view does not address the success of large stable states such as the United States, where citizens share a national, American identity but differ in individual ethnic identities. In some areas where state nationalities have not strongly developed, however, the goal of ethnic division appears to be happening. The breakdown of the Soviet Union, and parts of Eastern Europe into smaller states roughly along previously held national lines caught many who thought the state unit was secure by surprise. The mixture of ethnicities in states of Africa whose borders were created during colonialism for the benefit of Europeans, rather than Africans, have caused tensions that may produce future state divisions. The same appears possible in Canada, where votes by residents of Quebec for an independent state status grow with each referendum. If not accommodated within a state, powerful ethnic minorities appear ready to split off on their own.

One other possibility in a world of cultural pluralism is that members of the same cultures, isolated in different states, may join into a new state. The Jewish state of Israel is an extreme example, where members of the same religion created a homeland in an area of their heritage but largely not their current residence. The problems of relationships with the existing residents of the area hardly make this an ideal example of putting the cultural diversity perspective into effect. Other areas of the world, such as Amazonia, the Arctic, and Kurdistan where the majority of the people in each region have cultural unity (although intersected by state borders), seem more conducive to such new state creation. Even at their most idealistic, current states are unlikely to be eager to give up the lands in these potentially mineral-rich regions to ethnic groups that appear economically weaker and militarily unable to protect themselves. The ideal of cultural pluralists, which has not yet been reached, is a world where people do not attack others for land or economic gain.

Critiques from the Global Unity and State Primacy Perspectives

Advocates of global unity see the cultural pluralism perspective as virtually the opposite of their own. In their view global problems are universal and should be solved in a unified world. This perspective breaks the world into thousands of groups of people who all have unique interests. The possibilities for disputes are large, with no mechanism for solving them. This perspective also values all cultures as equal. Global unity proponents assert that some ways of life are more efficient or moral than others and those should be preserved while others should be absorbed.

The state primacy view would also reject the cultural tolerance perspective. It sees a world of thousands of small interest groups as unworkable. The system of the state, it asserts, is necessary to resolve problems in a fair and peaceful way. In the state, all cultural groups know the rules, and between states, governments are rational advocates in international debates. Disagreements between ethnic groups, without state intervention, can only lead to turmoil. The state is thus viewed as the defender of weak ethnic groups.

Synthesis

While the three perspectives discussed in this chapter are presented as if they are isolated, individuals can, to some extent, maintain ideas drawn from all of them. Synthesis is possible and, perhaps, sensible. Some people believe in the importance of human equality and personal choice but, at the same time, reason that strong state systems are necessary and can grant group rights in "the real world." Other people believe that the future will bring some form of political administration that unifies the peoples of the world. Global unity theorists can hold radically different views on human cultural diversity, however. Some picture a unified world in which the superior culture has prevailed and displaced all variations of the inferior type. Others picture quite the opposite: a world composed of small, independent, and equal cultural units that work together for a common good through a cooperative administrative model. Basically, however, the three perspectives presented here are common ways that modern scholars and other thoughtful individuals organize their views of human diversity.

CULTURAL DIVERSITY PERSPECTIVES APPLIED TO NUNAVUT

Matrix 3.1 summarizes the main points discussed in this chapter. To review, Nunavut is the name of the 770,000-square-mile eastern division of the Northwest Territories in Canada that will become an independent territory in mid-1999. The vast majority

Matrix 3.1
CULTURAL DIVERSITY PERSPECTIVES

	GLOBAL UNITY	STATE PRIMACY	CULTURAL PLURALISM
GOAL	Unified world system	State sovereignty	Cultural autonomy
KEY CONCEPTS	Assimilation	Patriotism	Tolerance diversity
STRATEGY	Political integration	Strengthen present system	Increase power of ethnic groups
SEES STATES AS:	Artificial constructs	Important to world peace	Artificial constructs
SEES CURRENT SYSTEM AS:	Overly differentiated	Good	Overly centralized

of the population is Inuit and 18 percent of the land of Nunavut will belong to them under a related but separate land claims agreement. Use of the rest of the land of the territory for traditional subsistence is guaranteed, as is a percentage of the profits for any mineral development from Nunavut Crown lands. All residents of Nunavut—Inuit and other Canadians—will have equal legal standing in the territory, but population ratios, official language designation, and cultural traditions will likely favor Inuit leadership.

The development of Nunavut is a major shift in the map and organization of Canada, and it stands as an experiment in designing a new state model for the twenty-first century. The status of Greenland, in Denmark, with its large Inuit population, can be seen as a predecessor to Nunavut but not a direct model. Nunavut is a contiguous part of a troubled state and its success is important to the long-term success of Canada. Nunavut will, therefore, be part of the international news for years to come. Different perspectives will create different analyses of the same situation.

A View from the Global Unity Perspective

Clearly, this experiment is rash and unwise. It further differentiates people rather than bringing them together into a global culture. It privileges people who are different rather than the mainstream culture. Also, rather than encouraging the Inuit to progress, it rewards them for their backwardness.

While few in this era of polite talk would speak as directly as the polemic above, the underlying attitude is widespread. The Inuit, especially those who continue to engage in traditional subsistence work, are often seen as quaintly primitive. They cause little trouble so there is no great campaign against them, but they do not seem to be full members of the modern world. Their language, Inuktitut, is seen, like Latin, as a historic language that no longer has a purpose on the international scene. The Nunavut plan to use Inuktitut as an official language would be interpreted as a crude method to keep the uninitiated out. English or French, depending on the inclination of the analyst, would be the only logical language of Canada. Encouraging hunting and fishing by ensuring Inuit free access to all animal habitats would be viewed as delaying the Inuits entry into industrial employment.

Acculturation is slow and selective in this situation and assimilation is discouraged. Certainly, leaders of the new territory will need to learn how to deal effectively with both government paperwork and non-Inuit elsewhere in Canada, and a good deal of Western training is envisioned as part of the transition. Others, however, should have less pressure to change. Additionally, and not to the liking of those holding this perspective, some acculturation of Euro-Canadians to Inuit culture seems likely in Nunavut. Those at the extreme of the global unity perspective who look favorably on subjugation would find this situation unacceptable—an unnecessary experiment in government that is apt to be used as a precedent for still more change empowering "inferior" people.

The problems that created Nunavut are not seen as problems from this perspective. Nunavut is, in the old cliché, fixing something that isn't broken. The troubles that individual Inuit legitimately face can best be solved with education for increased acculturation. Inuktituit language and culture study should be discouraged and governmental aid should be limited to those who live in towns and send their children to school. When enough Inuit obtain the proper skills and goals, there is no reason an Inuk cannot lead the territory or province. This leader, of course, would work for his or her people by promoting the same interests that any good leader of Euro-Canadian heritage would advocate.

A View from the State Primacy Perspective

Clearly, this experiment is extreme and more than a bit dangerous. It decentralizes power from the traditional government elite to the periphery, but, it does so in a manner that is established within the existing framework of the state. In the short run, it may help maintain the integrity of the state of Canada.

The Canadian form of government is far more decentralized than that of the United States. Canadian provinces have far more power relative to the central government than do US states. Danger to the sovereignty of the state, then, is found in the lessening of the power of Ottawa over the provinces and, perhaps, the territories. This is being seen in Nunavut. Canadian authorities have allotted Inuit representatives one-half of the seats on a number of administrative boards generally controlled by federal officials. Also, a good part of the land was removed from Crown control and all Crown land has been open to various uses by the Inuit. Control over mineral development is somewhat circumscribed by the claims of the Inuit.

A second concern, particularly acute in Canada, is the privileging of cultural groups. Given the history of French-English disputation in this nation and the increasing pressure for autonomy in Quebec, the public recognition of Inuit culture, as worthy of special status seems likely to affect Quebec's demands for autonomy.

Certainly, Ottawa would argue that Nunavut as a territory is given no more cultural privilege than other areas. Land claim settlements are separate from the territorial organization and they are based in prior First Nation claims. Nunavut territory is open to all Canadians, just as the Yukon and Quebec are. Language use, like in Quebec, recognizes majority use. Many Quebeçois advocates, however, see their issue as primary and due for first settlement.

State nationalists would applaud several aspects of the Nunavut plan. First, of course, it is built on the existing state structure. It creates a new territory, not a new form of organization. That this territory looks different than the others is true, but at its heart it is Canadian. It is open to all Canadians for residence and citizenship. In this way, it does not mandate a permanent dominance by Inuit residents. While the population remains heavily Inuit, it stands to reason that they will dominate, but if that changes in the future, then so will the power base. A contrast with the demands of Quebec is clear in this and might be suggested by state nationalists as a new model.

Nunavut allows the Inuit to be themselves while also recognizing the nationality of other Canadians. It does, however, divide the Inuit from Nunavut from the Inuit in other provinces. Settlements for the Inuit in Quebec, Labrador, and the western Northwest Territories are legally separate from those for these Inuit. Likewise, the Inuit of Greenland and Alaska have agreements of their own. The likelihood of a circumpolar nation or even an Inuit nation as a political reality seems dim. Nunavut might be different but it demonstrates a loyalty to the state.

From the state sovereignty position, the solution to the problems that led to Nunavut can be found within the Canadian system. The territory, either as the existing Northwest Territory or the proposed Nunavut, should be run as territories are today. The nature of the population may flavor the society but the law should not privilege any particular citizens. Rather than the Inuit language, English, the major language of Canada, should prevail here, although French, Inuktituit, and other languages should be allowed as second languages. Canada firmly retains control over this in Nunavat, like in all territories, and the Inuit, as citizens of Canada, should prosper. With these corrections, this solution should stand as a model throughout Canada.

A View from the Cultural Pluralism Perspective

Nunavut is an exciting experiment and one that is long overdue. Recognition of the special status of First Nations should be pursued throughout the Americas. It is unfortunate, however, that clearer, more permanent sovereignty is not vested in the Inuit and that other Inuit cannot join in a broadly Inuit national political entity.

At the heart of Nunavut is the recognition of the importance of Inuit culture to the people within that culture. Nunavut recognizes the right of the Inuit to pursue culturally meaningful subsistence activities and to adapt whatever Western customs they find meaningful. In other words, it values the traditional culture but does not confine the people to an unchanging system.

The Inuit were active in creating Nunavut politically. The fight for the establishment of the new territory and the land claims settlement took two decades of work and compromise. While in the end they did not receive all they asked for, their willingness to negotiate a final agreement led to the creation of the new settlement. A belief in cultural pluralism includes a trust that the desires of members of the culture are what are right for them. Paternalism should have no place in the analysis and, therefore, Nunavut must be defended as an Inuit creation.

While cultural pluralists will defend Nunavut, they may privately have some concerns. Nunavut may benefit the Inuit of the territory and be harmful to other First Nation people in Canada. The question of the future of the First Nations in western Northwest Territories is still open. While land settlements can be finalized, political power in the west is more problematic. Dene, Metis, and Inuit remain important populations there but even combined they do not have a solid majority of votes. Yellowknife, the capital, has a reputation of being a Euro-Canadian stronghold in the north and there is no reason to assume this would change with the loss of the Nunavut population. The future of Inuit in Quebec is also at issue. If Quebec leaves the confederation what happens to Inuit residents? Nunavut will complicate this problem.

Finally, there are concerns about the future of Nunavut itself. There is no guarantee of Inuit hegemony and no clear mechanism in place to ensure it. Rules for developing the legislature may well include clauses for length of residency and language restrictions to discourage outsiders from taking over this mineral-rich region. The development of the government structure is a profoundly important task that may well be the key to the success of Nunavut.

The solutions to Inuit problems should rest in the hands of the Inuit with the support of friends on the outside. Nunavut must be supported and help must be forthcoming to the other First Nations of the north. The successes and failures of Nunavut should be widely known far beyond the borders so that other First Nations around the globe can benefit from its experience. Nunavut is a culturally defined territory in a complex state and it must be nurtured.

As in all things, history will record the benefits of Nunavut for the Inuit and all Canadians. The future of the territory is yet to be told, but that it will be analyzed from a variety of perspectives is inevitable.

TERMS AND CONCEPTS

acculturation

alternative perspectives

apartheid

assimilation

ethnocide

national identity

paternalism

racism

subjugation

syncretism

tolerance

DISCUSSION QUESTIONS

1. This chapter poses an important question: Where does tolerance stop? Discuss how perspectives and cultural issues decide an individual's answer to this question?
2. If there were one world culture, what would it be? Who would decide? What would happen to those who disagreed with that culture?
3. If you were an official of the Canadian government, what position would you take on Nunavut? Why?
4. Can excess patriotism ever be a problem in a state? Why, or why not?
5. Consider the concepts of assimilation, acculturation, and ethnocide. The United States is a nation built on an immigrant ideal. How have these concepts been used in America?

RESEARCH PROJECTS

1. Choose one example of colonialism from history and use the perspectives discussed in this chapter to analyze the colonial situation at the time. Which perspective prevailed historically?
2. Take a contemporary case of ethnic dispute, such as the one in Northern Ireland, in French and English Canada, or in Cyprus. Using the concepts and perspectives offered in this chapter, explain the dispute, describe the situation surrounding it, and evaluate the proposed solutions.
3. Choose one perspective discussed in this chapter and apply it to three contemporary situations. Show how it works. Do any new problems appear?
4. Choose two front-page stories from today's newspaper. Learn the history of the issues and apply the alternative perspectives presented in this chapter. What perspectives do the reporters take on the issues?
5. Review a current political or economic issue in the news, such as international fishing or whaling treaties. What cultural issues are important in this seemingly noncultural topic?

INTERNET RESOURCES

Cultural Survival: *http://www.cs.org* This nonprofit organization focuses on the problems of indigenous peoples and oppressed ethnic minorities. Its homepage provides updates on its projects and links to other sites of interest.

Native Web: *http://www.nativeweb.org* This is a primary resource center for those interested in issues concerning Native Americans. It also maintains the Abya Yala Net relating to South and Meso American Indians at this site.

Nunavut Planning Commission: *http://www.npc.nunavut.ca* The homepage for the commission provides updated information on the formation of Nunavut in English and Inuit languages.

4

Economic Development

Modern technology offers the tantalizing prospect of enabling the world to produce enough food, shelter, clothes, clean water, and basic medical care for every person on the planet. Sadly, while this capability exists, its promise has not become a reality at the turn of the twenty-first century. Out of the world's population of well over five billion, about two billion people lead debilitating lives of desperation on the margin of survival. They seem to inhabit a different world from the planet's minority who enjoy a comfortable, consumer-goods lifestyle.

This chapter offers general explanations as to why a wide and growing gap exists between the world's rich and poor. This reality runs contrary to the image implied by *development*, which is supposed to provide an answer to the problem of poverty. Development is an economic process intended to enable increasing numbers of people to produce enough wealth to support an acceptable quality of life. Unfortunately, for those attempting to understand the process, this seemingly simple, straightforward definition masks major differences in strategy and in what an "acceptable lifestyle" actually means.

The dominant interpretation of development assumes that it means achieving a modern machine-based lifestyle, one measured by ownership of televisions, automobiles, and appliances, and characterized by plenty of food and leisure time. Yet an increasing number of people are adopting a different approach to development, one that emphasizes the fact that hundreds of millions of people on Earth have little hope of becoming part of a heavily industrialized society or of experiencing a consumer-goods lifestyle. These people must fulfill their basic needs for adequate shelter, food, clothes, and medical care by improving the productivity of their agricultural-based economies.

The industrial development strategy requires extensive economic growth. Such growth produces the extra earnings needed to invest in machines, the fossil fuel energy to run them, educated people to fix them, and the constant flow of new technology to update them. With industrial development, earnings from economic growth must be ongoing because energy and new technology costs continue as well. The alternative approach to development, however, does not accept economic growth as essential. It defines the process as one of "improvement" and "enrichment," of leading to a better life. Thus, achieving an acceptable lifestyle can mean having enough of life's basics without becoming part of a modern consumer-oriented, energy-guzzling, machine-dependent economy.

The two development strategies, one calling for economic growth and the other for fulfilling basic needs, propose different answers to the problems of the world's poor. Yet the adherents of both strategies decry the chronic, dispiriting, debilitating poverty that can kill hope and create desperation, disease, and dehumanization. One pitfall in analyzing development issues among the world's poor is that relevant information can seem too abstract, statistical, and unrelated to the actual lives of real people. Therefore, our discussion begins by introducing an individual whose lifestyle represents the majority of the world's population.

> Meet Lucia. She has good looks, not the prettiness of youth, but long-lasting, pleasant features with the high cheekbones typical of Andean peoples. It takes only a brief conversation to gain respect for this Quechua Indian peasant woman. She has a quiet confidence and speaks articulately. Choosing her words thoughtfully, she seems self-assured and refined. In her, life's hard experiences have produced a reflective composure.
>
> Lucia, her husband, and two children live in one of the farming sectors outside of Mollepata, a town about 9,000 feet high in Peru's Andes Mountains. Most of the over 900 town residents, and 3,000 people in its surrounding rural sectors, earn a living either directly or indirectly from subsistence agriculture. Potatoes, vegetables, grains, and some livestock are raised on slopes slanting often eight degrees or even more. The potato fields lie at the highest elevations allowing crop cultivation, around 11,000 feet. This food source was cultivated long before Europeans discovered it during their conquest. Dependent on what they raise themselves, Mollepata's residents remember well the drought beginning in 1982, when the seasonal rains did not come. Severe malnutrition was commonplace and starvation for many, but not all, was avoided only by the intervention of international relief agencies.
>
> In the early 1990s, Lucia organized a team from the women's committee in her sector to compete in a planting contest. Fourteen teams, twelve male and two female, entered the contest sponsored by a local non-governmental development organization. It took courage for the women to compete because in Quechua society men are responsible for raising the crops. The contest required three days of work. Not only did the teams plant a crop in their designated area of a large field, but also designed and dug irrigation channels. Lucia's team came in second. Upon receiving the prize of farm hand tools, she noted that her team's performance showed that women can contribute to the incomes of their families.

Lucia and her family are among the approximately three-quarters of the Earth's inhabitants for whom physical survival is a goal, not a given. Yet our short introduction to this peasant woman contradicts the assumption that the poor, out of necessity, always become beaten down, boorish, coarse, or devoid of hope and human feelings. If they can make decisions and meet their physical needs, low-income people can experience meaningful, useful, and fulfilling lives. People who live in poverty statistically may not always think of themselves as poor.

Poverty exists in virtually every country of the world and has common causes wherever it is found. Two worlds exist within the economies of most countries—one of privilege, the other of need. Statistics show that these worlds are moving farther away from each other in terms of living standards and productivity, but they remain intertwined economically in ways that most people do not realize. Even though rich and poor people live within the same state borders, the poor in industrialized countries are often obscured by a large middle class. Still, the overwhelming majority of the world's poor live in what can be called *developing countries* because of their desperate need for a successful development process. Industrial countries, in contrast, have achieved the economic growth it takes to move a majority of their people into the modern middle class. In these states, the poor live in pockets surrounded by people who, in global terms, live as part of the world's rich. Yet since most global poverty is located in states with primarily agricultural-based economies, tackling development as a global issue usually focuses on the situation of states in the *developing world.*

THE DEVELOPING WORLD

Many people first learn of the developing world through pictures of starving children in newspapers or on television. When a natural disaster, war, or both causes large-scale deprivation, the events make the nightly news. Such news stories often leave the impression that relief aid will fill the need until the unusual situation causing the problem works its way through. The episode is treated as an isolated emergency, with little attention focused on mitigating the underlying chronic poverty that allows one crisis to push large populations to the very edge of survival. The unspoken assumption—that such disastrous events are inevitable from time to time—is reinforced.

This sense of inevitability is strengthened by the data on global poverty, which make the problem appear so monumental that people reason nothing can be done to correct it in the foreseeable future. Such news articles typically begin by describing the differences between developing countries and industrialized countries in terms of economic performance. A key comparison uses the *per capita gross national products* of various countries. *Gross national product (GNP)* represents the total value (in US dollars) of all goods and services a country's economy has produced in a given year, including international transactions. The GNP then can be divided by the country's number of people to produce the *per capita GNP.* These admittedly very general figures, called *macroeconomic data,* provide a common measure of the relative wealth produced by each of the world's states.

One popular source of macroeconomic data, including per capita GNP, is the *World Development Report,* a book of comprehensive economic statistics published annually by the World Bank (an international governmental organization described in Chapter 1). The World Bank data shown in Table 4.1 report the per capita GNP for selected countries in 1995. In at least fifteen countries with low-income economies, per capita annual income was $300 or less in 1995. This represents very little purchasing power in any country. Overall, forty-two state economies with over

Table 4.1
PER CAPITA GNP FOR SELECTED STATES
AND GROUPS OF STATES, 1995

		GNP per capita (in US dollars)
Low-Income Economies		
Average:		$430
Examples:	Tanzania	120
	Pakistan	460
	Honduras	600
Lower-Middle-Income Economies		
Average:		$1,670
Examples:	Egypt	790
	Jamaica	1,510
	Poland	2,790
Upper-Middle-Income Economies		
Average:		$4,260
Examples:	South Africa	3,160
	Hungary	4,120
	Greece	8,210
High-Income Economies		
Average:		$24,930
Examples:	New Zealand	14,340
	United States	26,980
	Japan	39,640

Source: World Bank, *World Development Report 1997* (New York: Oxford University Press, 1997).

three billion people were classified as having a low-income economy. High-income economies included twenty-four states with a combined population of over eight hundred million.

Table 4.1 data show the wide disparity in wealth between the world's poorest and richest states. Many states that are classified as "middle income," are actually in the "lower-middle-income" range. While few middle-income states have experienced significant economic growth, Thailand and Botswana each had an average per capita GNP growth rate of over 6 percent a year in 1980–1993, while South Korea averaged over 8 percent during that time (World Bank 1995). Some states, such as Singapore, have moved from middle- to high-income status. While the economic growth of some countries has enabled them to move up in the income ranking, most states with small economies have not been as successful. In fact, a comparison of per capita GNPs shows that the disparity between high- and low- income countries has *increased* over time. Data from the *World Development Report* document the increase (World Bank,

1979, 1995). In 1977, the average GNP per capita was $170 for low-income states, $1,140 for middle-income states, and $6,980 for high-income states. This meant the ratio of low-income to high-income stood at 2.4 percent, while the middle-income ratio was 16 percent. In 1993, the comparable figures were $380 for low-income, $2,480 for middle-income, and $23,090 for high-income states. Thus, the ratio of low to high income dropped to 1.6 percent and that of middle to high-income was 11 percent. These data show that both low- and middle-income countries produced less wealth in relation to that produced by high-income countries in the 1990s than they did in the 1970s.

Yet even in countries with the lowest per capita GNPs, a small percentage of the population maintains a lifestyle similar to that of the majority in high-income countries. Conversely, high-income countries, such as the United States, have pockets of poverty, some of them fairly large. The economic data for Native American communities illustrate this point: Their combined per capita income in 1989 was $8,328, whereas that of the United States as a whole was $20,910. The poverty rate for Native American families was 27 percent in 1989, up from 24 percent in 1979; but the overall US family poverty rate was 10 percent in both 1984 and 1979 (Paisano 1997:2,3).

The *World Development Report* also includes data more directly illustrative of the poverty issue, as indicated in Table 4.2 on page 58. Poor people tend to have less access to nutritious food, medical care, and clean water, which is reflected in life expectancy and infant mortality rates.

Macroeconomic data thus tend to reinforce the unspoken resignation that little can be done to alleviate poverty in the world because the problem seems too large and continues to grow. Such a reaction could be interpreted as a contemporary version of the old aristocratic notion that "the poor will always be with us." To consider their condition as inevitable produces an attitude that is demeaning at best and debilitating at worst.

Using descriptive data to contrast the economic output of poorer countries with richer ones illustrates the problem, but does little to explain why poverty exists. The concept of development, discussed at the beginning of this chapter, is most usefully thought of as a process, not an end result. The key question is whether the process should aim to produce industrialization first, or whether it should initially concentrate on producing more food and other basic needs for daily living.

These objectives may not seem contradictory to development planners until they have to decide which projects to fund with chronically scarce investment resources. Should a large-scale project be built, such as a dam for electricity and irrigation, or should the money be used for projects that would enable villagers themselves to dig wells and irrigation ditches? One requires heavy machinery, the other shovels. If the industrial-based, heavy-machinery strategy is chosen, then those with access to large-scale financing get most of the benefits. If the pick-and-shovel-method is applied, poorer people can both participate in and have ownership of the project.

Both types of projects can be found in most countries, but the debate goes on as to what should be the primary or immediate goal of development—that is,

Table 4.2
LIFE EXPECTANCY AND INFANT MORTALITY RATES
FOR SELECTED STATES AND GROUPS OF STATES, 1995

		Life Expectancy (in years)	Infant Mortality Rate (per 1, 000 live births)
Low-Income Economies			
Average:		63	69
Examples:	Tanzania	51	82
	Pakistan	60	90
	Honduras	67	45
Low-Middle-Income Economies			
Average:		68	41
Examples:	Egypt	63	56
	Jamaica	74	13
	Poland	70	14
Upper-Middle-Income Economies			
Average:		69	35
Examples:	South Africa	64	50
	Mexico	72	33
	Greece	78	8
High-Income Economies			
Average:		77	7
Examples:	New Zealand	76	7
	United States	77	8
	Japan	80	4

Source: World Bank, *World Development Report 1997* (New York: Oxford University Press, 1997).

improving the daily lives of poor people or investing in the means to industrialize. The controversy, in turn, makes the problem of world poverty and the potential solutions to it difficult to analyze.

The dispute over development strategies exists in part because high-income countries historically have achieved their standard of living through industrialization. Thus, for many people planning and administering projects in the developing world, development means industrialization. Machine-based production may be expensive in the short term, but it is viewed as a proven path to reducing poverty in the long term. However, because it requires major economic growth and large-scale investments, advocates of the basic needs strategy alternative are increasing in number. Practitioners, academics, and some government and international aid agency personnel are coming to realize that for the world's poor majorities, the economic growth approach is not working. They focus on the need for a development strategy that will improve poor people's lives now, rather than later, when the industrial profits of the elite "trickle down." *Basic needs* development enables local people to produce more and better food and to provide basic medical care and literacy. These goals, it is argued, can be achieved in agricultural-based economies and are not dependent on industrial technologies.

The ongoing debate between advocates of the two general approaches of development—basic needs versus economic growth—recognizes that the two billion people living in poverty face a set of interrelated problems, which can be summarized as a *cycle of underdevelopment*. The leaders of many low-income countries oppose the use of the word *underdevelopment* arguing that it implies that their societies are "backward." Still, the term aptly summarizes the conditions that keep so many poor people from improving their lives.

Underdevelopment: A Vicious Cycle

As shown in Figure 4.1, a network of four interrelated, mutually reinforcing factors severely inhibit improvement in basic needs or economic growth in low-income and some middle-income countries. Breaking out of the cycle is extremely difficult, such that most low-income countries and communities have not been able to achieve a self-sustaining development process.

Dual Economy   A *dual economy* is one in which a small "modern" elite, comprised of people who live a consumer lifestyle, exists in a society where the vast majority of the population lives in poverty. The elite is composed mostly of large landowners, high-level government officials, a few businesspeople engaged in international trade and finance, and professionals such as physicians. A small middle class also exists, made up mostly of school teachers, managers, shopkeepers, and mid-level government workers. It remains virtually invisible when contrasted with the wealthy elite and the rest of the population, sometimes as high as 70 to 80 percent, who experience a very different way of life. Living in rural areas, most people eat what they grow themselves through backbreaking labor

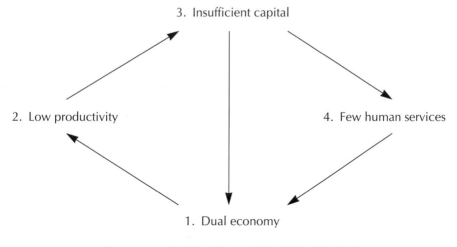

Figure 4.1   CYCLE OF UNDERDEVELOPMENT

performed without machinery. They lack social programs as a fallback in hard times. Economists refer to this lifestyle as *subsistence*, meaning people produce enough to live on and very little more.

Early economic growth development specialists in the 1950 and 1960s assumed a modern manufacturing sector would expand in low-income countries, albeit slowly, as the industrialization process became self-sustaining. As it had in industrialized countries, this process was expected to bring more jobs and educational opportunities to the poor in the subsistence sector. Yet steady growth has not occurred in most of the developing world. On the whole, countries with low per capita GNPs have experienced a few years of some economic growth but not enough to change the structure of their dual economies.

Low Productivity   A dual economy typically has low *productivity*, which economists define as the output of goods and services in relation to the number of work hours used to produce them. Low productivity results in low income and little savings because not much extra is produced beyond what people consume. This, by definition, is the case with those living a subsistence lifestyle. An economy with a large subsistence sector yields very little surplus and, therefore, does not grow. Hence, low productivity limits not only future growth but also the wages workers can earn, contributing in part to what economists call the *poverty trap*. Industrial development requires substantial economic growth over several years. Figures vary, but the countries increasing their per capita incomes have typically achieved growth rates between 7 and 14 percent during a five- to ten-year period. Such growth allows for the surplus produced as income and savings to be turned back into the economy as investment in capital.

Insufficient Capital   Economies with low per capita GNPs, large subsistence sectors, and low productivity have little capital. Physical capital, often called *infrastructure*, includes such things as factories, farms, roads, railroads, telephones, banks, and machinery, while financial capital includes bank deposits, earnings from international trade, and money. The goods an economy produces for immediate consumption, such as food, cars and clothes, are not capital. In sum, *capital* refers to the finances plus facilities needed to produce wealth. Wealth means goods and more capital.

Dual economy, productivity, and capital are closely related factors. As a result, the problems in low-income economies are interrelated and structural, meaning they are built into their situation. Such a mutually reinforcing combination of deeply rooted problems does not respond to a bit of tinkering here and there. A development project or two, however effective, will not change the basic structure of the economy. A subsistence economy with low productivity and little capital thus experiences great difficulty in generating enough growth to begin self-sustained development. It struggles with the cycle of underdevelopment, as indicated by the arrow closing the cycle in Figure 4.1.

Few Human Services   Low-income economies have little infrastructure and, by definition, lack the educational and medical care facilities of industrialized economies. Yet, as economists point out, "human capital" is needed for a successful development process. Schools, universities, clinics, and hospitals produce an educated and healthy population, which is needed for economic initiative and improved productivity to occur. Data reporting on people's access to education and medical care show the severe deficiencies in the world's poorer states as compared with richer ones. The figures in Table 4.3 are from the *1996 Human Development Report*, a compilation of statistics and explanatory narrative that is published each year by the United Nations Development Program (UNDP), an aid agency of the United Nations.

A lack of basic human services inhibits development and reinforces the existence of a dual economy. Thus the arrow that completes the cycle of underdevelopment in Figure 4.1 connects factor 4, "Few human services," to factor 1, "Dual economy." Without sufficient educational and employment opportunities the middle class remains very small, leaving virtually intact the polarized pattern of two main economic and social classes—namely, the high-income elites and the subsistence agriculturists. A dual economy lacks the large middle class that characterizes the industrialized world. A middle class is important because it provides not only a substantial domestic market but also new leadership and an educated voting public.

The cycle of underdevelopment presented thus far explains the unremitting set of obstacles faced by developing economies. Such problems would slow development even in a society with clearheaded and incorruptible leadership choosing enlightened public policies, a questionable standard even in countries with more productive economies. Advocates of both the economic growth and the basic needs development strategies recognize the problems associated with the vicious cycle of underdevelopment, but they diverge over what should be done about it. Economic

Table 4.3
POPULATION PER DOCTOR AND PUPILS PER TEACHER
RATIOS FOR GROUPS OF STATES

	Population per Doctor (1993)	*Pupils per Teacher (1992)*	
		Primary	Secondary
High human development	1,661	25	17
Medium human development	3,454	27	19
Low human development	14,053	43	24
All developing countries	5,767	33	22
Least developed countries	18,496	45	26
Industrial countries	344	18	14
World average	4,968	30	20

Source: United Nations, *Human Development Report 1996* (New York: Oxford University Press, 1996).

"Human development" is a classification from a statistical index that compiles data on life expectancy, adult literacy, school enrollment, and per capita gross domestic product (GDP).

growth strategists generally rely on international interventions to begin the development process. Outside aid and investments, for example, are designed to make up for the internal lack of productivity and capital. In contrast, the basic needs approach addresses the problem of a dual economy head-on by attempting to change the subsistence lifestyle. Once people produce more food and other essentials of life, so the basic needs reasoning goes, they can perhaps produce a surplus to invest. Some of the investment may well be in human services, yet some could find its way, via a reliable banking system, into the industrial sector. Either way, the central problem should not be considered in terms of productivity and capital, but as providing a better quality of life for ordinary people.

It should be pointed out that some states classified as having low- or middle-income economies have had occasional growth years, although they have not reached the 7+ percent sustained growth needed for substantial development. Yet people in the developing world expect more. The model of a better lifestyle is tantalizingly flashed on television screens in villages around the world. Seeing US situation comedies or soap operas, the most frequently televised programs worldwide, can raise expectations as to what constitutes an acceptable lifestyle. Many people in the developing world, as well as in the industrial world, seek answers to the question of why a majority of the world's countries face the cycle of underdevelopment.

The Colonial Legacy

As noted in Chapter 1, most developing countries were at one time ruled directly or indirectly by an industrialized state during the age of imperialism. A strong case can be made that global European domination has contributed to the deeply entrenched dual economies of the developing world. In this context, the United States is considered as "European" because its dominant population originated in Europe. The United States dictated policies in Central American countries and Cuba for decades beginning in the late nineteenth century. It also became the colonial ruler in the Philippines and Puerto Rico after the 1898 Spanish-American War.

In many parts of the world, some of the precolonial rulers had initiated economic development. In the Middle East, for example, factories and shops producing textiles flourished during the early 1800s in Egypt, Beirut, and Damascus. Great Britain at that time was the world's leading exporter of fabric and clothing. From Britain's point of view, textile making in the Middle East posed a threat to one of its main foreign policies—that is, establishing new markets for its own manufactured products. When it became the dominant imperial power in Egypt and in other areas claimed by the Ottoman Empire, Britain dismantled the local textile industry.

While it may be unfair to blame colonial rulers for all of the problems facing the developing world today, colonialization did initiate some of the problems while doing little to mitigate others. Subsistence agriculture, for example, was not forced on an unsuspecting and powerless people. It was already the economic mainstay before Europeans arrived. Yet the flip side of a dual economy, the elite, was superimposed by the Europeans after the precolonial rulers were removed from power. Establishing a new elite illustrates the fact that "progress," like other kinds of change, often has both positive and negative consequences. The new European-trained elite did learn the languages, management, and communication skills essential in today's international system. However, today this elite controls government as well as business decisions using the language and governing style of the ex-colonial power, be it French in Senegal or English in India, for example. This results in a separation between the elite and the larger majority of people. The gap is made even larger by differences in lifestyle and education. The elite decision makers often have earned advanced degrees in an industrialized country and live with all the conveniences available to people in high-income countries. This lifestyle gap is not simply one of quantity but of quality as well. It represents differences in culture as well as in the number of modern consumer goods one can enjoy.

Many argue that colonial rule helped to provide a transition from a traditional society to a more modern one and to initiate infrastructure development. Transportation systems such as railroads were built, as were educational facilities, in the capital cities. Mines and port facilities were constructed, and banking plus other capital expenditures were made by the imperial powers in laying the basis for a modern economic sector. When they left, the facilities remained in the control of the local elites, who also benefited from them.

Those emphasizing the negative legacy of imperialism hasten to note that the infrastructure investments served, and continued to serve, the economic interests of Europe and the United States. The transportation systems linked the sources of raw materials inland with seaports. While useful for the movement of commodities from mines in the colony's interior to the "mother" country for processing, such railroads, canals, and roads did little to develop the economy of the colony itself. They did not interconnect income-producing internal regions with each other. Angola in southwest Africa provides a case in point. Three railroads were built by Portugal, the colonial ruler. Each one connected an interior region producing trade products with a port city on the coast. The northern line carried coffee and diamonds, the center line moved cooper ore from the Congo, and the southern line transported iron ore. All three lines traversed east and west, moving roughly parallel to each other. None of the three interconnected.

The colonial ruler intended to provide new markets and sources of raw materials for its own companies, and to accomplish this with the least possible political and military expense. Economic development of the local economy was incompatible with both objectives. Local competitors within the colony would threaten the colonial power's domination of the market, and mass education would risk raising local nationalism and undermine colonial rule. Disputes will continue over the positive and negative legacies of the imperial age, but the fact remains that local development was not the colonizers' primary objective.

Finally, colonizers in the developing world introduced new crops, not for food but for income. Literally called *cash crops*, they included sugar, coffee, cotton, tea, tobacco, bananas, and other commodities wanted in Europe and the United States. Cash crops also include natural resources as well as agricultural products, such as tin and tea. Economists use the phrase *primary commodities* when referring to cash crops because, unlike manufactured goods, they are traded unprocessed or in their natural state.

The imperial conquest consisted of massive land grabs by European settlers seeking to produce cash crops. They used the labor of the conquered peoples whenever possible, or turned to importing indentured servants or slaves. On English, French, and Spanish islands in the Caribbean, for example, most of the indigenous people died within a few decades of the conquest. They were replaced with slaves from West Africa. Unlike the Europeans, previous empires had not always taken over the land of peoples they ruled. China's tributary system and the Arab and Ottoman Empires, for example, extracted taxes or tribute and obedience, but often left the existing economic and social system virtually intact. Contrary to this practice, European conquest changed not only the political leadership, but also the society's religious, economic, and social status practices. The continuing cultural impact of imperialism is discussed in detail in Chapter 2.

Today, many developing countries still earn a large percentage of their international trade income by selling the cash crops introduced during colonial rule. As with other continuing effects of imperialism, exporting primary commodities stimulates opposing arguments over whether it has had positive or negative consequences. Copper, sugar cane, cattle, hemp, and potash, for example, provide developing countries with some income in the postcolonial era. Yet exporting unprocessed products while importing manufactured goods produces a trade deficit. A deficit results because the prices of unprocessed products tend to decrease over time in relation to the prices of manufactured goods. Thus, developing countries find themselves in an unfavorable position in trading with industrial countries.

Outside Interventions

Virtually all the world's national economies engage in ongoing international economic interactions. Since World War II, the volume of economic transactions that cross national borders has increased annually for both developing and industrial nations. Economic interactions with other states, international organizations, and private corporations can assist in the development process. Such relevant outside interventions occur in four categories: trade, foreign aid, private investment, and technical assistance. As Figure 4.2 indicates, these interventions can provide machinery, financing, and expertise, but each brings problems of its own.

Trade   Trade in primary commodities, a legacy of colonialism, can earn income for a developing state in the years when prices in the international market are high. Trade earnings, called *foreign exchange* by economists, are used to buy machinery as well as to build roads, buildings, factories, and other infrastructure. Because foreign exchange is used to buy products imported from other countries, it exists as accounts in large banks with worldwide operations. These accounts are in US dollars, British pounds, or another currency that businesses in other countries will accept in exchange for their goods. Such a currency is referred to as a *convertible,* or *hard, currency.* Some development theorists believe that good planning can make up for annual fluctuations in cash crop prices. Others point out that the amount of money earned by the sale of primary commodities depends on processing and markets located outside of the developing country. Processing plants

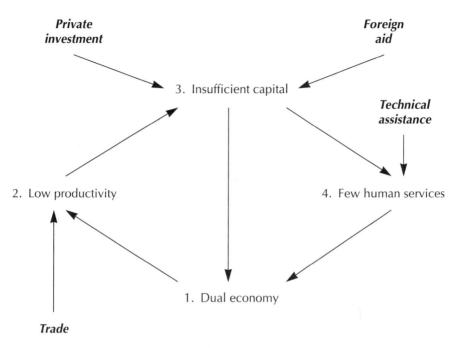

Figure 4.2
CYCLE OF UNDERDEVELOPMENT: OUTSIDE INTERVENTIONS

and market outlets are controlled by businesses in the industrial world, and it is their interest to keep the costs of raw materials as low as possible. They often play one source of primary commodities against another to keep prices down.

Foreign Aid The second type of international economic transaction, *foreign aid,* is designed to provide capital directly in the form of loans. Except for a small percentage of aid provided by private international agencies, foreign aid comes from either another country's government or an IGO such as the World Bank. For decades the United States was the leading state aid donor. But according to *World Development Report* data for 1993, Japan provided over $11 billion in official development assistance, while the United States contributed $9.5 billion (World Bank, 1995). As a percentage of donor GNP, the United States has always ranked well behind other industrialized states, and its rating has steadily dropped since 1960. In that year, the United States provided 0.53 percent of its GNP in economic aid. By 1980 the figure was 0.27 percent and by 1993 it had dropped to 0.15 percent—the lowest among the world's eighteen major aid donors. The Scandinavian countries have always led in the percentage of their GNPs designated for foreign aid. Denmark was the highest in 1993, at 1.03 percent of GNP.

Opponents of economic aid often make the mistake of thinking it is a give-away program. To the contrary, in virtually all cases foreign aid takes the form not of grants but of loans requiring repayment, often at commercial rates of interest. Missing loan payments affects a country's credit worthiness. Low credit ratings mean that subsequent loans (needed to finance international trade, for example) will cost more in interest because of the increased risk.

Foreign aid generally provides financing for specific development projects. Often a project will not produce income for some time, but loan payments come due right away. Also, the economic and political "strings" that accompany foreign aid can be a drawback. Most projects require the purchase of machinery, which generally must be made from companies headquartered in the country providing the aid. Thus, much aid financing never leaves the donor country. Not only does this practice help business in the industrialized country, but it also ensures continued earnings through a trade in spare parts. Foreign aid also produces a web of political strings, intangible but nonetheless real. Economic indebtedness brings with it political indebtedness, allowing aid donors to pressure governments in aid-recipient countries for diplomatic support.

Private Investment   As the third form of outside intervention, private investment has the virtue of avoiding government-to-government political ties and loan repayments. Investments by multinational corporations can bring income directly into a local economy through new employment opportunities. *Multinational corporations (MNCs)* are private businesses with holdings or operations in two or more countries. They are among the largest economic units in the world, as measured by a comparison of their revenues and the GNPs of states. A ranking of countries and MNCs according to the size of their annual product in 1991 showed the Sumitomo Corporation as the twenty-first largest producer of wealth, ahead of such states as Austria, Turkey, South Africa, and Israel. Mitsubishi was listed twenty-second and General Motors at twenty-fifth (World Bank 1994 and Mattera 1992: 704). Of the top seventy-five in 1991, twenty-seven were MNCs. Clearly, many of the world's largest businesses have much greater resources than most members of the United Nations.

The preponderant number of multinational corporations, and all of the biggest, are headquartered in the world's leading industrial countries: the United States, Japan, Germany, France, United Kingdom, Canada, and Italy. An MNC can exercise great policy-making influence on the government of a low-income country, especially when the MNC produces one of the few sources of foreign exchange earnings in a country. Multinational corporations are often promised a favorable business climate, such as low taxes, freedom from environmental restrictions, and suppression of unions. Like trade and foreign aid, private investment by MNCs is part of the dependent relationship the developing world has with the industrial world. Private companies bring in personnel with management and other skills needed for development; however, such people focus on work to be done to enhance the company's profitability and can be withdrawn at any time. They do not assist with projects prioritized to develop the local economy itself. Employing outside experts for this purpose is called *technical assistance*.

Technical Assistance   The fourth form of outside intervention, technical assistance makes up for the lack of local human resources by bringing in experts from other countries. Often these specialists do the planning and sometimes help make decisions as a project is carried out. Villagers, the intended beneficiaries of many projects, usually participate only as physical laborers. As a result, the villagers who are expected to carry on after the experts leave do not have a vested interest in the project and often are untrained in its upkeep. These "beneficiaries" may not even perceive the project as serving their needs because of their lack of participation in the planning. They did have to do the hard physical work to build the project, which meant less time in their fields. Such disregard for the human dimension of development has accounted for the failure of a large percentage of rural projects in past decades.

Other Factors

The factors contributing to the cycle of underdevelopment create structural problems that make development difficult. Outside interventions can either help or hinder the process. They can inadvertently reinforce the problems while purporting to provide solutions. Trade, aid, private investment, and technical assistance act positively on an economy when local elites have achieved stable economic and political decision-making processes. Such stability results from a social consensus. When people agree on the basics—for example, that they live in the same society and share a common future—they can develop ways of disagreeing without reaching an impasse. In extreme cases, an inability to work out problems can tear a country apart, as happened in Lebanon during the civil war of 1976–1989. Lebanon had achieved substantial economic growth and a relatively high standard of living and had become the banking center of the Middle East before internal violence destroyed its economy. Thus, in addition to economic factors, any analysis of developing world problems must account for the underlying social factors that may explain why some countries achieve ongoing growth and improved standards of living while others do not.

Overcoming economic deficiencies becomes much more difficult in a society pulled apart by people who do not share a common identity, value system, and commitment to an established political unit. Most states have multiple cultural groups within their borders. In some countries the groups share social and political commonalties, while in others they do not. Social cohesion enables people to continue on under one political authority in spite of severe economic downturns, resource depletion, and social tensions. When many groups are invested in one cohesive society, the country is more likely to survive the severe social and political dislocations of economic development.

Two other factors have proven important in providing a positive context for development: sufficient natural resources, either within a country's own borders or accessible through trade, and stable population growth (that is, growth that does not outrun an economy's ability both to sustain its population and produce capital investment). One caveat should be noted before moving into a discussion of each factor. All three do not apply in the same way to every country in the industrial world. Japan, the example most often cited, was relatively resource poor when it began industrialization, and this continues to affect the country's policies. Japan needs to sell industrial goods in order to make up for deficiencies in fuel by importing oil. The cohesiveness of Japanese society has helped the country compensate for being located on mountainous volcanic islands with little arable land and few natural resources.

Lack of Social Cohesion   The borders of developing countries often encompass various ethnic groups with no previous history of cooperation and, therefore, with no sense of common purpose prior to their colonial rule. When Europeans drew the borders of the present-day developing countries, they often forcibly brought together groups of people who had fought for generations. Even among groups who had interacted peacefully, tensions arose when they were merged into one state. Where they had been relative equals, now one was favored by the European ruler as its local elite. As a result, the country's identity, borders, and political institutions became sources of unresolved conflict when independence was achieved. The power of colonial rule had masked underlying tensions among ethnic groups, which surfaced with independence.

The postcolonial history of Nigeria provides an extreme example of interethnic problems subsequent to colonial rule. Like many other states in sub-Saharan Africa, Nigeria's borders date from the Congress of Berlin in 1884–1885, when European states met to settle disputes over the partitioning of Africa. No representatives of Africa's indigenous peoples attended the Berlin Conference, not even to provide information. Great Britain and France were the contenders for areas that now are part of Nigeria. France had moved down the Niger River while the British had moved up. A boundary was drawn as a compromise between them. The British consolidated their holdings around the delta of the Niger River and inland, calling the area Nigeria. It included many peoples speaking over two hundred languages, and three major cultural groupings with substantially different lifestyles and a history of conflict: the Hausa-Fulani in the north, the Yoruba in the west, and the Ibos in the east. The Ibos proved themselves the most adaptable to British practices and became civil servants and teachers, the core of a British-educated elite.

Nigeria became independent in 1960. By 1965, interethnic tensions had increased and were marked by a series of incidents resulting in Ibo deaths. Other factors contributed to the conflict, such as the fact that Iboland was rich in oil and Nigeria had virtually no economic integration among its internal regions. Consequently, many Ibos attempted secession. They declared their eastern region as the new state of Biafra. A brutal war ensued in 1966–1969, ending with Biafra's defeat. It is not possible to say with certainty that British colonial rule resulted in Nigeria's bloody war so soon after independence. Yet major factors contributing to the war derive from or were exacerbated by colonial policies.

When negative judgments about ethnic strife in the developing world are made by people in the industrial world, they ignore the fact that it took centuries of warfare for today's major European countries to arrive at a mutual consensus as to their borders. The United States has also fought wars—with Canada because it was part of the British Empire, with Mexico, with various indigenous peoples, and with itself in a bloody civil war—before its borders became unquestioned. It should not be surprising, then, that some developing countries have erupted in ethnic conflict to redraw international borders or to change which group rules within the existing borders.

Some commentators link the rampant corruption and government mismanagement in some developing states to their lack of social cohesion. Civic mindedness evolves from a sense of loyalty to the larger society. In its absence, rule becomes personalized, favorable to one ethnic group or the family and friends of the ruler. Vast amounts of capital have been diverted to personal use rather than invested in development projects. Mobutu, the former president of Zaire, renamed the Democratic Republic of the Congo, offers a glaring example of how a corrupt leader can drain and impoverish a state. Billions of dollars flowed out of Zaire and into personal accounts in international banks during the more than thirty years Mobutu was in power. Such "capital flight" and corrupt government policy making have proven formidable obstacles to development in several other developing countries.

Insufficient Natural Resources   This second factor contributing to development problems does not receive the attention it deserves. Most low-income countries lack the natural resources and moderate climates that industrialized countries possessed when they began a development process. Geographic location has much to do with the problems faced by today's developing nations. Almost all developing countries are located within the 37-degree latitudes north and south of the equator. Those outside of this region, such as Turkey, Argentina, Chile, and South Africa, are middle income or better. The heat in the planet's equatorial zone produces tropical, desert, or monsoon climates. Each of these climates presents problems for development. Deserts lack water, and tropical areas have thin topsoil that erodes quickly. In a monsoon region, rain comes down in destructive torrents during a short wet season, which alternates with many dry months. Such a rain pattern erodes and leaches nutrients from the soil. It contrasts sharply with the steady, easily absorbed precipitation of temperate zones. The bulk of Africa, for example, is located on both sides of the equator. Potential farmland makes up only one-fifth of the continent: 20 percent is desert and 57 percent is reddish, rain-washed, acidic soil. High in iron and aluminum, this soil does not produce thriving, cultivated plants (Harrison 1984:70).

Explosive Population Growth   Economists agree that optimum economic growth occurs when a population grows slowly and steadily. New markets are thus created at a pace that stimulates new production. Such a balance between economic expansion and population growth is not characteristic of the developing world. Overpopulation is a problem in low-income countries, where high population growth rates exist alongside low economic growth rates (see Table 4.4 on page 70).

States with higher-income economies tend to have lower population growth rates. They also report relatively lower economic growth rates but, since their economies are already industrial, they do not need to sustain high growth. In the long run, major population growth and stagnant economies pose insurmountable problems for the agricultural and industrial sectors of a developing economy. One

Table 4.4
POPULATION AND ECONOMIC GROWTH RATES
FOR SELECTED COUNTRIES

	Population Growth Rate (1990)	Economic Growth Rate (1989)
Low-Income Economies:		
Tanzania	3.66%	1.8%
Nicaragua	3.36	- 2.0
Bangladesh	2.67	3.5
Lower-Middle-Income Economies:		
Senegal	2.78%	2.2%
Bolivia	2.76	- 0.4
Jamaica	1.21	.05
Philippines	2.49	1.8
Upper-Middle-Income Economies:		
South Africa	2.22%	2.2%
Uruguay	0.56	-0.2
Greece	0.23	1.2
High-Income Economies:		
New Zealand	0.87%	1.9%
United States	0.81	2.6
Japan	0.43	4.1

Source: Allen, *Student Atlas of World Politics* (Guilford, CT: Duskin Publishing Group, 1994).

result is a strain on the social fabric of several countries. A solution could be capital investment in new machinery to increase the productivity of existing land, but this is prohibitively expensive in most villages.

The problem of exploding population growth did not face the already industrialized world. During their first decades of development, the populations of Europe, the United States, and Japan grew roughly parallel to increases in productivity resulting from the new machinery. Then, after achieving advanced stages of industrialization, a demographic transition occurred. This transition, illustrated in Figure 4.3, included certain changes in population growth in every industrialized country. Whereas before industrialization population growth was checked by a high death rate, now it is held steady by a low birthrate.

Before industrialization, populations generally had high birth rates and death rates. Thus explosive population growth did not occur. This changed during industrial development's early stages because more food, better sanitation, and wider availability of medical care substantially lowered the death rate. Since birthrates stayed high, the population increased. As industrialization advanced, it produced a higher standard of living based on employment in the manufacturing and service sectors. Having many children became an economic burden rather than a necessity. In a subsistence

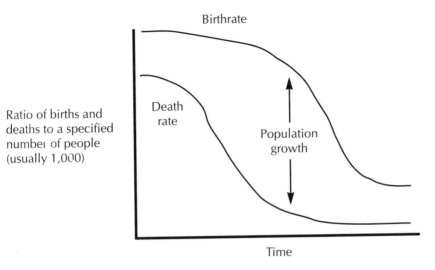

Birthrate

Ratio of births and
deaths to a specified
number of people
(usually 1,000)

Death
rate

Population
growth

Time

Figure 4.3   THE DEMOGRAPHIC TRANSITION

agricultural lifestyle, children are the work force needed to herd animals, carry wood, and take care of younger children. Industrial economies provide reasons for having fewer children as well as the technologies to achieve this result.

Unlike the population growth trends in the industrialized countries, developing countries find themselves stuck in the middle of the demographic transition with low death rates and high birthrates. In contrast to the past experience of today's high-income countries, economic growth in developing countries is not enough to absorb their growing populations. Colonial rule, and subsequent international aid programs, have brought lower death rates through increased sanitation and the eradication of some diseases. Ironically, the humanitarian work of missionaries and aid agencies has produced a long-term problem for the very people they have attempted to help. Using new medical practices, disease was attacked as the most visible cause of human suffering and the one most susceptible to an immediate solution. However, as discussed above, long-term development was not the objective, and even if it had been it would have taken longer to develop than it took to decrease the death rate. To put the problem in economic perspective, eradicating smallpox was relatively cheaper than building infrastructure. The present population explosion in low-income countries shows that unintended, secondary consequences can have major effects.

The problems facing developing countries can be summarized by contrasting their experience with that of an industrialized country. The United States, for example, began as a colony and after a successful war for independence became one of the world's leading economic powers in about a hundred years. Applying the factors explained in this chapter to analyze the US situation shows that most of the problems faced by developing countries today did not exist for the United States. Such an analysis points out why a similar development process has not worked for many developing states.

First, the territories that became the United States proved to be among the richest in the world, with arable land to feed a growing population and raw materials for an industrial economy. Second, the population and the economy grew roughly parallel to one another. Third, large-scale immigration and the existence of indigenous peoples did not, in the long run, threaten social cohesion. The peoples originally inhabiting lands ceded to the United States by Great Britain, Spain, France, and Mexico, proved weak opponents and only small numbers remained after their populations were decimated by new diseases, such as smallpox, for which they had no immunity. Generations of new settlers from Europe wanted to become US citizens and each contributed to the new country's economic growth. This process fostered stability. The one group brought by force, African Americans, was not able to make demands in the country's early decades since most of its members were slaves. This group was not allowed to assert political influence until the 1960s, when the United States was already industrialized and had a legitimized political system able to handle the stress.

Economic factors also favored US development. A dual economy never took root. Given the vast amounts of rich arable land, the frontier farmers who began with a subsistence lifestyle produced within a few years surpluses for sale in markets back east or in other countries. Such productivity allowed local communities to afford human services, schooling for their children, and health care. Investment capital, raised both domestically and from Britain in the early 1800s, built railroads and mines. The United States in its first decades had many advantages not characteristic of the typical developing country in the late twentieth century.

In spite of such a favorable situation, the country's population suffered a long civil war with a devastating loss of life. With over 500,000 casualties, the US Civil War was as grim as the internal conflicts experienced by developing countries in the late twentieth century. The extended struggle had its ethnic cause as well as deeply felt differences brought on by the process of economic development.

At the end of the twentieth century, the United States had the largest economy in the world, with a $6.4 trillion GNP in 1993 (World Bank 1995). In comparison, Japan's and Germany's second and third GNP rankings were reported at almost $4 trillion and $2 trillion, respectively, and the figure for all developing countries combined was $3 trillion. Despite such wealth, the United States still has pockets of developing economies in its rural areas and inner cities. The onrushing, ever-more complex industrial technologies have not swept every area of the United States onto the bridge to the twenty-first century, to say nothing of the majority of the world's population who remain poor.

THE INDUSTRIAL WORLD

The developing world and its problems are part of the international economic system. As the dominant states in the system, industrialized countries have had a different experience from that of developing countries as their high-income economies continue to become more interdependent by leaps and bounds. The international economic system, introduced in Chapter 1, has worked to produce startling growth. The

Industrial Revolution has greatly expanded world trade, producing surplus goods and an insatiable demand for raw materials. Refinements in machinery mean higher productivity and more goods, requiring larger markets. Thus the cycle continues. According to data provided by an international relations specialist, in 1913 world trade amounted to about $20 billion, but by the early 1990s about $3.7 trillion in goods were exchanged. The post–World War II era has brought a trade boom: Between 1948 and 1968, world trade increased from $53 billion to $350 billion, or 660 percent, and the pace in more recent years has not slackened (Rourke 1993:442).

A second category of international transactions, financial ties, have also greatly accelerated since World War II. Private bank lending in other countries totaled $4.78 trillion in 1990, with Japan as the largest lender at $666 billion and the United States the second largest at $527 billion. Another form of financial interaction is direct investment, or the purchase of capital in other countries. US international investments in 1950 amounted to $11.8 billion, which had mushroomed to $598 billion by 1990. The United States has also been the recipient of substantial investment capital, with direct foreign investment totaling $466 billion in 1990, (Rourke 1993:442). Unlike many developing states, increased trade and financial flows have contributed to the world's leading economies. They have achieved continuing economic growth over the long term and an ever-rising living standard.

A country's trade data and monetary transactions are totaled every year in its *balance of payments*. This summary of a state's international economic interactions with all other states shows credits minus debits in all categories of transactions: exports and imports, tourist travel and purchases, business investment and profits, loans and debt payments. If a country has to borrow heavily to bring its account into balance for several years in a row, doubts arise as to the future health of the economy. As with government budget deficits, investors tend to shy away from a country with chronic balance-of-payments problems.

Trade Issues

Trade generates about 15 percent of the world's total production of goods and services. For the United States and Japan, trade amounts to about 20 percent of GDP, whereas, for members of the European Union it averages about 50 percent (Balaam and Veseth 1996:113). Yet a basic, centuries-old policy argument within states goes on over whether and how to protect their own businesses from international competition. In their earlier stages of development, the leading industrialized states used *protectionism* to keep foreign companies from competing with their own "infant industries." Many of these policies are still in practice. They result in tariffs and other barriers to trade, including quotas and regulations on incoming products. Governments adopt a wide variety of regulations, such as subjecting imports to specific health and safety requirements, and limitations on where goods can enter a country.

In addition to restrictions aimed at keeping foreign goods out or increasing their price, a government may also use subsidies to make its country's products internationally competitive. The United States and some European countries, for example, buy selected agricultural products from their own farmers at a high enough price for the growers to make a profit. Then they sell these products in other countries at the lower prices dictated by international competition. Taxpayers take the loss. Subsidies can occur in other ways as well, such as in what is called parity payments in the United States. The US government pays farmers to keep land out of production and thus reduce the amount of corn, or wheat, or whatever the product. This can increase its price if sources for the commodity in other countries do not increase their production. Subsidies also exist for manufactured goods. One subsidy takes the form of government credits for overseas sale, which reduce the amount of interest that businesses pay for loans needed to finance trade. This, in turn, reduces the costs US companies must pass along to their customers in other countries, and they can charge lower prices than their competitors. The US Export-Import Bank handles such government-backed loans for US businesses.

Advocates of free trade disagree with protectionist policies. They say that mechanisms designed to enable a state to sell more than it buys cannot work in the long run because some countries inevitably have to be on the short end of the trade equation. In other words, everyone cannot sell more than they buy. Government policies that protect a country's businesses and markets have the effect of reducing the amount of goods flowing worldwide and thus limiting global economic expansion. Markets become constricted and economies of scale cannot be attained, so prices rise. On the other hand, if states adopt free trade policies, competition lowers prices for all consumers.

Free trade proponents argue that today's economies are so interlinked that for many industries it is outmoded to think of goods as from a single country. A decision made in one US town illustrates the point. Its local government decided to "Buy American" and chose a John Deere earth mover priced about $15,000 higher than one sold by Komatsu, a Japanese company. Unfortunately for the town's nationalistic objective, the John Deere machine was made in Japan, except for the motor, while the Komatsu was made in Illinois (Brown and Hogedorn 1994:162). A Boeing airplane provides another example of economic interdependence. Many of its important parts—rudders, landing gear, and computers—are made in Italy, Australia, Brazil, Japan, Korea, Canada, France, Ireland, Singapore, and the United Kingdom. Economists point out that because economic internationalization already exists, it should be allowed to become more efficient through free trade.

The debate over trade policy directly relates to people's daily lives because trade affects employment and living standards. A reduction in either exports or imports results in job losses. Fewer imports means some products become unavailable or more expensive and the standard of living drops. Also, ordinary people own shares in corporations in other countries through stock markets and mutual funds. In both the industrial and developing worlds, rural people produce cash crops, whether as laborers or landowners. Thus, their income fluctuates directly with the vagaries of international trade.

Monetary Issues

In addition to the exchange of goods through trade, states and their citizens interact in the world economy through the exchange of money for investments, aid, and personal transactions such as tourism and charity donations. The majority of these international financial flows are channeled through the world's largest private banks. They have subsidiaries in many countries and the size to handle billions of dollars worth of transactions every day. Each transaction requires the exchange of money, called *currency* by economists. Thus, the process of determining how much each state's currency is worth in relation to that of another state becomes very important, though it is often little understood by the general public.

News reports observe that the US dollar has become weaker or stronger. "Common sense" gives the impression that having a stronger currency is better, but such an assumption only sometimes proves true. Take, for example, a decline in the US dollar when compared to the German mark. This can be bad news for an American who intends to buy a German automobile actually made in Germany. But it would be irrelevant if the same person is going to buy a German automobile made in the United States. Or it could be good news if the American is working for a computer company that sells its products to Germany.

The worth of a country's currency in relation to that of another country is called the *foreign exchange rate*. This term is used when a person wants to know, for example, how many US dollars it takes at any point in time to buy how many British pounds, Japanese yen, Russian rubles, Ecuadorian sucres, Thai baht, Tanzanian shillings, Peruvian intis, Israeli shekels, or any other state's currency. To make the situation more confusing, exchange rates fluctuate, sometimes significantly, in relatively short periods of time. For example, Americans planning a trip to the United Kingdom months in advance may decide how many US dollars they will take based on the current exchange rate between the dollar and the British pound. Yet their trip could cost more if, upon arriving in London, they received fewer pounds for their dollars than they planned on because the exchange rate changed.

Applying the economic principle of supply and demand can help explain why the worth of a currency fluctuates. If Canada, for example, has a healthy economy, a growing demand for the Canadian dollar may well result. Banks and other multinational corporations would want to invest in a strengthening and stable economy. Since in the immediate term, the supply of Canadian dollars would stay about the same, their value will rise because demand for this currency has increased. It is not a coincidence that the four most internationally used currencies derive from four of the world's largest economies and more stable societies; namely, the US dollar, Japanese yen, German mark, and British pound.

A government's policies on interest rates and budget deficits can also have an effect on the worth of its currency. If a state's central bank raises interest rates, its currency often becomes more attractive because people in other countries will want to invest in an economy with higher rates. Thus, the currency becomes stronger when demand for it increases. Large, multiple-year government budget deficits, however, often have a downward influence on the worth of a currency. They cause investors in other parts of the world to question whether putting money into the economy of a government that cannot manage its own budget well is a sound, low-risk investment. High budget deficits mean large-scale borrowing. Demand for the currency sags, as does its worth. The United States, however, seems like an exception to this generalization because it continues to attract the foreign purchase of dollars for investment purposes. The reason is that the United States has been able to sustain huge budget deficits, larger than the whole economies of a majority of the world's countries. The gigantic size of the overall US economy, and thus the taxes paid to the government, has enabled it to afford paying the interest on the US national debt. Debt payments amounted to 15 percent of the 1995 US budget, or a little over $232 billion (Historical Tables, Budget of the United States Government, Fiscal Year 1997:103, 111). Actually, given the growth of the US economy over the years, the percentage of its budget deficit in relation to its annual GNP has actually decreased since 1992 and during most of the 1980s.

Economic internationalization has created a situation where an individual country, even one as wealthy as the United States, needs the help of other governments to establish effective economic policies. Take, for example, US efforts to steady the value of the dollar in relation to other currencies. A rising dollar means US imports are cheaper but exports drop because their prices rise. This occurs because it takes more of other currencies to buy fewer dollars, and the products valued in dollars. A falling dollar has the opposite effect. US exports increase but, since the dollar is worth less, imports cost more because it takes more dollars to pay for them. In the long run, economic transactions are aided by stable pricing and, therefore, stable currencies.

To steady the dollar, the US Treasury can buy and sell dollars. Buying dollars boosts their value by making them scarcer, whereas selling them puts more in circulation and thus decreases their value. The problem lies in the fact that the Treasury Department only has about $20 billion compared with the $750 billion to $1 trillion traded daily on the world's currency exchanges. This means the private currency exchanges have much more influence on the value of the dollar than any feeble response the US Treasury can afford. There is more hope of stabilizing the price of the US dollar if the world's leading countries together buy and sell dollars at the same time. Yet US citizens expect their government to manage the economy well and often do not realize this requires international cooperation.

Unfortunately for government policy makers in industrial states, their citizens often do not realize the extent to which their prosperity is connected to the international economy. Another complicating factor in establishing effective economic policy is the fact that a state's citizens exert opposite pressures depending, for instance, on whether they are employed by an importer or an exporter. They pressure government to act in their own interests. This can mean wanting the government to protect jobs by limiting imports of, say, automobiles. If quotas are set on car imports, or high tariffs levied to increase the prices of cars from other countries, such actions would invite retaliation from the countries affected. They could limit their imports from the protectionist state, thereby triggering a downward spiral of decreasing trade. In such a situation, everyone would suffer since trade wars produce economic declines in every country involved. Herein lies the paradox: Economies are internationally interdependent, yet their business and government leaders respond to demands from within their own country. Businesses must answer to stockholders, and democratic government officials must please voters.

A more sensible reaction would appreciate the delicate and difficult task of influencing trade and currency values. Many of the relevant factors remain outside of any single government's decision-making domain. Interdependence means mutuality. Whatever their position on their government's trade and monetary policies, citizens in states with high-income economies have difficulty realizing that the economic problems faced by their countries are not on the same scale as those impacting the developing world. Industrial states can do more to help themselves than can developing states. The consequences of economic downturns, enhanced by a global economy, have so much more destructive effects in developing countries that it sometimes seems as though they exist on a different planet.

Relations Between Industrialized and Developing Countries

As pointed out previously, increasing international trade and financial flows since the Second World War have fostered sustained economic growth over the long term in the world's high-income states. Some with middle incomes have prospered as well, but low-income economies generally have not made significant gains. The growing world economy has not produced balanced, healthy economic growth in the poorer states. Instead, the cycle of underdevelopment more aptly describes their plight. In the context of weak economies, the negative effects of international trade and foreign investments have been devastating. Issues of trade and currency values preoccupy the economic policies of states with low-income economies even more than those with high incomes because the downturns are far more debilitating. Government decision makers in weak economies have less ability to counter the negative effects. To be poor means having few choices for both individuals and governments.

One of the reasons low-income states suffer enhanced trade problems is that they produce mainly primary commodities. The prices paid for these raw material exports tend to increase more slowly over time compared with the prices of industrial goods. The problem is greater in the many low-income economies that produce only a few commodities for export. They are more vulnerable because an annual fall in the price of one commodity can cause a depression for that year. These states do not have the cushioning effect of income from a variety of other products.

In addition to trade difficulties, developing countries suffer severe monetary problems. Since their currencies are not in demand outside of their own borders, their governments and citizens wanting to make international transactions must buy another country's currency, one accepted on a worldwide basis. The value of these convertible currencies—the US dollar, British pound, Japanese yen, and German mark—generally increases in comparison to the developing state's currency. One of the reasons is that the poorer countries have chronic budget, trade, and balance-of-payments deficits. They borrow heavily from other governments, all in the industrial world, or from international aid organizations, whose policies are set by industrialized countries, or from multinational private banks, all of which are owned by people in the industrialized world. Borrowing by developing states incurs liabilities that even further undermine the worth of their currencies. Thus, they need to exchange more of their own money for the world's international convertible currencies to pay for imports and to repay loans. This puts additional inflationary pressure on the local currency, and the cycle continues its downward spiral.

Because they have little impact beyond their own borders, the problems of most developing economies do not inspire much concern in the industrial world, except for a few creditor banks. However, economic decisions made in the industrial world have direct effects in the developing world. This decision-making inequality, sometimes called *dependency*, may be illustrated by an example. The worth of the US dollar is not just an issue in the United States. More often than not, when businesses and governments want to buy and sell goods they use US dollars for the transaction since there are more of them available and acceptable around the world than any other currency. So stabilizing the value of the dollar is important to virtually all the world's countries, and vital to the indebted ones whose payments are calculated and paid in dollars. What the US does to strengthen or weaken its own currency can help or cost a country dearly. In the early 1980s, for example, the US government decided that fighting inflation deserved the highest priority. To strengthen the dollar, interest rates were set at their highest level since World War II. As the worth of the dollar rose, it added literally billions to the loan payments of the developing states. In contrast, the worth of the Ecuadorian sucre or Jordanian dinar, for example, has no measurable effect on the United States.

Citizens of industrial states are beneficiaries of their countries' favorable economic position. They should realize that their governments have worldwide economic responsibilities. Only the governments of the leading industrial states can set policies beneficial to the global economy in the long run. Interdependence means that income increases in the poorer regions will benefit the whole international economy. The United States, for example, sold over 40 percent of its 1993 exports in the developing world. If steady growth were achieved in more economies, markets and investments would expand for industrial world businesses.

Thus far, this chapter has introduced general concepts and analysis explaining international economic interdependence and development issues. In the process, it has pointed out the relationships between the industrial and the developing worlds. Now the discussion moves on to consider a case study of a specific, successful development project. It illustrates the applicability of many of the concepts introduced throughout this chapter. In so doing, the case study accomplishes two tasks. First, it makes real heretofore abstract concepts about the pressing global issue of economic development. Second, it demonstrates the fact that projects designed to improve the daily lives of the poor can succeed.

FROM PEASANTS TO FARMERS:
DEVELOPMENT IN THE PERUVIAN HIGHLANDS

The successful irrigation project described here took place during the 1980s in four of the agricultural sectors outside the town of Mollepata, Peru. Lucia, who was introduced at the beginning of this chapter, lives in one of these sectors. The project shows how peasants took responsibility, made decisions, worked hard, and changed their lives for the better. It also illustrates that outside financial assistance and technical expertise can be effective when development professionals work with village people as partners and not as experts who make all the decisions. The peasants participating in the project seem to have changed with their experience. Assertive and proactive in meetings, they project confidence in their own decision making. They no longer wait for fate or some outside power to take action, such as a rich landowner or the government. In assuming responsibility for their own future, project participants have changed from peasants to farmers.

A Tale of Two Canals

In 1981, the Andean Center for Development, Education, and Promotion (CADEP) began work in Mollepata. A local NGO, CADEP had been working with peasants in several Andean towns since its founding, in 1968, by the Archbishop of Cusco. As in other locations, CADEP workers began by organizing peasant committees, which decided the actions they would take to improve their daily lives. Then the CADEP leadership located international NGO funding for the planned project.

Months of peasant meetings in Mollepata finally crystallized into a decision to rebuild La Estrella, "the star." This irrigation channel had been built in the early years of the twentieth century by a local *hacendado*, the owner of a large estate. La Estrella had brought water to some of Mollepata's agricultural sectors from a rapidly falling stream several kilometers away. The Committee to Rehabilitate La Estrella (CORES), was organized with CADEP's assistance to plan and make decisions about the project. CORES was made up of the men who would do the actual work because they lived in the agricultural sectors downhill from La Estrella and would benefit directly from its rebuilding.

The La Estrella rehabilitation project addressed the central factor of the vicious cycle of underdevelopment—that is, the existence of a large subsistence sector in developing world economies. As a basic needs development project, it focused on food production. The CORES committee members worked hard and long because they clearly saw the connection between La Estrella and improving their daily lives. In addressing subsistence directly, the project was less entangled in the cycle of underdevelopment's other interrelated factors. It did not try to change one while the rest remained constant.

La Estrella avoided another pitfall inherent in the cycle, because increasing productivity was not taken to mean producing products for international trade. The

CORES committee began the project for more food to avoid famine. If enough extra food was grown and could be sold, much the better, but rebuilding the irrigation channel was not specifically intended to increase productivity for marketing purposes. This point may seem too fine a distinction since solving the food problem would produce more crops from the same land and thus increase productivity by definition. But development projects focusing on increasing agricultural productivity often target cash crops, not food. Cash crops require favorable circumstances well beyond the villagers' control, involving the country's elite and the international market. The state's elite, such as exporters and the makers of government trade policy, affect cash crop prices paid to villagers. Also, price fluctuations in the international market can have a direct effect on the livelihoods of local cash crop producers.

The La Estrella canal suffered from years of disuse and severe deterioration. Many sections were buried by landslides, a common occurrence in the rugged Andes. Previously, the *hacendado* had paid for the canal's upkeep. This ceased with his "retirement" when the new leftist military government carried out a land reform policy after coming to power in a 1968 coup. Peasants benefiting from La Estrella had tried to keep it clear and repaired on their own, but finally gave up. They needed to cooperate with one another but lacked practical experience in making decisions and taking action together for their mutual benefit, having lived for so long under the *hacienda* system. They also had no resources.

Mollepata's residents had suffered through a severe drought in the early 1980s. Given this fact, the decision to rebuild La Estrella may seem obvious with the clear vision of hindsight. Yet when put in the context of when it was made, it took courage and more than a little desperation. Ahead were years of extraordinarily backbreaking labor, even more than the CORES committee members anticipated. Their work on the channel was in addition to that already needed for sustenance, such as raising crops.

The decision was made more difficult by the dismal failure of another canal project in Mollepata, this one sponsored by the Peruvian government in the 1970s. Called Canal Nuevo, meaning "new canal," this project had squandered years of peasant time and effort. Originally, it was to have been bigger and better than the old *hacendado* channel. Canal Nuevo symbolized the progress promised by the new Peru. Unencumbered by a feudal past, the government would ensure a bright new future. The new canal would be wider, at about four feet across, and straighter, enabling it to carry water at 1,000 liters per second, contrasted with La Estrella's 200.

Funded by a $5 million Inter-American Bank loan, Canal Nuevo was built using modern heavy equipment moved from the coast at great expense, as well as peasant labor. The contractor chosen to design and construct the project was from Lima, Peru's coastal capital city, and had no prior experience in the mountains. Work began in 1974, and was to take fifteen months. Six years later Canal Nuevo was completed, but within three weeks water ceased flowing due to a landslide. After two more years of futile efforts to clear rubble and repair damage from landslides, the government quit the project.

La Estrella's peasant planners and workers started from where they were with their own skills and technology. When outside technical assistance and aid were brought in, they supported what already was available. In contrast, the Canal Nuevo, while having increased agricultural production as its aim, was designed not by the people who would have to use and maintain it. Canal Nuevo was planned and built as a capital formation, an infrastructure project by outsiders. It was defeated by the next factor in the cycle, the human services factor, because the construction firm from the coast had no experience building irrigation channels in the Andean highlands. It did have heavy equipment and well-educated engineers, but this human and physical capital proved ineffectual.

Local Initiative

In 1984, the 105 families committed to rebuilding La Estrella began the task. They negotiated how much work time each person would contribute using Andean cultural practices dating from before the Spanish conquest. Called *ayni* in Quechua, this mutually agreed-upon reciprocal work arrangement applied when cooperation was needed, such as during harvests. Each month a group of men would climb to 13,000 feet where the canal began diverting river water. This took about eight hours. They carried hand tools and enough food for the three days or more they would spend away from home. The men slept in the canal itself, their only shelter from the cold Andean nights.

By 1985, after months of work, the men of CORES decided the undertaking was too great for them to complete on their own. In 1986, CADEP found funding from AGROACCION, a private German international aid organization. Jan Hendricks, an irrigation engineer who spoke Spanish and had built irrigation projects in mountainous regions, was hired to design and work on the La Estrella rehabilitation project. Unlike Canal Nuevo, several varying construction techniques were used given the differences in terrain; for example, in one section unusually susceptible to landslides, large pipes were connected and buried underground over a 400-meter stretch. Getting each pipe to the site required tying it on logs and having it carried uphill several kilometers by twenty-four or more men. Another technology, in this case Incan, provided the precedent for braking the destructive force of rushing water in those sections where it plunged for hundreds of feet. Large rocks were set in the canal bed and held in place not by cement, which would erode, but by moss. As a tribute to such traditional construction techniques, some Incan canals still function elsewhere in Peru.

As one of the additional factors affecting development, social cohesion depends on mutual respect among a society's multiple ethnicities. That such respect can help development is illustrated by the importance of traditional Quechua cultural practices to La Estrella's success. They clearly and concretely illustrate that applying traditional methods can prove positive in an effective development strategy. Proud of their Incan heritage, the villagers used their ancestors' canal construction techniques appropriate in the Andes. *Ayni*, Quechua work-sharing practices, also proved necessary since it took years of labor to complete the project. Canal Nuevo, in contrast, was designed and built by Peru's Spanish-speaking elite with Mollepata's residents only supplying hand labor. Treating the local people like peasants contributed to the New Canal's failure by ignoring their fears of landslides.

As work continued, men from two additional local sectors were asked to join CORES. Because their fields lay downhill from the planned route, they too could benefit from the completed canal. After much discussion, one sector accepted while the other cited the failure of Canal Nuevo as its reason for refusing. The mostly pick-and-shovel project took until 1990 to complete, and since then La Estrella's water has never ceased to flow. Two farmers from each of the four sectors in CORES have been trained as technicians to clear and maintain the canal. They also regulate the water's increased volume during the rainy season by opening sliding outlet hatches built into the sides of the canal (an engineering design not built into Canal Nuevo). For the first time, the farmers of CORES produced two crops, in 1993, because they had a source of water lasting throughout the growing season.

The Mollepata case study illustrates points made in this chapter, but with a positive twist. Previous information and concepts have explained why development remains so difficult to achieve in many parts of the world by pointing out the factors contributing to the cycle of underdevelopment. However, applying the same concepts to the rehabilitation of La Estrella can explain its success. In the context of local decision making, outside aid and technical assistance proved vital to the rehabilitation project. Rebuilding the canal became a full partnership among CORES, CADEP, Jan Hendricks (the European engineer), and a German-based international NGO that provided funding. The fact that the technicians have kept La Estrella in repair years after the canal began functioning shows the effectiveness of a local, regional, and international partnership.

Analysis

The La Estrella case study illustrates the fact that a basic needs strategy can result in effective development projects. Clearly, the economic growth strategy has worked over time in high- and some middle-income economies. Yet in the contemporary context of poverty characterized by underdevelopment's multiple factors, a strategy designed to meet basic needs provides viable, low-cost options. As Canal Nuevo shows, technologies that work in the industrial world must be applied selectively, with caution, and only on a scale appropriate to the local context. In contrast, CORES and CADEP used outside help as needed, such as huge pipes to carry water underground in a landslide-prone section of the canal. This example illustrates that industrial technology is not necessarily incompatible with a basic needs strategy. But the La Estrella case study also crystallizes differences between the two approaches to development. Understanding economic growth and basic needs development strategies provides the basis for the contrasting perspectives people use in responding to the global issue of economic development, as explained in the next chapter.

TERMS AND CONCEPTS

balance of payments

basic needs strategy

capital

cash crops/primary commodities

demographic transition

dependency

developing countries/world

development

dual economy

economic growth strategy

foreign aid

foreign exchange

foreign exchange rate

gross national product (GNP)

hard/convertible currencies

multinational corporations (MNCs)

per capita gross national product (per capita GNP)

private investment

productivity

protectionism

social cohesion

subsistence

technical assistance

DISCUSSION QUESTIONS

1. What reasons do you think best explain the success of the irrigation project in Mollepata, Peru?
2. What problems preoccupy industrial states about their international economic relations? How do these problems compare and contrast with those of developing states?
3. Why are the following indicators used to differentiate levels of "human development": literacy rate, infant mortality rate, and life expectancy? What other indicators would make sense?
4. Given their historical role, what case would industrialized states make about economic development during the age of colonialism? What case would developing states make?
5. What factors account for world poverty? How could development strategies bring about constructive change?

RESEARCH PROJECTS

1. Choose a country and make an assumption about its level of economic development. Then do some research to find the country's macroeconomic indicators (some good sources of information include the *World Development Report*, the *Human Development Report,* and the *Almanac*). Use the data to write a brief economic profile of the country. Do the data support your initial assumption?
2. Survey the media's coverage of the developing world for a month. What images are conveyed? What, if any, information is provided on the underlying economic and social problems in developing countries?
3. Compare and contrast the population growth rates and economic growth rates for several countries in the low-income and lower-middle-income categories in various years over the course of at least two decades. What trends do you find?
4. Visit a local mall or department store. Choose a category of goods and systematically determine the percentage of goods that is imported. Repeat this procedure for another category of goods. Compare and contrast your findings.

5. For a country with low-income indicators (such as per capita income and economic growth), but high human development indicators (such as literacy and infant mortality rates), discuss the factors that may account for this seeming anomaly.

INTERNET RESOURCES

Care: *http://www.care.org* A development NGO, Care, provides information about its projects, data about major world issues (such as hunger, poverty, health, environment, and education), and maps and other information about the countries in which it works.

The Central Intelligence Agency Factbook: *http://www.odci.gov/cia/publications/nsolo/factbook/global.htm* This CIA site has maps, economic data, and some demographic data about all the world's countries.

UN Development Program: *http://www.undp.org.* Some data from the annual *Human Development Report* are available at this site.

5

Perspectives on Economic Development

The ideas of economic liberty, a free market open to the world, and private initiative as the motor of progress have become embedded in the people of Chile.
—Novelist and politician Mario Vargas Llosa
(quoted in Goodwin 1996:74)

Creating a sustainable society will require fundamental economic and social changes, a wholesale alteration of economic priorities and population policies.
—Environmentalist Lester Brown (1981:8)

Reasonable people with different perspectives can come to very different conclusions about the same events. Adequate explanations as to why an international problem exists must, therefore, include an analysis of the alternative perspectives people use to decide on viable responses. In the case of development as a global issue, three perspectives offer contrasting explanations of how the international economy operates and what should be done about its problems. The *liberal economics*, *dependency*, and *participatory development* perspectives organize the debate over how to respond effectively to poverty and economic downturns.

LIBERAL ECONOMICS

Liberal economics prevails as the leading economic theory in the world today. Otherwise known as *market economics*, this theory's core concepts, such as supply and demand, free trade, and laissez-faire government, were formulated in the late eighteenth century by Adam Smith and were later refined by his successors. Today, at the threshold of the twenty-first century, liberal market prescriptions have become the main economic policies of most governments and IGOs, while their main competitor, socialism, is on the defensive. In general, socialist strategies prescribe a dominant role for government in the economy.

Liberal economists generally respond to the problem of worldwide poverty by advocating economic growth strategies. They agree that economic expansion produces higher incomes, which in turn generate more demand for products, greater growth, and more jobs. This pattern of mutually reinforcing supply and demand produces an upward growth spiral that enables an economy to break out of the cycle of underdevelopment. Economic growth is best achieved with a minimum of government intervention and a maximum of people willing to invest capital.

Comparative Advantage

Applying market strategies to the international economic system is accomplished through what is called *comparative advantage*. An economy has a comparative advantage in the production of a good or service when it can produce that good or service at a lower cost than its competitors. Any state's economy should aim to export those products in which it holds a comparative advantage and import those that other states can produce for less. Figure 5.1 illustrates this concept by using a simple trading system—two products (wine and cloth) traded by two countries (Portugal and England) to compare labor costs (one of the factors included in a product's price). It is a classic example reflecting the international system of a couple of hundred years ago, developed by the early nineteenth-century economist David Ricardo.

A cursory look at the figure may result in an obvious question: Why would Portugal trade with England when it could make both wine and cloth at a lower cost than could England? The answer comes from a careful reading of the definition of comparative advantage and a closer look at the figure. The phrase *relative comparison* provides the clue. If, on the one hand, Portugal was self-sufficient and traded for neither wine nor cloth, where would it get any savings? If, on the other hand, it specialized in wine and traded it for cloth made in England, Portugal would save ten labor hours. Then it could use the surplus to invest in making wine more efficiently and become more competitive with, for example, the French wine-making industry. In response, the French would have to reduce the cost of making their wine. Due to such competition over time, the price of wine will come down and consumers in all free trading countries will benefit. The same reasoning will produce lower consumer prices and growth for the cloth-making industries in states within the free trading system.

Figure 5.1
COMPARATIVE ADVANTAGE

	Portugal	England
Wine (y barrels)*	80 hours of labor/year	120 hours of labor/year
Cloth (x yards)	90 hours of labor/year 10 hours of labor/year	100 hours of labor/year 20 hours of labor/year

*y barrels = x yards

Needed Policies

Free Trade   Comparative advantage leads to the conclusion that people in every economy will benefit from policies of *free trade* and specialization. Liberal economists maintain that imports and exports should be unrestricted by tariffs and other barriers. If governments impose regulations artificially increasing the cost of their imported goods, the benefits of competition in bringing down prices for consumers will disappear. Also, the protected domestic producers have no incentive to become more efficient by updating their plant and management practices. Over time, they get farther and farther behind their competitors in other countries.

Specialization   Countries should specialize by trading those products in which they have a comparative advantage and not artificially subsidize exports. This further encourages cost efficiencies because of *economies of scale*. This economic principle refers to the fact that the per-unit cost decreases when a company produces more of a given product, since the plant, personnel, and other overhead costs remain about the same. Also, specialization produces efficiencies through reinvestment and increased knowledge of the production process.

Benefits for All   All economies can benefit from comparative advantage, albeit not always equally. In the wine and cloth example illustrated in Figure 5.1, England will benefit more initially because it can save twenty labor hours, while Portugal will save only ten hours. Yet for both countries, specialization produces savings that can be reinvested, thereby further increasing the level of efficiency. The resulting lower prices increase demand for the products of both countries and, therefore, stimulate further growth in imports and exports. As more and more states adopt policies encouraging comparative advantage and specialization, liberal economists assert that the international economy will grow. That is, consumers worldwide are encouraged to purchase more goods at lower prices, which, in turn, stimulates further growth. Policies inhibiting free trade, such as those based on the goals of self-sufficiency and protectionism, stifle growth and harm all states within the trading system.

In summary, liberal economics theory prescribes economic growth through trade as a development strategy. Every country, whether developing or industrialized, should lower tariffs, with the ultimate goal of eliminating them and other trade barriers (such as quotas and subsidies) entirely. This also means that the government's role in economic decision making will be reduced as much as possible. Developing countries that adopt free trade and other liberal economics policies have achieved substantial economic growth. Such policies have included the privatization of government-owned economic enterprises and the establishment of an open economy—one that is free of restrictions on both trade and financial flows. Chile provides an often noted example of the potential success of such strategies. In the 1970s, Chile's military government opened the economy to foreign investment, emphasized exports, and greatly reduced health and social welfare programs. By 1995, the Chilean economy had grown for eleven consecutive years, often with an annual growth rate of over 7 percent, such as in 1988 (Goodwin 1996:72).

DEPENDENCY

Dependency theorists contend that liberal economics theory ignores the particular problems faced by poor economies. Brazilian economists Raul Prebisch and Fernando Cardozo, who developed dependency theory in the 1950s, were at the time responding to an increasing gap in earnings between primary commodities producers and manufactured goods producers. These economists turned descriptive information into a theory by formulating general principles derived from the relationship between industrial and agricultural-based economies.

The core principles of dependency theory directly challenge those of liberal economists, who see the international trading system as capable of benefiting all states through free trade and specialization. In contrast, dependency analysts argue that free trade is in the interests of businesses in the industrial world and that they use their size and wealth to keep primary commodity prices low by playing suppliers in various countries against each other. Dependency advocates accept the necessity of using developing world governments to counter the established power of the industrial world's firms. A government's policies can help its citizens compete with foreign companies by limiting imports and subsidizing exports. A government also should redistribute at least some income within its society so that the poorest, most dependent citizens, can improve their lives.

Structural Inequality: Neocolonialism

Dependency theory recognizes the inequality in the relationship between the industrial world and the developing world. Decisions made by businesses and governments in the industrial world affect the developing world more than the other way around. This inequality is referred to as *neoimperialism,* or *neocolonialism,* because developing world countries have achieved political independence but not economic independence. Poor countries need the rich much more than vice versa. Developing economies depend on the industrial world for markets, capital and capital goods, consumer goods, refined fuels, processed food, and just about everything else that characterizes a modern economy.

Industrial economies, in contrast, import mostly primary commodities from the developing world, which adds only a small amount to their total production costs. This unbalanced economic relationship has international political implications. A developing world country does not have much of a bargaining position when negotiating with the government of or a business in the United States, for example. Nor do its interests figure prominently in the actions and policies of IGOs, such as the World Bank.

One attempt to redress this sense of powerlessness was the formation of new IGOs in the late 1960s and early 1970s to coordinate the production of and trade in primary commodities in order to negotiate higher prices. Most were not particularly successful. The Union of Banana Exporting Countries (UBEC), for example, tried to take on the three US companies that dominated about 70 percent of the world's banana trade—United Brands, Del Monte, and Castle Cook. Facing such a concentrated control of marketing and transportation systems, and possessing a perishable food product that cannot be withheld from sale for long, UBEC's members could not gain a decided negotiating advantage.

Dependent economic relationships also exist *within* countries. In a developing state's dual economy, the subsistence sector is dependent on the modern consumer and trading sector for jobs, consumer goods, fuel, capital, markets, and so on. Similarly, chronically poor urban and rural areas within industrial states are dependent on the state's high-income economy. Native American reservations in the United States, for example, bear not only the burden of economic dependency, but also of their history as losers in a colonial struggle.

Because poverty means having very few choices, wherever it exists the poor tend to act like dependent people. The well-to-do often view them as either excessively deferential or too demanding. However they are perceived, their condition relative to that of the wealthy has humanitarian, economic, and political consequences that cry out for action.

Government Intervention

Dependency theorists oppose the liberal economics prescription for breaking out of the vicious cycle of underdevelopment. Free market advocates advise developing economies to open their local markets and allow foreign investment as well as imports of manufactured goods. Also, so say the liberal economists, the production of cash crops in which the developing economy has a comparative advantage should be encouraged. They are needed to pay for imports. Dependency theorists counter that such prescriptions will only increase dependency by perpetuating the developing states' unequal relationship with the industrialized world, which uses the developing world as a source of raw materials and cheap labor.

The liberal economics and dependency perspectives share at least one common development goal; namely, economic growth leading to industrialization. To this dependency adds the goal of decreasing the power gap between the industrial and developing worlds. Substantial economic growth cannot be achieved by mainly primary commodity-producing states without some wealth redistribution and shared decision making, both internationally and within the developing states. This goal implies a positive role for governments to act together within IGOs, such as the United Nations and World Trade Organization. Dependency theorists realize that even when they work together, developing countries face an uphill struggle.

Concerning internal economic policies, developing world governments should establish tariffs, quotas, and other trade restrictions to protect their infant industries from unfair competition with established MNCs headquartered in industrialized states. Developing world governments can also provide some funding for plant, equipment, and infrastructure, such as transportation and communication systems. Subsidies may be needed in the fragile early stages of development.

Dependency theory recognizes that large companies with multiple sources of raw materials and markets and large amounts of capital often employ a common business practice: They lower the prices of their products below costs in one of their markets in order to drive out competition. They can sustain losses in this market because they charge higher prices in markets where they control a large market share. New industries with only one or even several small markets cannot match the giant company's low prices and are driven out of business. After the demise of their smaller competitors, the large company raises its prices.

The international economic context has changed significantly since the late nineteenth and early twentieth centuries, when most industrialized countries began their major growth process. Today, huge multinational corporations dominate the international market and are serious competitors to small businesses in newly developing economies. Whereas a nineteenth-century small operation could make a profit, the present-day international economy requires a minimum of multiple markets and access to worldwide transportation and communication systems. There are many ways a small, local company can be cut off and driven out of business. In this context, dependency analysts argue, it is impossible to create through free trade any semblance of a level playing field in the way advocated by liberal economics theorists.

The International Economic System

Positive government action can occur externally, in the international economic system, through resolutions passed by IGOs. Developing countries recognize that they share interests and often cooperate with each other in international trade negotiations by adopting common negotiating positions (for example, by withholding support for international tariff reduction treaties until they include decreases in the tariffs industrial states can impose on primary commodity imports from developing states). In the 1970s, the developing world attempted a major change in how the international economic system functions. As noted in Chapter 1, the year 1973 was a banner year for developing states. Because of the oil embargo, members of the Organization of Petroleum Exporting Countries (OPEC) had negotiated with the industrial world as equals. Partially as a result, a 1974 special session of the UN General Assembly passed a series of resolutions called the *New International Economic Order (NIEO)*. According to the developing countries, they constituted an attempt to level the international economic playing field. The required two-thirds majority vote occurred because, during the 1960s, most countries in Africa gained their independence and joined the United Nations. A total of forty-two developing countries were admitted into the UN during the 1960s. Thus, the poorer states outnumbered the industrialized states by three to one.

Two of the 1974 proposals show how the NIEO reflected the dependency model. The first proposal set a target for the amount of foreign aid industrialized states should provide to the developing world; the second, called *indexation*, attempted to fix primary commodity prices in relation to those of manufactured goods. The aid resolution proposed that industrialized states earmark 0.7 percent of their annual GNPs for foreign aid. Since imperialism was one of the main reasons the less developed countries became trapped in the cycle of underdevelopment, the wrong could be redressed through increased aid. Added to this reasoning was the fact that industrialized states had used outside capital during their early stages of development (for example, British capital helped finance railroads in the United States and Canada). Indexation addressed the core of the dependency perspective's analysis; that is, why the world trading system works against developing countries, resulting over time in declines in the prices of primary commodities in relation to those of manufactured goods. The NIEO aimed to establish an index each year, combining the price of specified manufactured goods. When the index rose a certain percentage, then the price of primary commodities would automatically increase by the same percentage. This mechanism was designed to stabilize the income developing states would earn for their primary commodities.

The NIEO resolutions never went into effect because they required implementation by the industrialized countries. This result was predictable, given dependency theory's basic assumption that the industrial world has much more power than the developing world. Today, dependency is used less as a strategy for change and more as a critique of the existing world economic system and the economic plight of developing economies.

Earlier, during the 1940s to 1960s, primarily in Latin America, another strategy had been tried in an attempt to overcome dependency. Called *import substitution*, the goal was to produce domestically at least some of the products imported from the industrial world. Latin American governments adopted policies to protect new businesses by subsidizing them and raising tariffs on competitive imports. The governments also limited capital investments by multinational corporations. In the 1980s and 1990s, the policies restricting imports and international investments were dismantled due to pressure from private multinational banks and the International Monetary Fund. Countries needed additional loans from these sources because they faced severe debt crises in the 1980s, and deep, multiple-year recessions. Although the import-substitution strategy raised the level of industrialization, it also created a few problems. For one, domestic markets were not large enough for economies of scale and, therefore, new businesses could not compete in the international market against similar products made in the industrial world. In addition, because import substitution requires a sizable investment, it often involved borrowing internationally the capital that was not available in the domestic economy.

Open market competition makes sense if gains are possible at least once in a while, but according to the dependency perspective the cards remain so stacked against developing economies that they have little hope of doing so. Some exceptions have occurred due to their particular circumstances; for example, South Korea has industrialized and achieved a per capita GNP of $7,660 in 1993. Its distinctive circumstances include an extraordinarily cohesive society and much aid from the United States. These have enabled decades of centralized control by the military to produce major surpluses from year to year and substantial investment. Some South Korean companies such as Hundai have become so dominant domestically that their low costs, economies of scale, and profit margins have enabled them to compete in the world market. Unfortunately for liberal economics prescriptions, however, decades of economic data indicate that the large majority of developing world states will not emulate South Korea's relative success.

It may be something of a surprise to realize that industrialized countries, the most fervent advocates of free trade, still impose tariffs and other restrictions on imports. They also subsidize the local production of some products; for example, the US Department of Agriculture's price support program for agricultural products includes cotton. This puts US cotton farmers in a favorable position as they compete with several developing countries including Egypt and Tanzania. However, while cotton represents less than 0.5 percent of total US export earnings, it produces about 6 percent of Egypt's and 11 percent of Tanzania's exports (United Nations, *International Trade and Statistics Yearbook 1994*).

Current US government support for its own producers violates the free trade principle, though such policies are not new. Economic development in the United States during the nineteenth and early twentieth centuries used tariffs as a way to protect domestic markets. Also, the US government provided generous subsidies in various forms; for example, free western land seven miles on either side of the tracks was given to railroad companies in the nineteenth century.

Dependency theorists point out that examples of free trade hypocrisy on the part of the industrial world may undermine its propaganda but not the pressure it exerts on the developing world. The dominance of industrialized states occurs in bilateral negotiations with developing governments as well as in multilateral governmental organizations such as International Monetary Fund. To receive an IMF loan, a government must sign an agreement to open up its domestic markets to foreign imports and investment, increase its exports, and privatize and otherwise reduce its budget deficit by spending less on social programs. In other words, developing states must adopt liberal economics policies that will enable businesses in the industrial world to take advantage of what are called *emerging markets*. Thus, dependency is not only perpetuated but also expanded by IMF policy.

A Critique from the Liberal Economics Perspective

Free trade advocates point out that activist economic policies, such as protective tariffs, provide artificial assistance that, over time, will discourage new businesses in developing countries from becoming competitive. Free trade is necessary for comparative advantage to lower consumer prices in all economies. When governments intervene in economics they make mistakes whether they are in industrial or developing countries. Economic efficiency is not their main purpose because political demands take precedence, such as pressure from subsidized companies and their workers to continue subsidies long after they could compete in the free market. Such political pressure makes it extremely difficult to have flexible pricing policies in response to changing market conditions. Therefore, subsidized companies and industries react sluggishly, remain uncompetitive, and even worse, discourage growth. States that subsidize the price of bread, for example, undermine their own farmers' ability to grow wheat at a profit. Farmers have no incentive to increase wheat production since they cannot earn more money. Sometimes they cannot even earn enough to meet increases in the cost of production, so they turn to other crops or occupations. For years, Egypt has had to use scarce foreign exchange or aid credits to import US wheat because of shortfalls in its own production. When it attempted to reduce bread subsidies in the late 1970s, street riots ensued. Introducing free market remedies is always politically unpopular in the short run but needed for a healthy economy in the long term.

Liberal economists concede that over years many primary commodity prices do fluctuate in the international market, sometimes severely, and that they are often not a solid basis for raising development capital. Yet, this cannot be seen as a sufficient explanation for why poor countries face insurmountable problems that put them permanently at a disadvantage. It is true that agriculturally-based economies do not have the purchasing power needed to industrialize quickly. They must gradually build a reliable basis for economic growth and accept investment and advice from the industrial world.

Sustained free market policies will work in the long run. Unfortunately, most developing states have had to abruptly change strategies, making stable growth difficult. Many had socialist policies exacerbated by mismanagement and mistakes. Only recently have sizable numbers of developing countries begun dismantling their elaborate and inefficient government bureaucracies. It is possible that many of these countries will experience positive growth in the future. Some states that recently achieved years of substantial economic growth were once mainly primary commodity producers. Thailand, for example, in its early stages of development, earned large percentages of its foreign exchange through the sale of rubber and rice. In the mid-1980s, however, its liberal economic growth policies had paid off in GNP increases of often over 10 percent a year.

The need for foreign investment remains obvious. In the case of Thailand, billions in Japanese investments have spurred economic growth. Outside capital has been a catalyst in the development of many industrial countries. It can help today's developing world as well if allowed to move freely from state to state. In attracting such investment, developing economies have a comparative advantage in several product categories, not just in primary commodities. The production of textiles, for example, is labor intensive; therefore, clothing manufacturers are attracted by the lower wages in developing countries.

PARTICIPATORY DEVELOPMENT

Advocates of participatory development argue that relying on economic growth and industrialization to alleviate the problems of the world's poor has not worked for the vast majority of developing countries. The focus should be on directly raising their quality of life using strategies available now, rather than waiting until industrialization has produced a trickle-down effect. Often termed a *basic needs approach* or *sustainable development*, participatory development produces more and better-quality food to reduce malnutrition, and improves primary medical care, education, and housing. While economic growth may occur as a result of meeting basic needs, it is not a goal in and of itself. In fact, making growth the primary objective has often reduced the poor's quality of life because scarce resources are redirected and invested in increasing the production of cash crops instead of food.

Since industrialization requires very high levels of capital investment, participatory development advocates question why it is viewed as a goal. It sets a standard that invites failure, given the overwhelming problems developing economies must overcome. Why emulate the process used and advocated by the already rich, one that enables them to become richer by creating investment opportunities in developing economies? Ordinary people can improve their lives without industrializing first. The definition of participatory development has emerged from practical experience, by noting through trial and error what factors account for success. First, development projects are designed to meet basic needs. Second, local people who will benefit and maintain the projects must participate by making decisions as well as providing labor. Third, locally available resources and technologies must be used which do cause harm to the natural environment.

Local Decision Making

Local people not only determine which development projects to undertake, but they also make daily organizing and allocation decisions. By participating in project planning and implementation, local leadership becomes established, which is needed to make the change permanent. To be most effective, outside aid workers act in support of local initiatives. The outsiders make recommendations, provide technical expertise, and secure outside funding. If the project is completely designed by outsiders, its permanency may well be doomed from the beginning. It may take months or even years longer to complete a project when committees of local people make key decisions, but this process greatly increases the chances that it will continue after the external support stops.

Available Technology

Village-level projects are more likely to become permanent when they use locally available tools, fuel, knowledge, and skills. The less that has to be imported, the better. Beneficiaries will have to know how to run and repair the needed technology and afford the resources it requires. Often this means using picks and shovels instead of heavy earth-moving machinery. *Labor-intensive technologies* take more time but cost less and can be used in repair work.

The road to economic development is littered with failed projects that did not last past the first few years after outside financial and technical expertise had ended. One oft-cited example is said to have occurred during development's early stages in a west African country. Tractors financed by loans from the United States ended up unused and rusting. Large tractors built in the United States need acres of relatively flat land to be cost efficient. Such terrain exists in few places outside of the US Midwest. Also, fuel to run the tractors, and their spare parts, had to be imported. The repair manuals required the ability to read English at a fairly sophisticated level. All these factors meant continued use of the machines depended on a constant supply of outside expertise and financing. Even if all these factors had been in place, there was no guarantee that markets existed to return enough profit to pay for all the expenses of a capital-intensive production process. Often enough profit cannot be made because domestic markets are small in developing world countries. The international market cannot be relied on either, because cash crop prices fall just as often as they rise.

Environmental Compatibility

In any given village, the natural environment dictates what lifestyles can be sustained over long periods of time. To maximize the chances for success, grass-roots development projects should maintain an equilibrium with available resources. Expensive oil imports, well beyond the earnings of most villagers, are required to operate machines. Therefore, participatory development strategies often apply *labor-intensive technologies* using human and animal power, wind, or water instead of modern machinery. Pick-and-shovel technology poses less threat to the natural environment, a problem that faces most developing world villages at the end of the twentieth century. Growing domestic animal and human populations have produced chronic erosion and deforestation. Labor-intensive answers include planting trees to replace those used for firewood. Also, villagers can raise fodder for their animals instead of letting them forage and destroy the plants needed to retain soil during the rainy season.

Participatory development advocates do not decry all of an industrial economy's technologies. Those based on renewable resources can prove useful, such as solar collectors for heating water and providing electricity. In addition, improved seeds and organic fertilizers produce more food. Technologies for controlling human fertility provide another example. Yet, these illustrations demonstrate the fact that technology by itself cannot work unless local people decide to use it; for example, technologies limiting population growth will only lower the birth rate in those villages where there is a good chance children will survive. This is not the case where infant mortality rates remain high. Therefore, birth-control methodologies must be introduced as a part of a total, holistic strategy emphasizing improvements in primary medical care and food production. Such multifaceted programs in Bangladesh and India have proven that development can happen, and on a large scale, without industrialization. Kerala, a region at the southwestern tip of India, has carried out participatory development strategies for over three decades. The result has been an improvement in the region's quality-of-life indicators to levels of high-middle-income countries; literacy has reached 100 percent, life expectancy stands at 70 years, and infant mortality has declined by 37 percent. These achievements have occurred even though Kerala's per capita income has remained very low, lower even than that for India as a whole, at around $330 in 1991 (Franke and Chasm 1994:ii).

Critiques from the Liberal Economics and Dependency Perspectives

Liberal economics theorists point out that, unlike machine-age technology, village-level sustainable development has not demonstrated the capacity to produce ongoing improvements in the standard of living on a country-wide basis. Economic growth projects will prove necessary at some point. Single village, or even regional improvements in daily living, are limited in their ability to distribute benefits and could lead to an economic dead-end. In the long run, local needs and products must become part of a large-scale, ongoing demand-and-supply cycle where increased demand stimulates greater production thus lowering costs, which, in turn, increases demand. So far, participatory development has proven only to have scattered local benefits. It can help if it does not detract from major investments. It will not produce the needed economic expansion in and of itself and, therefore, will take too long to improve the lives of people in large numbers.

Dependency perspective proponents applaud the goal of improving the poor's quality of life. Yet they hasten to point out that it is not possible to escape, in the long run, the world market economy's negative effects. Limiting the goal to providing improvements in daily living, village by village, constitutes a "cop out." It ignores the basic reason why the poor can only marginally improve their quality of life. The main problem is the stranglehold the world's rich and powerful elites have on local markets.

Sooner or later the products of local self-help projects, whether handicrafts or surplus food, will be undercut by multinational corporations that will use their size to charge lower prices in selected local markets. One example of how international firms drive out locally produced goods has occurred in Peru. For centuries, Andean women have used large squares of cloth to carry everything from babies to firewood. Village women weave the material with wool from their animals. The most energetic would supplement their families' incomes by selling the products of their own work in local markets. Now the vast majority of these carrying cloths consist of brightly colored acrylic material produced by a Japanese-owned subsidiary. This has resulted in further dependency on the industrialized world.

ECONOMIC PERSPECTIVES APPLIED TO DEVELOPMENT IN THE PERUVIAN HIGHLANDS

Matrix 5.1 summarizes the main points discussed in this chapter. The discussion so far and the matrix contrasts the three perspectives. They also complement each other in explaining reasons for the success or failure of specific development projects. The case study of Mollepata's irrigation channel provides an example.

The case study in Chapter 4 describes villagers' different experiences with two irrigation projects in Mollepata, Peru. One produced a failure and the other produced more food crops. The first project, Canal Nuevo, was a failure due to the misapplication of resources, which is common in all too many development projects. The other, La Estrella, produced more food crops. Its success demonstrated that major accomplishments can result from the combination of effective local leadership and dedicated development workers, supported by outside funding and technical expertise. As the remainder of this chapter will show, the three economic perspectives—liberal economics, dependency, and participatory development—provide varying explanations for the success in Mollepata.

A View from the Liberal Economics Perspective

La Estrella illustrates how effectively privately designed and organized projects can work without government regulation and intervention. Yet the canal does not provide a model for country-wide development. Large-scale industrialization remains the only proven method for lifting whole populations out of poverty.

Matrix 5.1
ECONOMIC PERSPECTIVES PERSPECTIVES

	LIBRAL ECONOMICS	DEPENDENCY	PARTICIPATORY DEVELOPMENT
GOALS	Economic growth	Self-determination Economic growth	Quality-of-life improvements
KEY CONCEPTS	Comparative advantage	Dependency	Sustainable development
STRATEGIES	Industrialization Private funding Free trade	Industrialization Some public funding Stabilization of primary commodity prices and aid	Labor-intensive rural development, locally controlled Self-sufficiency Equilibrium with natural environment
"BEST" TECHNOLOGY	Capital intensive	Capital intensive	Appropriate
MAJOR PROBLEMS OF EXISTING SYSTEM	Mistaken policies Over population	Maldistribution of wealth and power (domestic and international)	Blind use of industrial technology Maldistribution of wealth and power (domestic and international)
SEES CURRENT INTERNATIONAL ECONOMIC SYSTEM AS:	Potentially benefiting all countries	Favoring the industrialized world	Favoring the industrialized world

Free market principles could explain the success in Mollepata by pointing out that its rewards went directly to those residents who took the initiative and worked hard for years digging the irrigation channel. Now that the steady supply of water enables them to produce a surplus, they can sell it in the Cusco city market at a price they negotiate themselves. Thus, those who did the work on the canal are earning the profits. Since the land they work is their own, they had an incentive to invest in it and built the channel. It was not a government project. La Estrella's success emphasizes private, individual initiative without government interference. Supply and demand determine the price for Mollepata's surplus potatoes and other products and thus their producers can make a profit. An observer should question, however, whether to invest scarce investment capital for many local projects while there is such a need for large-scale development.

A View from the Dependency Perspective

The irrigation project avoided the debilitating effects of cash crop production, which benefit the rich and powerful both domestically and internationally. It proves the poor are capable and competent, thus dispelling the myth that elites are needed to provide leadership.

Dependency theory highlights the fact that the village of Mollepata is relatively isolated. It lies in the Andes, a three-to four-day drive up winding roads from Peru's port of Lima. Its residents are not enmeshed in producing cash crops for sale overseas nor heavily in debt to a large local landowner. The two local *hacendados* moved out as a result of a leftist government's policies in the 1970s and, after a failed attempt at communal ownership, the land was turned over to its residents. Therefore, the negative effects of a domestic dual economy do not apply. Neither does its parallel in the international economic system based, as in a dual economy, on the unequal exchange of cash crops for industrial goods. Mollepata's residents experience less of the oppressive polarization between the powerless and the powerful than elsewhere in the developing world. In the context, outside help was directed by and in the interest of the villagers themselves. International NGO financing and technical assistance supported decisions made by CADEP and the project beneficiaries. Inequality did not distort the relationship between who did the work and who received the benefits.

A View from the Participatory Development Perspective

The contrast between Canal Nuevo and La Estrella shows that basic needs projects are the only kind that make sense for the majority of the world's people. Industrialization with its long-term promise of trickle-down benefits has not and will not solve the problems inherent in global poverty.

Mollepata's experience fits all participatory development principles; that is, beneficiary decision making to improve their daily lives, available technology, and environmental compatibility. CADEP, the non profit private development organization based in Cusco, helped organize the residents of the agricultural sectors into a decision-making committee. They argued, debated, decided, and carried out their own plan, advised all along by CADEP development workers. Local leadership emerged from this process.

For a project to remain in operation, village people will have to maintain it without outside help. Therefore, the second principle of participatory development emphasizes using technology currently available to villagers. This applies to La Estrella, since most of the work was done with picks and shovels. In addition, ancient Incan building techniques were used; for example, large stones were dug into the channel bed to break the fall of water when it cascaded steeply downhill.

This was vital because fast-flowing water will erode the sides of even concrete-lined conduits.

The irrigation canal's success can also be attributed to participatory development's third principle: that it was designed to have a minimum impact on the natural environment. Upkeep of the canal does not require pumps or other machinery that need fossil fuels. The technicians, village people trained to monitor and maintain the canal, regulate the flow of water by using sliding overflow hatches. These are operated by pulling up on a handle. The overflow outlets diminish the danger during the rainy season of fast-flowing water that could erode the channel.

To summarize, each of the three perspectives highlights different reasons for La Estrella's success. Yet some of the reasoning overlaps, such as the point that the people who planned and worked on the project also received the benefits. Advocates of all three perspectives would see this as a reason for success but have differing explanations: Participatory development emphasizes local decision making, dependency aims to redress inequality, and liberal economics assumes the efficiency of personal financial incentives and private, nongovernmental decision making. The analysis indicates that the design of development projects would benefit from taking all three perspectives into account.

TERMS AND CONCEPTS

comparative advantage

economies of scale

free trade

import substitution

labor-intensive technologies

neoimperialism/neocolonialism

New International Economic Order (NIEO)

DISCUSSION QUESTIONS

1. Which perspective do you think best explains the success of the irrigation project in Mollepata, Peru—liberal economics, dependency, or participatory development? Give reasons to support your answer.

2. What do the liberal economics and dependency perspectives have in common? The dependency and participatory development perspectives? Explain your reasoning.

3. Choose a current problem facing low-income states, such as indebtedness or population growth. How would each of the three perspectives discussed in this chapter explain its cause? What would each suggest as a solution to the problem?

4. List some of the common assumptions about world poverty made by people you know. Which perspective does each assumption reflect?

5. In your opinion, should US development policies be based on liberal economics, dependency, or participatory development? Why do you think so? What assumption does your view reflect about the US role in fostering world development?

RESEARCH PROJECTS

1. Read several articles about world poverty, and determine which perspective each author takes on the issue of economic development.

2. Write a short list of questions about the causes of world poverty from the point of view of each perspective. Pose the questions to at least five people and record their answers. What perspectives do the respondents seem to take?

3. Research the position of the United States on a current trade issue, such as copyright ownership. Which perspective does the US position reflect?

4. Choose a country and gather some information about its trade pattern: What are its major trading partners? What does the state import and export? Given the trade patterns and economic interests of the state, which perspective would its people be most likely to support?

5. Find several examples of development projects (successful or unsuccessful). Which perspectives do they reflect? How can you use the perspectives to explain the success or failure of each project?

INTERNET RESOURCES

Japan International Cooperation Agency: *http://www.jica.go.jp* The Japan International Cooperation Agency, a unit of Japan's Official Development Assistance Program, provides an extended explanation of participatory development in its report, "Participatory Development and Good Governance."

US Agency for International Development: *http://www.info.usaid.gov* In addition to providing maps, charts, and other data, this colorful site includes information on the agency's projects.

"Talking About Development," an interview project by Vera Britto: *http://www.personal. umich.edu/~fiatlux/td* This site includes a series of interviews with practitioners in various countries about their experiences with development.

6

Human Ecological Sustainability

Homo sapiens is one of the most successful species on Earth in a number of respects. They can live in virtually all climatic zones—from the Arctic to the tropics and from deserts to swamps. They are omnivorous and have developed technologies, or tool kits, that allow them to build shelters, process foods, and provide elaborate health care. Consequently, the number of people on Earth has grown to a historic level, but population growth is not the only consequence of this success. The human race has also changed the planet. The human impact on the natural environment has effects not only on the biological reality of humans, but also on their cultural, economic, and political realities. With this awareness, the research of biologists, chemists, and geoscientists becomes a key to understanding these relatively new issues.

This chapter looks at typical human adaptations to nature in order to analyze their effects. People, in their respective adaptations, can either work the land without using it up or work the land and cause a myriad of problems. Pressing problems of health, food, and pollution have plagued the twentieth century and caused widespread human misery. The case study involving the Amazonian rainforest in Brazil, presented at the end of this chapter, illustrates and defines many of the world's ecological concerns. It must be remembered that humans are very much part of their environments.

ECOSYSTEMS: THE NATURE OF ENVIRONMENT

In 1859, Thomas Austin, an Australian farmer, imported twenty-four rabbits from his native Britain. These common European animals are placentals, meaning that they give birth to developed young. Placentals were unknown on this continent which is home to an entirely different form of mammal, the marsupial, which give birth to immature young which grow in external pouches. Soon Mr. Austin's rabbits were loose and breeding "like rabbits." With the local predators, dingoes and eagles, decimated by European hunters, the descendents of Mr. Austin's rabbits spread throughout the southern half of the continent killing small mammals and much of the plant life in the semi-arid areas that had been damaged by the sheep (also imported). Foxes, brought from Europe for fox hunting, also went free and followed the tasty rabbits. Soon the region was denuded of much of its plant life, birds, tortoises, and small marsupials, leaving a decimated landscape behind. In the twentieth century, myxomatosis, a virus fatal to rabbits, was spread throughout the continent as a means for control. While this limited the population for a while, the disease spread to Europe and killed valued rabbits there. Currently Australian government scientists are experimenting with new biological controls including the virus, RCV (rabbit calicivirus), which is deadly to infected rabbits, but offers concerns for long run consequences and efficacy. (Vandenbeld 1988:252–55, Anderson and Nowak 1997:34–37)

This oft-told tale of nineteenth-century Australian history illustrates several concepts of ecological importance. First, Thomas Austin did not set out to destroy the ecosystem of southern Australia with rabbits. He was merely trying to re-create the environment of his birth in this new world, and the small, nonaggressive animals were not seen as an environmental threat. More important was the "fit" of the rabbits within the existing environment, which was either unknown or not considered by Austin at the time. These rabbits found a niche in their new home that was virtually void of predators and filled with food. They thus became aggressors in this particular setting. Most important, however, was the concept of system or interconnectedness, in that the rabbits became a particularly dangerous threat to the plants. Similarly, the rabbits were protected from predators, since farmers had killed off the dingoes and eagles that they believed were killing their domesticated and economically important sheep. The increasing loss of plants allowed rapid erosion, further threatening animals and plant life in the area. Then the solution to the problem created new problems, spreading disease to other areas that became connected to the previously isolated continent through human development. The introduction of the twenty-four seemingly harmless rabbits thus upset an ecosystem and had far-reaching consequences.

The Interrelationship of Environmental Systems

All environments are composed of complex interconnections among plants, animals, and physical and chemical factors, which are called *ecosystems*. The most important part of an ecosystem, as the term implies, is the interrelatedness of the elements within the system. When one element changes others may be modified in turn. For example, a change of the acidity of the water in a stream will affect the plants that depend on that water, the animals that depend on those plants, and the people who depend on the plants, animals, and water. The interrelationship of all plants and animals and their physical and chemical environment within a region is a specific ecosystem. In the larger sense, the Earth is also an ecosystem since no part of the world is truly isolated from the other parts.

Many of the changes in ecosystems are begun by human agency but end in consequences well beyond human expectation or control. It is apparent that ecosystems are finite arenas. In some places, human populations appear to be nearing a critical level and, perhaps, their *carrying capacity*—the number of people who can be supported indefinitely in a given environment with a given technology and culture. For example, in India or Bangladesh, where the huge population has decimated forests, polluted waters, and consumed soils, poverty and disease are uncontrolled and the capacity to feed and house the number of people who are born is seriously strained.

The world's resources are finite, yet all people share the resources. We know that the *Commons*—areas publicly owned and opened for general use—are not typically well tended. Often individual interests override the common good. Environmental changes that bring short-term benefits for individuals or communities can often lead to long-term devastation for many more people. Biologist Garrett Hardin described this trend as "The Tragedy of the Commons" in an article by that title published in the journal *Science* (1968:1243–48). As an example, people using public land for grazing animals or similar economic gain will overuse these areas while protecting the lands they privately own. In this view, individual self-interest triumphs over communal good and the common areas of the globe steadily degrade. The full impact of such a view is most vivid in the use of the oceans as a dumping ground for garbage and the atmosphere as a recipient of chemical pollutants. A more complex issue is the need for the conservation of areas, such as temperate and tropical rainforests, that are located within individual states but whose environmental stability is crucial to the well-being of people well beyond the borders of those states. Clearly, abuses of all these Commons have become global issues.

HUMANS AND THE ENVIRONMENT

The major cultural and economic adaptations that humans have used to survive in their environments include foraging, pastoralism, agriculturalism, and industrialism (see Chapter 2). Each of these adaptations has advantages and disadvantages in terms of its ecological effects on Earth's environments.

Foraging

Foraging depends primarily on the hunting of wild animals and the gathering of wild plants. As the sole means of human survival for over a million years, it has been a successful form of adaptation. It is also successful ecologically, since its form of human food procurement is in balance with the natural environment.

The traditional strategy of the Inuit, the San of the Kalahari, and the Aboriginal Australians, among others, foraging is characterized by low populations that are dispersed over large areas. Foragers are constantly moving and, therefore, cause little disruption of the natural environment. There are no centers of pollution since there are no permanent houses or garbage dumps. People have simple forms of technology and use little energy because humans provide most of the labor themselves. Shortly after foragers move their camps, the actions of other animals and natural forces remove what they have left behind. While there is little permanent damage to the natural environment through this way of life, foraging cannot support large populations, and many such societies have been forced to practice infanticide in order to stay below the carrying capacity of their environment.

Pastoralism

Pastoralists—people who focus their economies on specific domesticated animals—include the Bedouins (camels), the Nuer (cattle), the Sami (reindeer), and the Kurds (sheep and goats). These cultures can support larger and more dense populations than can foragers, but the numbers are still far below those of agricultural societies. Pastoralists are often migratory, leading their animals to new pastures. Compared to foragers, their technology is more specialized but not complex, and their energy use includes animal power as well as human labor. Their environmental uses, however, are more demanding in an ecological sense: Herd animals exploit plants and pollute water, and large animals demand abundant quantities of land to survive.

Agriculturalism

People who focus on domesticated plants are horticulturalists, or if they use complex technology, agriculturalists. They share in kind, if not degree, the exploitation of the environment and the susceptibility to diseases that comes with plant cultivation.

An essential element of agriculturalism is the ability of the group to develop large and dense populations that are sedentary. A large number of people can live using a much smaller region than foragers. Horticulturalists using slash-and-burn techniques can destroy large areas of forests, leach the nutrients out of used fields, and pollute the air with smoke. The carrying capacity of this technology is very low, and increasing populations have driven many societies back to foraging, into extinction, or into agriculture. Agricultural techniques increase the yield of fields and can feed far more people in smaller areas, but there are environmental costs. The use of fertilizers and plow animals increases the pollution of the lands dramatically. The denser human settlements produce more garbage and human waste that must be disposed of to prevent health disasters. Water is also an issue because irrigation techniques often pollute water supplies just as they increase crop yield. Technology in these societies can be quite complex and some of the new tools, from metallurgy to fossil fuels, create their own forms of pollution.

Industrialism

Industrialism is the primary subsistence strategy of the world system today. While many people still live in less technologically complex societies, millions of people live in industrialized societies. But all people are influenced to some degree by industrialism. It is the only known economic strategy that can support the current population of the world.

This form of the subsistence strategy depends on the production of goods through the use of fossil fuels. From the coal that fueled the beginning of the Industrial Revolution to the petroleum base of contemporary industry, carbon-based fuels have allowed technological advances previously thought impossible. Humans with animals and rudimentary tools could not match the speed and efficiency of work that fuel-powered machines allowed.

One social result of the development of industrialism is a vast inequality between those who can use fossil fuels and those who cannot. This is true both within industrialized societies and between industrial and nonindustrial countries. In either case, a significant percentage of the population must still be involved in intensive agriculture or agribusiness in order to feed the large population of people that this type of society can maintain. A broad societal difference between rural and urban life is thus created. Between countries, the nonindustrialized states are generally poor and dependent on industrialized states for technological improvement. While there are signs of serious problems in parts of the world, the upper limits of the carrying capacity of industrialism as a world strategy have not yet been reached.

However, the long-term sustainability of industrialization, as it is currently practiced, is a serious concern. The ecological threats include extensive pollution from fossil fuel use, high-density human waste, and chemical contamination. In addition, as finite amounts of oil and coal are depleted, the extraction techniques bring more environmental change. Parts of the world appear incapable of growing enough food for their increasing populations. The rush to promote economic growth through industrialization and cash crops has increased the use of agricultural lands for other purposes, such as housing developments, shopping centers, and light industry.

THREATS TO CRITICAL RESOURCES

As mammals, humans, cannot survive without numerous, basic environmental resources, including breathable air, potable water, and arable lands. Without these resources, humans and other animals on Earth would die. Humans also need heat, clothing, and the plants and animals of the planet. Some animals and plants are used directly as food, while others are vital to the continuity of the ecosystem. Industrialism has improved the lives of millions of people, allowing increases in food, populations, and technological goods. This has a cost, however. Globally, industrialization has threatened all of the ecological essentials of human life. When looking individually at issues of specific environmental domains, it must be made clear that each is interlinked with the other. Earth's ecology does not respect state boundaries. Air, water, land, plants and animals exist throughout the globe, and environmental threats to any one of these resources are carried from one state to many others.

Air

The air, perhaps, is the ultimate common and is often taken for granted. The atmosphere that envelops the globe is essential to the survival of all living things. This unique blend of elements has no barrier walls and so the modification of any part of it can alter all its other parts and negatively affect the world. Air pollution comes from industry and urban life, such as from automobile emissions, factory outflows, and oil-, coal-, or wood-burning fuel. National and regional laws restricting the type of fuels that can be used and limiting the amount of allowable discharge of pollutants are now common in industrialized states. Most of these rules look at the local environment and react to immediate problems since there are higher concentrations around, and downwind of, the sources of emission. However, global issues that threaten the future of the world's environment remain largely unchecked. Increased levels of carbon dioxide and other gases in the atmosphere and the depletion of ozone are among the long-term challenges to the well-being of the planet.

Carbon Dioxide   Carbon dioxide (CO_2), is a colorless and odorless gas that makes up over 350 parts per million of the atmospheric gases. It is a natural part of the atmosphere, used by plants as a necessary part of their respiration. The mere existence of CO_2 does not pose a problem; in fact, the world as we know it depends on this gas. The relative increase in CO_2 in the delicate mix of the environment, however, is a problem. The burning of carbon-based fossil fuels in factories, automobile emissions, and power plants spews massive amounts of CO_2 into the atmosphere. Chemists estimate that there has been a 30 percent increase in CO_2 concentrations in the atmosphere since 1800 (Hileman 1995:19).

An additional factor is the loss of plant life from the mass destruction of rainforests, decreasing the rate of breakdown of carbon dioxide into oxygen and carbon. More CO_2 is produced and less is removed from the atmosphere through photosynthesis. Therefore, the percentage of carbon dioxide in the air has increased. One major threat of CO_2 buildup is the so-called *greenhouse effect* which many scientists fear will advance a climatic change involving increased global temperatures.

Global Warming   Global warming refers to small but regular and significant increases in the temperature of the Earth. Atmospheric gases, including CO_2, methane, ozone, and chlorofluorocarbons, which scientists call *greenhouse gases*, allow the short-wavelength radiation from the sun to pass through the atmosphere and reach the Earth. Like the glass in a greenhouse, short-wave radiation passes through and warms the inside. The greenhouse gases, however, absorb and trap infrared radiation that is emitted from the planet. With increased amounts of greenhouse gases in the atmosphere, less energy escapes back into space. The buildup of this increased capture of light energy warms the general atmosphere. Scientific models largely support an increase in this phenomenon in the foreseeable future if fossil fuel emissions continue at their present levels (Hileman 1995:18). The United Nations Environment Program (UNEP), the World Health Organization (WHO) and the World Meteorological Organization (WMO) issued a joint report in 1996 that warned against a "wait-and-see approach," since health problems from increased heat waves and insect-carried diseases could quickly follow global warming. They have estimated that three to six times as many deaths from severe heat in cities like New York could be expected by 2050 (Cushman 1996:2).

To the average person, an increase of three or four degrees Celsius in a century seems hardly a call for alarm. After all, humans have survived through the ice ages with far less complex technology. It is humans' dependency on technology, however, that has made this a serious concern. Not only has industrialization caused the problem, but it also makes the human consequences far more severe. The estimated change in temperature within the complex climatic system would also trigger a rise in sea levels (flooding low-lying lands), severe heat waves, and the disruption of agriculture in tropical and subtropical areas (Hileman 1995:19).

The potential effects of global warming on ice packs in glaciers and Antarctica, on storms and prevailing wind streams, on changes in ocean circulation patterns, and on particular periodic climatic events such as the Pacific El Nino are still being debated by some climatologists. To be sure, the rise in sea levels would threaten such urban regions as New Orleans, the delta of Bangladesh, and other densely populated areas, causing the dislocation of millions of people. The loss of agricultural potential would also be devastating in a heavily populated world, as would the destruction caused by more frequent and more violent storms and other severe weather patterns.

Virtually all of the proposed solutions to global warming lie in the realm of prevention. International guidelines limiting the release of greenhouse gases into the atmosphere and the use of fossil fuels in industry and automobiles are advanced as essential first steps. It is a truism of science that putting any system that has been modified back into a former state takes both great skill and good fortune. Once a system as complex as global warming is fully underway, it would be nearly impossible to reverse. Carbon dioxide released into the atmosphere will remain there for decades and sea levels will fall only with the refreezing of water into glaciers. Modifications in plants, land forms, and waterways would create their own climatic events. Clearly, in a systemic change like this, using technology to fix individual problems as they arise will not do much to reverse the pattern of global warming.

Restrictions on the use of fossil fuel, then, seem necessary but such limits would restrict the economic growth of the developed and the developing world. The vast volume of fossil fuel emissions comes from the developed world, particularly the United States. *The United Nations Environment Program* (*UNEP*) reports that the United States, is the world's greatest polluter, emitting four times as much CO_2 as Japan. Russia, the second most-polluting country, emits 73 percent of the US total, and China, the third, emits 52 percent (United Nations 1995a:37, 91, 154, 194). Since restricting the use of fossil fuels would mean a significant slowdown in US industrial growth, neither global warming nor the necessary steps for its solution will be easy for the world.

Some progress has been made in developing international limits on the emission of greenhouse gases. The 1997 Kyoto Protocol on Climate Change, which came out of an international meeting held in Kyoto, Japan, sets emissions targets for the developed nations. Between the years 2008 and 2012, the industrial powers are mandated to decrease their emissions of six greenhouse gases, including carbon dioxide, to an assigned percentage below their 1990 emissions levels. The US goal is 7 percent, and the EU's is 8 percent. The protocol also encourages the development of such projects as reforestation that will clean the atmosphere. While the results will be less far reaching than many environmentalists want, the conference establishes an agreement that global warming is a critical world problem that needs international action.

Ozone Depletion   The depletion of the ozone layer is another atmospheric issue that has captured many headlines in recent years and has been the subject of important international agreements. While high ozone levels in the atmosphere often cause health care officials in big cities to announce "ozone alerts" and to recommend that people with respiratory problems remain indoors, the opposite problem exists higher above the Earth. The ozone level in the lower stratosphere has thinned dramatically, especially in the outermost areas of the world, near the poles. These decreased concentrations are called *holes* in the ozone. These have begun to form in the protective layer that protects life on Earth from destructive ultraviolet rays. Without protection, radiation can cause skin cancers, cataracts, problems in the immune system, and increased mutations in animals. It can also disrupt photosynthesis in plants. The problem is of particular concern in very sunny areas, such as much of Australia. Maintaining the ozone layer is necessary for the continuation of the contemporary way of life on Earth.

Scientists Mario Molina, Paul Crutzen, and F. Sherwood Rowland shared the 1995 Noble Prize in Chemistry for their work in explaining the process of ozone depletion and predicting its repercussions. Chlorofluorocarbons (CFCs) chemically break down ozone (O_3). The ultimate proof of the problem is the expanding hole in the ozone layer first noticed in 1985, over Antarctica. More recently, a similar weakening in the north has also become quite severe.

Many world leaders, scientists and politicians, believe that damage to the ozone layer is happening and that it has potentially deadly results. Once again the solution seems to lie in the prevention of further damage. In 1987, the industrialized nations signed the Montreal Protocol on Substances that Deplete the Ozone Layer. The treaty mandates the end of the production of CFCs that account for over 70 percent of the chemical damage by 2000. In 1992, the date was moved up to January 1, 1996. In the developed world, CFCs had been widely used in refrigerants and aerosol-spray propellants. It has been estimated that the United States alone will spend about $100 billion to end CFC use (Alder, Cazamias, and Monnack 1995:428). With a successful ban, the level of CFCs should slowly decline in the atmosphere in coming years, and protective concentrations of ozone could slowly be regained.

Water

In addition to clean air, human survival depends on clean water. The surface of the planet is covered with more water than dry land and, consequently, the Earth appears as a blue sphere from outer space. The problem is not the quantity of water, but its quality and distribution.

Oceanic Pollution and Overuse   The oceans are an integral part of the human commons, covering about 70 percent of the Earth's surface. A healthy ocean is important for climatic stability, adequate food supply, healthy tourist industries, and access to new sources of minerals and other resources for potential medical cures. As former chief scientist of the National Oceanic and Atmospheric Administration Sylvia Earle summarizes: "The *living* ocean drives planetary chemistry, governs climate and weather, and otherwise provides the cornerstone of the life-support system for all creatures on our planet, from deep-sea starfish to desert sagebrush . . . If the sea is sick, we'll feel it. If it dies, we die" (1995:xii).

Two major, but conflicting, problems stand out: (1) The oceans are being used as dumping grounds for industrial wastes, and (2) oceanic resources are being overutilized. The oceans serve as dumps for the world's wastes both incidentally and intentionally. Incidentally, runoff from urban regions located near ocean shores and from nearby farms and industries goes into the oceans and creates pollution in coastal regions. Some of the urban-area beaches in New York and New Jersey have been closed to summer swimmers due to high fecal contamination of the waters or dangerous medical wastes on the shores. These problems endanger the health of millions and the economic livelihood of many others as well. Oil spills from accidental tanker collisions and leaks in drilling operations add to the pollution.

Intentional dumping of hazardous wastes, sewage discharge, and garbage from coastal cities into the seas has long been practiced under the mistaken notion that the vastness of the oceans would allow relatively small amounts of waste to dissipate and harmlessly disappear. Until recently, coastal sludge has been dredged and redeposited further out at sea on the assumption that doing so would protect the shore. Obviously, the fact that the ocean is a complex ecosystem dooms such actions to failure. Some parts of the Atlantic, just east of the New Jersey shore, have been labeled "dead" as a result of dumping practices that were outlawed in the United States in 1992. Even nuclear wastes have been discarded in the oceans by such industrial countries as Russia and the United States. Only very recently has France agreed to end its nuclear testing in the Pacific Ocean. On a much less pernicious level, even trash from ocean going vessels has caused damage to oceanic life. Such vessels have added to the pollution of the oceans. For years sea mammals have been found starved and strangled by plastics thrown off boats. Some cruise liners, including those of the Holland America line, have recently stopped the classical luxury ship recreation of skeet shooting because of concern over the dumping of lead pellets in the sea. These ships also have added pollution devices that restrict the discharge of waste products and oil into the water. Even a thin layer of oil inhibits the evaporation of seawater to water vapor, replenishing the oxygen in the atmosphere. The loss of greater amounts of oil from wrecks of oil tankers and leaking oil rigs has smothered shorelines, killed seabirds, and brought the issue to public awareness.

The United Nations, working through the UNEP and the International Maritime Organization, has taken a lead in promoting rules governing the uses of the oceans and advising techniques for limiting pollution (Carroll 1996:46). The Regional Seas Program of the UNEP has enabled states that share ocean resources to work together to protect them. The 1994 treaty that addresses these and other problems unique to the oceans is called the *Law of the Sea*. This long-debated UN-supported treaty establishes general rules for conduct in the oceans. It also codifies the definition of a twelve-mile limit of state control over coastal waters and an exclusive economic zone in which the state has rights over natural resources. Like all such international agreements, however, the good will of the signers is essential to the success of the mission and few sanctions exist that fully counter national interests.

Potable Water   Clean drinking water is the last problem in this category, and it is the one that comes closest to home. Life cannot continue without access to usable water. Not all water can be used, however, and most of the water on Earth is located in the oceans or frozen in the poles. Available nonsalt water is found in rain, lakes, rivers, and underground aquifers. Rain that replenishes streams, reservoirs, and underground reserves provides most of the potable water that people drink. Acid rain and air pollution can taint the water before it ever reaches the ground. In the rivers and lakes this water can be further contaminated by industrial wastes, chemical and biological fertilizer runoff from agriculture, human wastes from urban communities, and numerous other pollutants. Illness, and even death, are the results of drinking such untreated water.

Aquifers—caches of water found in rock cavities underground—provide the spring and well waters that are valued for their purity. Throughout most of human history, aquifers have supplied a seemingly endless source of drinkable water. Today, however, the same types of pollutants that affect surface waters seep into the soil and aquifer, and wells in many parts of the world have become contaminated. Another threat to the aquifers is overuse. The demand for water for industries, irrigation, and urban populations has ballooned since the Second World War, and water shortages are becoming commonplace even in the wealthiest areas. Irrigation water is rationed in part of the western United States. Also, demand for water from the Colorado River, which flows through the southwest United States and northern Mexico, has caused disputes between the two countries and among cities, in the United States.

Industries have emerged that search for technological solutions to the problems of water shortage and pollution. Techniques for converting saltwater to drinking water have been developed and used in a number of communities. The major problem with these desalinization techniques is their high cost. Water-treatment plants use physical, chemical, and biological techniques to bring urban waters to acceptable quality standards, but these methods are too costly for many parts of the world. Therefore, despite technological advances, the need for conservation of water supplies and limits on pollution remain primary concerns.

Acid Rain   Rain is a major source of fresh water. Evaporation and rain are two aspects of the natural recycling of water, as runoffs from melted snows join with rain and replenish lakes and streams. When the rain turns toxic, the entire system is in trouble. There are varieties of pollutants that have tainted rainwaters but one of the most commonly discussed is sulfuric acid, which causes acid rain. Sulfur dioxide (SO_2) is an acidic chemical that is emitted from factories burning sulfur-containing coal and from diesel fuels. The sulfur dioxide in the smoke chemically reacts with the water in the atmosphere to create sulfuric acid (H_2SO_4). This is maintained in the clouds and falls to earth in the form of *acid rain*. The high acidity of this chemical can weaken or kill plants and animals that have adapted to less acidic environments. Additionally, fish and other aquatic life can be endangered by increasing the acidity of water in small lakes. In the 1970s, the Adirondack Mountain area in New York was plagued by dying trees in the forests and lakes with dead fish, both poisoned by acid rain. Similar incidents in Germany,

Russia, and Canada made this one of the first ecological issues brought to international attention.

Solutions to acid rain were sought in the industries that produced the sulfuric acid. One solution that factories had used to protect the areas surrounding the plants from the dirt and pollution of coal burning was the construction of extremely tall smoke stacks, but these only intensified the problems of acid rain (Odum 1993:121–122). Mandates for the use of alternative fuels, or so-called cleaner coals, sprung up in regions and expensive refitting of plants did take place. In the 1980s, Western Europe restricted levels of SO_2 emissions and many factories in the former Soviet Union switched from coal to natural gas or oil. Within a decade, reports of decreased pollution in the Arctic seemed to reflect success (Facts on File 1993:1).

A curious problem in the attack on this problem is that the solutions are often limited within state borders while acid rain shows little respect for international boundaries, sometimes falling hundreds of miles from the polluting plants. Disputes between the United States and Canada over acid rain continue today, although the rain that falls in northern New York and southern Quebec is the same rain and the climatic zone is a common. In 1984, the European nations finally agreed to work together to decrease the SO^2 that pollutes their rains.

Land

While dry land covers a minority of the Earth's surface, it is the home of virtually all humanity. It also provides the breeding ground for most human food and the resource base for most industry. With the growth of human populations and industrialization, demands on the land have increased exponentially. Most lands, unlike the oceans, are not commonly owned. Private and state ownership of specific lands has become the norm, despite global implications of land degradations. The destruction of land through erosion, including deforestation and desertification, and toxic pollution continues to affect the world's climate and productivity.

Erosion   While poets have seen the Earth as eternal, scientists see the destruction of large parts of it through overuse or inappropriate use. Although it does seem to be increasing, this ecological devastation is not an invention of the twentieth century. Erosion, from deforestation and intensive agriculture, in inhabited parts of the American Southwest had already occurred by the thirteenth century. In Chaco Canyon, ancestors of the contemporary Pueblo people moved away from their cities and irrigated fields in the canyon after a dry spell made their modified environment too difficult.

The most vivid picture of devastating soil erosion, however, was that of the dust-bowl conditions of the American Midwest in the 1930s. Photographs, works of literature, and individual life histories remind us of the human pain those environmental changes created. The drought and loss of soil in one of the world's most important grain-growing areas caused population dislocations and added grief to the already stricken Depression years.

Fertile soils are delicate. The organic materials in soil are easily eroded by water and wind. Overgrazing, inappropriate farming techniques, and other disruptions leave land open to erosion without the protection of vegetation that could rebuild the fertility. The fact that the grain fields of the United States once again have become bountiful should not be taken, however, as proof that past harm can be easily overcome. Fertilizers can make up for soil depletion, but they create new problems of their own. Many scientists believe that the long-term health of the US Midwest is threatened by destruction of the aquifer, overuse of fertilizers, and urban growth. At this point, by nature and by human intervention, only one-quarter of the Earth's soils is suited for modern agriculture without intensive irrigation and fertilizer (Odum 1993:139).

A major threat in many parts of the world today is *desertification*. Areas of the great deserts, including the Sahara, are growing and grasslands, and similar marginal areas, are becoming deserts. The UNEP reported in 1984 that 35 percent of the Earth was in danger (Amstutz 1995:438). The reasons for this include overgrazing and changing weather patterns after deforestation. The extensive grazing of cattle or other herd animals on such grasslands has destroyed the protective vegetation. In some areas, these lands can be purchased cheaply, and used intensively for a finite amount of time, and then abandoned by, often foreign, enterprises such as cattle ranching. Similar damage is done with *deforestation,* where tropical forests are cut in order to create grazing areas for animals. In parts of Asia and South America, this has accounted for major soil degradation.

Toxic Pollutants The pollution of the air and seas also extends to the land. Modern industries, which by their nature create extensive amounts of potentially dangerous wastes, must be able to dispose of those wastes. In the past, landfills or waste dumps were widely employed. The garbage was simply buried in out-of-the-way lands and left to disintegrate.

The problems with this practice are evident today. Many of these wastes do not fully disintegrate, nor do they necessarily stay in place. Frequently, chemicals from these materials leach into the water supply and pollute areas far from the original dumps. In addition, many of the out-of-the-way areas are no longer remote with the extension of urban or suburban areas. The famous case of Love Canal in Upstate New York made the international news and promoted judicial review and legislation. A development of homes, built on a toxic landfill, had to be abandoned when the residents' health was clearly jeopardized.

Laws in many wealthy countries now mandate that industries assume responsibility for the proper disposal of their pollutants. Cleanup is now part of the price of doing business, when the laws are enforced. In poorer nations, however, local and international industries function under no such laws or have no means for enforcing the ones they enact. Consequently, this can lower the price of doing business in these countries and attract foreign corporations. In at least one case, this did not free a multinational corporation in the face of an extraordinary disaster. Union Carbide paid about $0.5 billion in compensation for the deaths of over two thousand people in 1984, in Bhopal, India, following a leak at its insecticide plant. Despite this occasional reckoning, the pollution tragedies of the past in the industrialized world continue largely unabated in today's developing world.

Plants and Animals

Extinction, the complete loss of a biological species, is normal in the world ecosystem. The nature of evolution argues that animals and plants that "fit" in a particular environment continue to breed, while those that have changed and become unfit, or those that have not changed in a changing environment and become ecologically unfit, do not successfully reproduce and become extinct. While each extinction might be a loss, each is not a threat to the world or an unnatural occurrence. The fate of most species that have existed on Earth is eventual extinction. The loss of dinosaurs, mammoths, and giant sloths is part of the natural history of the world. The contemporary ecosystem would not exist if extinctions had not occurred. Obviously, this does not mean that extinction is inherently good, but it clarifies that extinction by nature is not inherently bad. The problem of the contemporary era is that human actions have created an artificial world environment that has dictated a broad and massive loss of plant and animal life without replacement. In other words, human interference with natural systems has created the world as it is now. The diversity of life on the planet is thus threatened, and it is this type of extinction that is both new and frightening.

Extinctions: Plant Species   Like animals, thousands of plants species have become extinct throughout history. It seems likely that the original type of grass, later domesticated into modern maize (a major grain crop), has become extinct, perhaps because of competition with its domesticated offspring. Three issues are raised by the destruction of plants today: the effects of such losses to the ecosystem, to potential uses of endangered plants, and to local cultures.

A major focus of this concern involves deforestation, and especially in the tropical rainforests, which are decreasing at an alarming rate. The loss of trees negatively affects the soil and, in tropical regions, the soil level is particularly thin and fragile. The trees and the ecosystem that the soil supports are themselves very important. Temperate and tropical rainforests in the Americas, Asia, and Africa have been called the lungs of the Earth. They absorb huge amounts of carbon dioxide from the atmosphere as part of normal photosynthesis. Conversely, when the forests are burned, as they often are in clearing for agriculture, they release CO_2 back into the atmosphere. The relationship of the care of tropical rainforests and the greenhouse effect is well documented. It has been calculated that 45 percent of these forests have been lost to deforestation (Amstutz 1995:438).

Another international need for the preservation of these forests has only recently been recognized. The plants and animals of the rainforests are not well known by most people outside of their environs. In many ways, they represent an unknown library of new knowledge. The application of Western science and technology to these new raw materials may well produce discoveries valuable to business and health. Questions of the ownership of these materials and the importance of knowledge of them have raised questions about ownership and intellectual property rights. The United Nations is currently establishing principles for the recognition of and payment for the use of these rights. Some NGOs, such as Cultural Survival, have taken the lead in demanding that the rights of indigenous rainforest people be taken seriously. Some businesses, such as the cosmetic firm the Body Shop, have negotiated with local people for the use of tropical goods that have been used by the firm. They have also found it good business to advertise themselves as a multiethnic business.

One important discovery has come from the temperate rainforest of the Pacific Northwest, where the bark of the local yew tree was found to be a source for taxol, an effective treatment for ovarian cancer and perhaps other cancers. In 1991, Bristol-Meyers Squibb contracted with the US government for yews on federal lands. Since Pacific yews are the only known source of natural taxol, and these trees are found in old growth forests, the rapid reduction of old growth forests in Oregon, Washington, and British Columbia nearly destroyed this rare, and now very valuable, resource, even though semi-synthetic taxol is now produced.

A final important issue concerning the rainforests is a local one. While much of the world sees these forests as resources, people and endangered animals see them as home. Many of the last horticultural and hunting people of the world live in these forests. The destruction of the forests inevitably means ethnocide as well. The cultures of the Yanomamo and Bororo, among many other groups, cannot be relocated elsewhere. These people lack power in the national and international political scene. The reason their plight has reached the international press is due largely to the publicity that musicians, including Sting, have brought to them through rock concerts and other benefits.

Other people are effected as well in different but important ways. Rural women in many parts of the world spend hours each day collecting firewood for cooking and heating. As the forests recede, the women are forced to go further. United Nations (1995b:55–56) figures confirm this, showing that in some tree-poor areas in Africa, Asia, and Latin America women spend two to four hours a day collecting wood for their homes.

Extinctions: Animal Species   Every year animal species become extinct. Most go largely unnoticed, others, such as the Dodo bird and carrier pigeon, become metaphors for finality. In the contemporary era, the plight of tigers, elephants, rhinoceroses, spotted owls, and the great apes has been addressed in national legislatures; international accords regulate hunting them, destroying necessary territories, trading in animal parts, and exporting animals out of their natural areas. While all continue to be endangered, and some undoubtedly will become extinct in the wild, public interest and the growth of ecotourism have shown governments the importance of these resources.

Many endangered animals live in the sea, and the issue of the Commons is a complicating factor. The endangerment of two types of sea animals illustrates the interaction of economics and politics in the preservation or destruction of natural resources. One prominent call of ecologists is to "save the whales," and clearly, the human awe of the great whales is very real. One of the authors remembers being in a small boat crossing a strait in southeastern Alaska when she noticed an island she had never seen before. As she pointed it out to a friend, her "island" moved, spouted water, and dove under the surface. A local naturalist told her that she had seen a blue whale that was being tracked in the area. Her island, this animal, can weigh one hundred tons. A whaling factory ship could process this animal in an hour.

The story of the exploitation of whales is historically enlightening. Before 1860, whaling was a major industry in the United States and Europe, with whale oil and bones being lucrative products. As whales became harder to find, substitutes were developed, including new oils, steel-bones for corsets, and gas lighting. The decline reversed at the turn of the century, with a demand for oils for soaps and margarine. In 1900, two thousand whales were taken, and a decade later ten times as many. By the end of the Second World War, Norway and Britain, using technologically advanced factory ships, became the leaders of the industry. At that time, the International Whaling Commission (IWC) was formed to research the situation of whales and recommend limits. By the 1960s, Japan and the Soviet Union had become the titans of whaling, with whale meat their main economic product. In 1967, the IWC completely protected blue, right, gray, and humpback whales, and quotas on others followed. In 1983, it mandated, despite the objections of Japan, Norway, and the Soviet Union, the end to commercial whaling by 1986. While Iceland and Norway have withdrawn from the IWC to resume whaling and while Inuit and some others may take some whales for cultural purposes, the pressure on the whale populations from hunting is well reduced. The products of the whale are no longer in high demand and the reputation of the industry is bad. The grey whale population has increased to the point that it is no longer defined as endangered. Many coastal communities have turned to tourism using whale watching as a main source of recreation to compensate for the losses in the fishing industry. Today, the pollution of the oceans presents the greatest threat to whales.

Fish are less romantic than whales, but far more important economically. Seafood is the major animal protein for many millions of people (Carroll 1996:43). Until the Second World War, fishing was largely a local and low-technology industry. More recently, however, fishing has become a high-technology industry, with drift nets and factory ships able to harvest vast areas of the sea far from their harbors. Some of the most productive food-fish areas of the world have become overfished. The outerbanks of Newfoundland that provided cod and Atlantic salmon for hundreds of years are essentially fished-out. Strict restrictions on fishing off of Canada have led to disputes between that nation and the European Union. Likewise, the depletion of many Pacific salmon runs has caused serious political disputes between indigenous and nonindigenous fishers, between Alaska and Washington, and between Canada and the United States. Similar international disputes center on fishing areas off South America and Africa. Aquaculture, especially fish farming, has been promoted as an answer to the wild fish shortages and is well established in parts of Asia. It is not equally successful, however, in all areas or with all species, and disease and serious pollution appear to be growing problems. Recently in Washington State, farm-raised nonindigenous salmon that had escaped were declared a "pollutant."

Resources in Balance

It should be clear that all of the issues discussed in this chapter are interrelated. Carbon dioxide affects land, water, and plants and animals. Deforestation, erosion, desertification, plant and animal extinctions, and atmospheric pollution are interrelated. Changes in one element causes changes in others, and the cycle of environmental deterioration continues. They all also illustrate the reality that scientifically it is far easier to prevent environmental problems than to fix them with technology. The focus remains on the importance of environmental changes for people. A personal and profound attack on human well-being by an environmental system out of balance is disease.

HUMAN HEALTH ISSUES

One of the great wonders of the twentieth century has been the improvements in health care. A child born in an upper- or middle-class household in a high-income country can expect to live about eighty years. Never before in history has this been true. Much of this good health results from improvements in medical knowledge and technology joined with improved nutrition and safer working and living conditions. Unfortunately, this is not a universal reality. Another child, born into a poor, rural household in another part of the world, faces much bleaker prospects. Poverty creates an environment of poor nutrition, lack of health care, unhealthy living conditions, and dangerous or unhygienic work conditions. Additionally, in many parts of the world, overpopulation has caused intense stress on available resources, and lack of pollution regulations has allowed deadly environmental conditions.

Disease

Many diseases that were considered deadly at the turn of the century now can be routinely cured by Western medicine. As importantly, many diseases can now be prevented by vaccines. Smallpox, a previously deadly disease, has disappeared completely. The technology of Western medicine, led by the discovery of antibiotics and the lessons of sanitation, has increased the normal life span of people in high-income countries. But there are two major difficulties that come with this good news. First, the progress has not been universal. Second, the nature of development has created new health problems and allowed older ones to spread widely.

Diseases of Development: Health and Economic Systems   The health concerns of gatherers and hunters are quite different from those in more complex cultures. Accidents including food poisoning and hunting mishaps, infanticide, and childbirth are major causes of death. Lack of pure water and malnutrition can also be problems in some environments. Chronic and epidemic diseases, however, and diseases spread by pollution are rarely a concern since the small populations and regular movements do not provide conditions for the survival of such diseases. The major health issue for foragers is their lack of health care technology so that, despite often extraordinary knowledge of the medicinal herbs of their region, serious ailments can be disabling or fatal.

Health issues among pastoralists differ from those of foragers. While accident and childbirth are still killers, there is an increase in deaths from diseases. The hardship of a migratory lifestyle is difficult for the elderly and the extremely young. Humans are susceptible to many diseases carried by animals as well. For the first time in human history, then, epidemics and plagues have been introduced in pastoralism.

Health in farming communities is conditioned by sedentary living. Accidents are less frequent, but injuries from violence are more numerous. Illness from pollutants in the water supply and food are common and epidemics become constant threats with both dense populations and settlements contaminated by wastes and pests such as rats. Health care may slightly improve, but the diseases often overwhelm people's capability to cure. The Black Death of 1348–1352 in Europe illustrates the depths of disease and human suffering that such societies could reach.

The specific diseases of industrialization are discussed later in this chapter, but it is worth noting here that accidents, pollution, and new diseases have challenged the spectacular growth in health care technology that has also emerged. Culturally, the growth of a class system leads to an uneven distribution of health care that takes its toll on the health of the poor. Issues of technology take center stage as both the cause of illness through pollution and the preservation of health for people in the industrialized world.

Diseases of Development: Sickle-Cell Disease and Malaria Sickle-cell disease (sicklemia) and malaria are diseases with different symptoms and causes. Human changes to the African environment, however, have spread both diseases in that area and brought them into a symbiotic relationship. This case demonstrates the complex set of circumstances that might be set off by human design without any understanding of the outcome.

Sickle-cell disease is a genetic condition in which the red blood cells take a crescent, or sickle, shape and produce severe anemia. Without recently developed and expensive treatments, sickle-cell disease proves fatal before the victim reaches adulthood. Victims of sickle-cell are homozygous for this trait, which means that they inherit this abnormality from both parents. What is peculiar about the disease is that it occurs at far too high a rate for such a deadly disease. Normally, a fatal genetic disease of this sort kills its victims before they have children or before they have many children. Such diseases continue as a very rare condition in the population. This is not true of sickle-cell disease, which became common in some populations. This observation led researchers to look for the reason for the high incidence of the disease. As it happened, the map of its distribution was a clue: areas of sickle-cell turned out also to be areas of uncontrolled malaria.

Malaria is a parasitic disease that is spread by mosquitoes. It has been estimated that 300 million to 500 million people get malaria each year and that about 1.5 to 2.7 million people die annually from the disease (Wade 1997:4). The majority, who survive, may live with symptoms of ill health throughout their lives. Conditions that spread malaria have blossomed in the modern world. In the parts of Africa where sickle-cell is most severe, deforestation and irrigation have been used to increase agricultural production. These areas have proven to be prime breeding grounds for the malaria-carrying mosquito.

Thus, those who are most prone to sickle-cell are also highly endangered by malaria. The relationship between the diseases is somewhat complex. People who are born with sickle-cell traits have a natural immunity to malaria. Unfortunately, people with sickle-cell disease die of that malady. Those who inherit sickle-cell traits from only one parent, however, do not have that disease and are immune to malaria. This explains the high incidence of sickle-cell disease. The abnormal trait is beneficial in areas where malaria is common.

The Centers for Disease Control in the United States has worked for many years on the problem of sickle-cell disease because many Americans descend from inhabitants of the infected areas. New treatments have lead to extended life spans and reduced suffering. Yet, if victims live long lives and have children, the disease will continue to exist in high numbers. Countering this, however, is genetic testing and effective birth-control techniques, both a result of medical technology, that can now help couples know their own genetic makeup in order to make informed decisions about reproduction. These medical responses, however, are expensive, complex, and, not available worldwide.

Responses to the problem of malaria have focused on insecticides that can kill the mosquitoes, but they leave their own health consequences; the draining of wetlands, which kills the mosquitoes but modifies the general environment; and preventative medication, which works in many cases but is now being rendered ineffective by new resistant forms. If the malarial mosquitoes became extinct, the disease would follow, and after many generations, without medical intervention, there would be no advantage to those with sickle-cell genes and sickle-cell disease would become extremely rare. This complex interaction of disease, development, and environment would finally become harmless, but at an environmental cost.

Transportation and Disease Transportation, another component of industrialization, literally has far-reaching implications for health. The transportation of goods is essential to successful industry, and the twentieth century has seen unprecedented success in connecting people around the globe. All but the most remote communities are tied to others by roads, and even the most remote areas can be reached by air travel. If there ever were truly isolated regions in the world, there are none now. Theoretically, a sneeze in the Arctic can spread a cold around the world. More seriously, deadly diseases, such as AIDS, can move swiftly from their sites of origin to become universal scourges. Sleeping sickness, a disease spread by tsetse flies, recently expanded throughout western Africa after the opening of new roads there (McElroy and Townsend 1996:332). Few states like to set roadblocks to human mobility, but many countries do set border regulations in order to combat such diseases.

A New Epidemic: AIDS During the 1990s, a new entry into the genre of horror fiction emerged in best-selling novels and films. Replacing the monsters made huge by radioactivity, the new horror feature was the out-of-control epidemic. In the plot, a newly mutated or laboratory-synthesized virus escapes into the general population and rapidly kills millions around the world. Like the radioactive giant lizard that eats Japan, killer viruses of this ilk are not plausible, but like the monster, they reflect real environmental threats. Atomic energy is a real danger, as has been seen in the nuclear reactor disaster at Chernobyl and in many cases of improper medical-waste disposal. *New epidemics* are also real and can also be deadly; but their spread is far more complex than popular fears might suggest.

Perhaps the best-known epidemic in the contemporary world is AIDS, or acquired immunodeficiency syndrome. Caused by HIV, human immunodeficiency virus, AIDS is a contagious and deadly disease that has spread throughout the world. When it was first made known to the public in the United States, in the mid 1980s, it was thought to be largely limited to homosexuals, a discriminated-against population, but AIDS was in fact already spreading as a heterosexually transmitted disease in Africa at that time. The early sufferers of the disease were shunned and some HIV-infected children were physically barred from attending school. Even though it was known that the disease can be contracted through contact with the bodily fluids of an infected person, the public generally feared any type of contact with AIDS sufferers and even suspected that authorities were not telling the whole truth about the contagion. It took a number of years before the public began to see the disease as serious, but not out of control. A major concern initially was the safety of blood available for transfusions. In France, a government scandal followed the awareness that unsafe blood had been made available and had caused hundreds to be infected with HIV.

International relations have been strained by this new disease. China and France demanded AIDS tests for Americans and others from high-incidence areas seeking to enter those countries. In parts of Africa, where the disease probably developed, the percentage of infection is among the highest in the world. In some villages in Uganda and its neighboring states, only the children and the elders remain uninfected. Men who work in cities or drive trucks along the roads and who use the sexual services of infected prostitutes have carried the disease back to their homes and communities. Similarly in Asia, particularly as a result of sexual tourism in Southeast Asia, the disease has spread from there to both Japan and Europe. Even though the spread of AIDS was feared early in the epidemic, few countries were able to protect their citizens.

Scientific research on AIDS is an international-based effort. Four institutions lead that effort: the World Health Organization (WHO), the US Centers for Disease Control, the US National Institutes of Health (NIH), and the French Pasteur Institute (Grmek 1990:13). Laboratories around the world are involved in the search for a cure and a preventive vaccine for the disease. While no cure is at hand, there have been encouraging advances in drug treatments that have lengthened the lives of AIDS sufferers. However, these medicines are expensive and, as a result, limited in use.

Health Care

While the most complex successes of modern health care are found in the industrial world, many people around the world have been introduced to Western medicine. Governments and NGOs have built clinics in poor and rural areas. WHO has been involved in organizing worldwide research and care since 1948. Many nongovernmental agencies, including numerous medical missions, have focused their work in developing areas, opening clinics and educating local people. The most important successes of these clinics have been related to sanitation. Teaching parents how to care for their children by giving them clean water and food and protecting them from contamination has saved millions of lives. One of the largest killers of the world's children, diarrhea can usually be overcome with a little knowledge about clean water and inexpensive foods. Similarly, the clinics' introduction of the use of vaccinations and antibiotics now prevent or cure diseases that would have likely become epidemics in developing states.

The clinics' mission is based on the most easily accepted elements of Western life: people wish to be healthy and to see their children thrive. However, two factors can discourage people's use of the clinics. The first, is money; many people cannot pay the slightest amount for medical care or even to travel to a clinic. The other is culture; successful cures are only those that make cultural sense in ethnic communities.

Malnutrition

The major underlying condition of poor health worldwide is *malnutrition,* which is caused by both insufficient caloric intake and a poorly balanced diet. While starvation is a reality that has made the international news often in recent times, there is a much broader problem. Poor diets make people increasingly susceptible to a wide range of diseases that they might otherwise have avoided. The relationship of homelessness to tuberculosis is a clear demonstration of the problem. Likewise, the death of children from diarrhea is largely the result of diet deprivations. Why, in such a rich world where food production is at an all-time high, are so many people deprived of healthy foods?

The answer to this question lies in an understanding of the economic world. The world's wealth is unequally distributed. The wealthy and the middle class live healthier and more comfortable lives than their ancestors, whereas the poor do not. In fact, some economic innovations that have lead to increased wealth have had negative effects on the poor. One example is cash crops. Many farmers and ranchers who had formerly grown food for use by their families and communities are now producing food for a distant market. Moreover, they produce one or two cash crops for this market, rather than the broad variety of crops needed for a healthy diet. Many grow major cash crops, such as coffee and sugar, that add nothing in the way of nutrition to a diet. Furthermore, if the world price of a crop falls below the amount farmers need to feed their families, they cannot keep the crop as food for their own use. In earlier generations, rural farmers may have produced less but fears of poor nutrition or starvation were dependent on things like severe weather patterns and insect infestations that could destroy an entire crop. Today's farmers still fear these things, but they also must deal with the caprices of a world market over which they have no control.

The modern economic situation has also had an impact on the most basic of human foods, mother's milk. In many parts of the world, men migrate to cities in order to earn money for their families and women remain in the countryside to run the farms, tend the fields, raise children, care for the elderly, cook food, and everything else that needs to be done at home. In addition, because it has become increasingly difficult to obtain fire-wood in parts of Africa and Asia, women must walk long distances to gather fuel, adding to the physical toll of their way of life. As mothers that value large families, they work while pregnant and while nursing to ensure the survival of their families. Nursing is a problem, however. The physical condition of a mother affects the quality and quantity of her milk. Young children are left with older ones, and their mothers often cannot be available for regular feedings.

Some corporations see the situation as an area of opportunity. In a now-famous example that occurred in the 1970s, the Nestlé Company used hospitals in Africa to promote its dry infant formula. Mothers were encouraged while in the hospital to use the free formula with their newborn babies, but when the women left the hospital many had no breast milk to feed their infants and no money to purchase the formula. Often mothers used too little formula for good nutrition and used unsterilized bottles. Many children suffered, and an international boycott of Nestlé and censure by the World Health Organization followed. Nestlé changed its policy, and UNICEF and other organizations advocated breast milk as the best infant food. But the larger issue—that of a mother's ability to feed her child in the contemporary economic situation—was never fully addressed.

It is also important to recognize the political reality of hunger. The displacement of millions in Africa during the 1980s and 1990s, which produced heartbreaking pictures of children scarred by malnutrition and dying of starvation, was a result of both natural droughts and political turmoil. People fleeing genocide in Rwanda and Burundi, for example, were unable to feed themselves. Their farms were left as they fled for their lives and they had no surplus cash to buy food. International relief agencies often meant the difference between life and death for thousands, and some of the international workers were driven away by death threats. The crossing of international boundaries by starving refugees causes a host of political problems; some states, including the Democratic Republic of Congo in this case, have attempted to close their borders to limit the political turmoil within their countries.

Many people throughout the world remain hungry. Not all of them die, but millions suffer. Environmental disturbances, including drought and severe storms, are temporary problems that have been aggravated by human interaction. The destruction of productive food lands in the interest of cash crops and urban sprawl has also been an important factor. The politics and economics of food distribution have sometimes pitted the rich against the poor.

CASE STUDY

BRAZIL AND THE TROPICAL RAINFOREST

The complex relationship between people and their changing environment is played out in all societies. In rare cases, however, one state can control a unique environmental region that is necessary for the health and well-being of people around the world. Brazil is such a country.

Brazil is one of the largest and most modernized nations in the world. On June 3, 1992, a global assembly of states, called the Earth Summit took place in Brazil, where 178 countries met to discuss the world's environment and agree on regulations to protect it. Brazil was making a statement by its hosting of the meeting.

Earlier, at the 1972 Stockholm Conference on the Human Environment, the Brazilian delegation had been one of the least interested in ecological protection (Stone 1985:155). In the twenty years following that conference, the expense of ecologically destructive development became evident in Brazil with the collapse of the so-called "Brazilian Miracle" and a massive international censure. The Earth Summit thus represented Brazil's public commitment to ecological responsibility. It is a significant commitment because Brazil is a nation of vast resources, some of them with worldwide importance, and monumental ecological problems. This also makes Brazil an important case for illustrating environmental threats and related concepts.

Brazil is an enormous country, the fifth largest in the world. It is also a highly urbanized country; 79 percent of the over 161 million Brazilians live in cities (United Nations 1995a:25). The rest of the people live in thinly populated regions. Almost half of Brazil is located within the Amazon Basin, one of the last remaining great tropical rainforest terrains. In this region lies Brazil's future and its greatest problems. It is also a region of global interest since it contains countless rare and unknown species of plants and animals and has great stands of trees that, given their role in the carbon cycle, are vital to the health of the Earth's atmosphere. Furthermore, the fires of burning timber, resulting from slash-and-burn agriculture, are associated with the depletion of the ozone layer. Consequently, an important national resource is also seen as a critical international resource. Clearly, in the Amazon issues of state sovereignty and global necessity often clash.

Amazonian Environment

The Amazonian rainforest is an area where thousands of plants and animal species interact, creating a complex matrix. The sheer numbers of species of plants and animals in the rainforest overwhelm those in temperate areas. The most obvious plants are the tall trees that form a high, dense canopy that shades the rest of the rainforest. Commercially, the lumber from these trees, including cedar and mahogany trees, are obvious resources. In addition, rubber trees made part of the Amazon a commercial boom area at the start of the twentieth century, and coffee trees, have provided significant Brazilian exports. Major mammals found in the forests include howler monkeys, tapirs, capybaras, and jaguars. Innumerable tropical birds and insects join the amphibians and reptiles, creating a mosaic of animal life. The loss of an individual species immediately threatens the long-term existence of many others.

Within this plentiful environment it seems odd that the forest could also be fragile, but that it is. It is one of the most delicate environments on Earth. In the dark on the forest floor the soil that exists has been slowly eroded away by rainfall over the centuries. A lack of rocks in the forest means that there are no new minerals eroding into the soil. New nutrients come largely from rain carrying minerals from the rich rivers. Insects and other life forms in the forest use the dead vegetation that enriches temperate soils. Little is left to form rich soil (Denslow 1988:33, Buckley 1992:4-5).

From a distance, Europeans and Americans see global prosperity, and even global survival, in the maintenance of the rainforests. The plants and animals of the rainforest, left undisturbed, protect and regulate global climatic and atmospheric conditions, promise resources to improve the health and well-being of people throughout the world, and protect the cultures and lives of the indigenous people who first owned this area.

Although Brazilian environmentalists and indigenous people work for the protection of the Amazon, many other Brazilians—from entrepreneurs and cattle ranchers to the urban poor and the rubber tappers—see their future prosperity and survival in the development of the Amazon. Many see the destruction of parts of the forest as necessary to produce timber, create pasture land for cattle, and to open lands for settlement. Highways and railroads are cut through the forest to move people and goods far into the Amazon. Miners, by the tens of thousands, seek to make their fortunes in the extensive mineral reserves. In places, the unrestrained gold-mining areas resemble historic pictures of nineteenth-century California and the Yukon. Just as national and international goals clash, so do those of the people who seek to preserve the Amazon and those who seek to destroy selective parts of it.

Economic Uses of the Amazon

Rubber Tapping   The first rush to exploit the Amazon was not for gold or timber but for rubber. During the 1850s, an international market for rubber exploded with the advent of rubber bicycle tires and, soon after, automobile tires. The rubber trees of the Amazon were the sole supply of rubber at the time. Manaus, a town that served as an inland port for access to large ships, became the capital of the rubber region in Brazil. In the rubber boom days of the early 1900s, Manaus had a population of about fifty thousand and an international reputation. European companies performed in the ornate opera house that was the city's pride. The rubber boom also brought to Manaus roads, polluting ships, unsanitary urban sprawl, extreme exploitation of rubber trees, and abuse of its indigenous people.

The bust that followed the boom came to Manaus soon after Amazonian rubber tree seeds were smuggled to Malaysia and cultivated there. It thus rapidly became cheaper and more efficient to use the Malaysian rubber. Manaus reverted to a smaller community and rubber tappers worked for subsistence wages rather than great wealth. Since 1967, Manaus has been a free trade zone and today is full of factories and shops. However, this economic strategy has not been completely successful in improving the standard of living. Now a city of about two million, Manaus is polluted, has no sewage system, and has an unemployment rate of 30 percent (Dostert 1996:58).

Rubber tapping has continued with many tappers now active in environmental protection. Rubber trees, if treated correctly, can produce rubber for extraction without harming the trees. Indeed the clear cutting of forests to obtain other trees in the forest means the destruction of this renewable resource and rubber tappers are aware of the danger to their industry. Union organizer Chico Mendes became an international voice in environmental conservation. He also reached out to the indigenous people of the Amazon to join in common interests. On December 22,

1988, Chico Mendes was murdered by local landowners. In a century, rubber tappers had changed from symbols of environmental destruction to martyrs for environmental survival.

Cattle   The chief opponents of Amazonian environmentalists are developmentalists of the interior. The Brazilian government has actively encouraged Brazilians from coastal cities to relocate into the interior. The building of the national capital, Brasilia, in the southern interior symbolizes this internal movement. In 1970, the military-controlled government designed what was called a "Program of National Integration," which would build roads and settlements in the interior for the new inhabitants. While the plan envisioned that 75 percent of the migrants would come from the northeast where drought was severe, only 30 percent actually came from there; the others came from the cities and knew nothing of rural life or farming (Moran 1988:157). The Transamazon Highway was built in 1971, and other highways were built later, to encourage migration (Prance 1990:61). But when the rural population did not grow as anticipated, the government used the infrastructure for other purposes, especially cattle ranching (Stern, Young, and Druckman 1992:70). In the early 1990s, the annual population growth was -1.5 percent in rural areas and 2.3 percent in urban areas (United Nations 1995a:25).

Until the mid-1980s, the government offered loans and tax incentives for entrepreneurs to clear sections of the Amazonian forest in order to create pasturelands for beef-cattle raising. The incentives were so lucrative that individual investors could make the success of the cattle operation a secondary concern. This was important because, due to the poor soil conditions, most of the pastures that were created became unusable for cattle within a few years, and many areas were soon after cleared and then abandoned. According to Bob Reiss, "of the 135 million cattle in Brazil, half lived in the Amazon, eating the place to death. Each bull needed one hundred times more pasture to live here than in the South of Brazil where the soil was better" (1992:131). Without the government's financial encouragement, then, the industry would not have grown because it was not an economically sensible or desirable industry in this area. Yet the cutting and burning of the forest for pastureland contributed significantly to depletion of the rainforest.

Dams   Another government plan for Amazonian development involves dams. Over seventy dams are planned to be built in the Amazon by 2010 (Reiss 1992:20). Dams are needed for electricity to run the industries and light the cities throughout Brazil. The environmental impact of such dams is of great concern. The flooding of lands could kill plants and animals, and, in some cases, destroy the traditional lands of indigenous people. Further, the acidity of the water is expected to corrode the machinery and make the dams difficult to maintain. The Balbina Dam, built with World Bank support in the area north of Manaus, illustrates the potential threats: Rich forestlands were flooded, the lands of the Waiami-Atroari Indians were destroyed, and little energy was produced (Prance 1990:62).

Mining   Mineral extraction is also a factor of the new Amazon, where gold, iron, bauxite, diamonds, manganese, copper, nickel, and other minerals are available in commercially viable amounts. The control of such wealth has been important to the Brazilian government. Mines have recently been developed with environmental safety in mind and are run cleanly (Stone 1985:140ff).

Gold mining, however, remains a problem for the government and the people in Brazil. Gold rushes are notoriously rowdy, and the Brazilian case follows suit. Stories of murders over claims were reported daily in Brazilian newspapers in the late 1980s and early 1990s. The clash of gold miners and indigenous Brazilians also brought scenes reminiscent of the American Old West. Miners and Indians both died from homicides while massacres of Indians were also reported. The Brazilian government legally barred gold miners from Indian-reserved lands, but implementing the law was difficult and it was frequently ignored. In all mining areas, the customary practice of using mercury to separate gold from waste metal has poisoned miners, local residents, and the plants and animals of the rivers. In 1993, nineteen Yanomamo, indigenous people from the Venezuelan-Brazilian border, were reported killed by environmental mercury poisoning (Sponsel 1994:43).

Indigenous Peoples

The role of Indians in Brazilian society is a complex one that goes beyond both the Amazon and environmental factors. Amazonian Indians, however, are important in any environmental understanding of the region. These people have adapted so well to life in the Amazon that any environmental change would immediately challenge their ability to maintain their culture and a catastrophic change would threaten their very survival. These indigenous people, more than anyone else, understand the resources and dynamics of the healthy Amazon. Globally, their knowledge is important, but it is being lost. Their ability to hunt, gather, and farm for subsistence is threatened in many areas. Dams and roads cut into their lands. Outsiders steal their lands and kill them by bringing pollution, disease, and violence. A road across Yanomamo lands brought epidemics of influenza, tuberculosis, and measles in 1974, killing large numbers of Yanomamo and destroying several villages (Commission for the Creation of the Yanomami Park 1989:45).

The Brazilian government agencies that deal with Indian problems have been notoriously ineffective. Today, reserves are set aside for individual indigenous nations but the government vacillates on protecting these regions from outsiders. One notorious case occurred in 1988, when two Kayapó men, including leader Paulinho Paiakan, traveled to the United States to speak at a rainforest symposium. They expressed their concerns about rainforest development in general and about a proposed dam in particular. While in the United States they were also invited to visit Washington, DC, to speak of their concerns to members of the World Bank and the US government. On their return to Brazil both men and Darrell Posey, an anthropologist who acted as an interpreter, were indicted under a Brazilian act that forbid "foreigners" from denigrating the government. Although the charges were eventually dropped, the status of Indians and their relationship to the government in Brazil were made clear to the world, to Brazil's embarrassment.

Health Conditions

The health conditions that plague inhabitants of the Amazon include those new diseases introduced to the Indians, among others. Pollution problems, such as the lack of urban sanitation and the mercury poisoning mentioned earlier, are severe threats to basic health. Malaria is a widespread and increasingly severe threat in areas where the forest has been cut and the waters made stagnant. The increase in standing water reserves allows for the breeding of malaria-carrying mosquitoes in areas where they previously had been less of a threat. Reiss reports that in the Amazon "health officials watched the number of reported cases grow from eighty-nine thousand in 1975 to seven hundred thousand in just the first six months of 1989" (1992:113). Diseases and deaths connected to development lifestyles also plague the inhabitants of the region. Sexually transmitted diseases spread with prostitution. Alcohol abuse, homicide, and other crimes exist at high levels throughout the new communities of the Amazon.

Analysis

The Amazon is an example of the wealth that a large, healthy region can offer a growing nation. At the same time, it reflects the harm that ill-considered development can inflict on plants, people, and other animals. The Amazon is important to the future of the people of Brazil and of the world. Fortunately, it appears that the views of the Brazilian government and the international public on unchecked development are changing and that the importance of this international treasure is being recognized.

The Brazilian Amazon provides a laboratory for understanding the complexity of an ecosystem. The relationship among the trees, soil, animals, water, and human health is quite clear. Even the ordinary practice of road building has brought deforestation, plant and animal extinction, soil erosion, water pollution, and disease. But this ecosystem is globally important in that the Amazon is a necessary part of the world Commons. The burning of forests has not only added CO_2 to the atmosphere; it has also reduced the number of trees on Earth that take in CO_2 from the atmosphere. The stand of trees in the Amazon is therefore essential for the good health of the atmosphere, and the conservation of the Amazonian ecosystem is a priority for all the world's nations.

TERMS AND CONCEPTS

acid rain

carbon dioxide

carrying capacity

the Commons

deforestation

desertification

ecosystems

global warming

greenhouse gases

Law of the Sea

malnutrition

new epidemics

United Nations Environment Program (UNEP)

World Health Organization (WHO)

DISCUSSION QUESTIONS

1. Celebrities often campaign for ecological causes, raising money to support rainforests or local rivers through a rock or folk concert. What issues are raised by these celebrity campaigns? What additional questions should be asked?

2. AIDS, a relatively new epidemic, is widely known and feared in the United States. What changes has this disease brought to the communities where it is found? What steps have been taken to prevent new diseases?

3. What has been done in your community to protect the environment? Which strategies have worked and which have not? What do you think it will take to convince people to do more?

4. The end of the production of chlorofluorocarbons (CFCs) has been seen by most Americans in changes in spray cans and air conditioners, but this effort has cost businesses far more. Has it been worth the expense and inconvenience? What would increasing ozone depletion have cost?

5. Since the world is an ecosystem, changes in any major element would be expected to change others in significant ways. How would a change in the water temperature of a local river, the extinction of a species of whale, or the drying of a broad savannah be expected to change other environmental factors? Do these changes actually occur?

RESEARCH PROJECTS

1. Many articles have appeared in newspapers and scientific journals about the increasing ecological problems near the poles. Rising temperatures, ozone holes, animal extinctions, and ice-pack melting are among the warnings for the Arctic and Antarctic. Choose one of those areas and warnings, and review the problems and solutions that have been explored.

2. Several new diseases have been reported from Africa in the 1990s. Choose one of the diseases and track the progress of its discovery, identification, and treatment since it was first reported.

3. Diseases such as cholera have been reappearing throughout the world in areas of extreme poverty. Review two or three recent cholera outbreaks in different geographic areas and analyze the common elements that might contribute to the spread of the disease.

4. Brazil is not the only country with rainforests. Review the literature on rainforests in another part of the world, such as Indonesia or Central America. How have the people

and governments of this region dealt with the rainforests of their country? What major themes emerge?

5. Choose one major ecological issue in your local region, and research the underlying problems and issues associated with it. What international components or lessons are relevant to the local issue?

INTERNET RESOURCES

Centers for Disease Control: *http://www.cdc.gov* This US government site contains up-to-date information on health concerns throughout the world.

National Wildlife Federation: *http://www.nwf.org/nwf/home.html* The homepage of this well-known environmental group focuses on environmental issues in the United States and offers good links to other sites.

Pan American Health Organization: *http://www.paho.org* The homepage of this organization includes country health profiles for member states.

UNAIDS: *http://www.unaids.org* The homepage of this joint UN program on HIV/AIDS contains important information on the status of the disease and the search for treatment.

UN Division for Sustainable Development: *http://www.un.org/esa/sustdev* This searchable site includes information on the environment and on sustainable development.

World Health Organization: *http://www.who.org* The homepage for this UN organization contains details of the WHO's mission and international health projects.

7

Perspectives on Human Ecological Sustainability

It is expected that the frontier will continue to expand in Amazonia in the years to come as people from across the country migrate to the region in search of land and livelihood. The challenge is to meet the needs of a growing population while promoting forms of production adapted to Amazonia's unique environmental conditions.
—*Marianne Schmink*
(1988:163)

Brazil's planning minister from 1969–1974, J. P. does Reis Velloso, was overheard commenting about the possible negative environmental impact of Japanese investment plans: "Why not? We have a lot left to pollute. They don't."

—*Werner Baer*
(1995:325)

The Earth is home to all people. No one wants to destroy it. Having said that, it is clear that there is a wide discrepancy among the views of intelligent people about how the resources of the Earth should be used and conserved. It is equally clear that everyone cannot live the conserving life of gathering and hunting. It would not satisfy most contemporary people, nor do they have the skills to survive in this way. More globally, the technology of foragers has a low carrying capacity and could not accommodate the current world population. At the same time, it is possible that mixed forms of subsistence may comfortably coexist on the planet and that different environments may be better suited for some rather than others. As Chapter 4 demonstrates, it is equally true that the pressure for full industrial utilization is strong and growing throughout the world.

This chapter focuses on three perspectives that describe how different people view the world and how they respond to issues that often place conservation and progress in economic conflict. Called the *high technology, shared technology*, and *appropriate technology* perspectives, each presents a different view on how people and governments can best approach development.

HIGH TECHNOLOGY

Advocates of the high technology perspective are optimistic about the ability of humans to overcome obstacles through their intelligence, technological innovations, and hard work. Humans are in this view the masters of nature. Moreover, nature exists for the use of people and provides the raw material for progress. There is little romanticism about the nobility of nature, nor of the people who live closely attuned to it. Proponents share a pragmatic view that is supported by economic development over the centuries.

The basis of the high technology view is that human creativity is equal to any challenge. Problems can be solved and new technologies can be created to overcome any obstacles to progress. Progress, furthermore, is viewed as inherently good for all people. Visions of hunger cured by genetically created crops, of diseases eradicated by vaccines, of polluted waters cleaned by new chemicals, and of the atmosphere purified by technological manipulation are seen by advocates to be future realities that will make the concerns of today short-lived and insignificant.

Problems not only will be solved, but the fact that problems are noticed by concerned people will hasten their solutions. This is due to the nature of the market system. There is a lot of money to be made or saved in the solving of ecological and health problems. Technologies that effectively clean polluted waters or reduce particulate emissions from machines or factories are, or will be, in high demand in the marketplace. Similarly, drugs that cure common diseases not only save the lives and end the pain of hundreds of thousands of people, but they also can make millions of dollars for the producers. According to this perspective, problems become the economic opportunities on which capitalism thrives.

There are many examples of such successes that can be used to support this optimistic view. Green industries, those that concentrate on being nonpolluting, are expanding throughout industrialized nations. Processes that are polluting and not essential for the integrity of products, such as the bleaching of paper, are eliminated at the expense of superficial appearance. They are then able to advertise their products to an increasingly ecologically aware public that values the anti-pollution efforts over luxury.

Other industries have arisen in the quest for cleaner techniques for existing facilities. Most factories in the United States and other Western nations now employ extensive technology to clean up the emissions in smoke and water that used to escape into the wider environs. Disposal of this waste is now a profitable industry in itself. Photographs of American cities taken early in the twentieth century contrast markedly with contemporary pictures. Dark soot from the smokestacks of neighbor-hood factories once covered buildings while today this type of urban pollution has been significantly reduced. Many urban rivers, including the Hudson River that flows by Manhattan Island, have been similarly cleaned to the point that fish species, which had disappeared, are returning. The free market has thus played its part in cleaning the environment.

While such examples support the high technology perspective, it is also true that other forces contributed to their success. Government regulations, not private market forces, have played an important role in forcing much of the industrial cleanup in the United States. Also, the flight of factories from the urban North to less expensive areas in the South and other countries eased the pollution at the cost of local unemployment.

In the realm of health care, the power of technological innovation is apparent. New treatments for diseases appear daily in the news and the idea that modern med-icine eventually will be able to cure all ailments is common. Organ transplants, vac-cines for childhood diseases, fetal surgery, and genetic testing, which would have seemed impossible a generation ago, are now almost routine. This means that some fatal diseases have been cured, dangerous children's diseases have become rare, and fewer children are born with fatal conditions.

On a global scale, the most extraordinary success has been the eradication of smallpox through large-scale vaccination. Smallpox, a highly contagious and deadly disease, once killed millions of people yearly around the world. In 1967, the World Health Organization directed a worldwide vaccination attack on the disease. Individ-uals in the most urban and the most remote areas of the globe were injected with the smallpox vaccine. Countries barred their doors to travelers who could not prove they had been vaccinated. Within a decade most countries could declare themselves smallpox-free, and in 1979, after two years with no report of the disease, the vacci-nations ended. Since then the only smallpox virus remaining was kept in laborato-ries as a guarantee against its return. All samples are scheduled to be destroyed before the year 2000.

The destruction of smallpox and the control of poliomyelitis (more popularly termed polio) support the vision of a world in which sophisticated technology can overcome deadly diseases. Less optimistic scientists point to the fact that both of these diseases resist mutation and need human hosts for survival, and these rare characteristics made them more vulnerable than most contagious diseases (Karlen 1995:154). Some proponents of the high technology perspective might regret the fact that it was the United Nations, rather than private business, that led the attack against smallpox. They can point to more extensive private enterprise in the polio campaign, however, to show that these programs need not be the exclusive domain of states or international organizations.

The most significant agenda attacking the problems of world agriculture with a high technology perspective is called the *green revolution*. Promoted by the Rock-efeller Foundation and championed by the Nobel Prize-winning agronomist Norman E. Bourlaug, the core concept of the green revolution involves the transfer of high technology farming techniques to the developing world. By increasing the production of crops in the less developed areas of the world, world hunger might be dramatically reduced or eradicated and developing states could use exports to improve their positions in the world market. In the 1960s and 1970s, concentration was placed on new grain hybrids that had been created for high production. This meant the wholesale replacement of local varieties with imported, genetically engineered crops. To prepare the soils for these new plants, the intensive use of water, chemical fertilizers, and pesticides was required. An immediate increase in wheat and maize output in a number of countries dramatically highlighted the claims of success, and many predicted the end of world hunger (Bodley 1996:138).

The promise of this beginning soon gave way to grave doubts about the universal applicability of the green revolution. Both ecological and cultural factors worked against the long-term success of the operation in many areas. Local people did not like the crops that were imported and rejected them in favor of local crops. The new crops had no immunity to the diseases in these environments. Even where there were no inherent local barriers to success, in many areas the intensive use of delicate soils led to erosion and loss of water supplies.

Most criticism of the green revolution, however, focuses on the intensive use of fertilizers, herbicides, and pesticides. The dangers that such chemicals bring to an uncontrolled environment were made clear. The runoff from fields to water supplies threatened the health of local residents and negatively affected the plants and animals that were necessary elements of the local ecosystem. Some of the chemicals used early in the green revolution are now widely banned. Other critics cite the economic problems associated with a dependency on petroleum-based resources. With the increases in the price of oil since the 1970s, only the wealthy can afford the crucial resources needed to continue this form of agriculture. Many individuals, and even states, were drawn into heavy debt in their attempts to maintain high crop production.

Other economic concerns soon became apparent. The green revolution fostered a dependency on the industrialized nations that forged the techniques and produced the necessary tools and chemicals, as well as a growing dependency of peasants on the rich. Not only did wealthy countrymen purchase peasant farms when peasants could no longer afford the fertilizers and pesticides, but the peasants, themselves, could no longer work in the agricultural field. Because the new farming techniques were not labor intensive, fewer people with sophisticated machines could handle farms that had employed many others. The displaced farmers were forced into low-paying wage labor or destitution in the cities. According to Richard Franke, in a review of the program that spent over $100 million in Indonesia, "For the poor, the Green Revolution in Java offers only the choice between servitude and homelessness" (1974:87). At best, the green revolution caused an increase in the number of large farms owned by elite families, who produce food that the unemployed peasants cannot afford to buy. At worst, the green revolution has destroyed formerly fertile lands and clean waters and decreased overall food production in the area.

From the high technology perspective, the green revolution remains a work in progress. The technological failures of the past were to be expected as with any new complex technology. Improved technology can overcome this. New disease-resistant high-yield seeds and more careful use of new pesticides and fertilizers will solve most of the previous problems of technology. The social and political difficulties that have deterred the success of the program can be overcome by the efficient work of dedicated governments. The rise of an agribusiness elite is not an inherent concern since this educated elite can lead the transformation from peasant to modern farming.

SHARED TECHNOLOGY

While proponents of the shared technology perspective also see technology as a major tool in the fight against human hunger and planetary pollution, they hold that such technology only works in an open and cooperative social association of world groups. Ecological problems are global and must be solved globally. Social factors, in this view, are not unfortunate distractions; rather, they are central to any successful project and often the reason behind the failure of others. The key words in this perspective are *cooperation* and *sustainability*. First, projects should be created with the input and agreement of all parties affected. The goal must be the equitable distribution of resources and technology throughout the world. All states, ethnic groups, classes, and genders have played roles in creating ecological problems, and they should all be agents in creating solutions. As an end, all people should benefit from modern technology. Second, new industrial projects must be sustainable and must be designed for long-term success. It should be demonstrated that there are planned solutions to the problems the project will inevitably cause. This is notably different from the high technology perspective, where each step is taken one at a time and any problems caused by the first solution will encourage research to solve them. Affective incentives, in this view, are assumed to be private, individual, and financial. For shared technology projects the solutions to foreseeable problems should be devised before the first step is taken and designed for the general good.

The major philosophical requirement for the global success of such a perspective is a universal agreement on the importance of ecological stability as a central human priority. Hope for such a consensus depends largely on education. It is assumed that, given all the facts, only one conclusion could be reached by an intelligent person: without a healthy environment, the human race is in peril.

Within the last two decades a number of international events have spurred the creation of a state-based international ecological movement, joining hundreds of existing ecological NGOs. In 1983, the United Nations established the World Commission on Environment and Development to investigate the state of the world's environment and propose solutions. Named after the prime minister of Norway, the *Brundtland Commission* issued its report in 1987. Called "Our Common Future," the document affirms the validity of concerns about the fragility of the world environment and stresses the importance of broad actions that address the issues of the poor rather than the rich. Fully embedded in this document is the concept of sustainable development. Successful development is defined here as improving not only the lives of contemporary people but also those of generations to come. While the concept of development as a purely economic issue (as seen in a state's statistics) is directly challenged, the document affirms technological development as a means to attack poverty.

The World Commission on Environment and Development held conferences again in 1989 and 1992, to formulate policies that would address the challenges of the report. At the Rio Earth Summit, heads of state from over 100 of the 178 states represented attended; but the summit was largely ignored by the United States, a critical state in development. The conference ratified Agenda 21, a blueprint for sustainable development, as a plan for the twenty-first century. It explicitly mandates the inclusion of all people in development programs and emphasizes the need for full participation of the poor, women, youth, and indigenous people. The agreement is broad and difficult to enforce. The ideals of the document, however, form a moral core that has international support.

Concerns over the practical protections of the documents from the Rio Earth Summit arose almost immediately. The right of indigenous people is recognized, for example, but their rights to the resources of their lands and their knowledge of the uses of these resources are defined as "intellectual property rights," which may be exercised by states rather than ethnic groups. While some businesses contract with indigenous people for using their inventions and knowledge and promote their products to the public as "ethnic" and "green," most businesses do not. The Body Shop, a lotions and cosmetics chain, has contracted with the people of the Santa Ana Pueblo of the US Southwest for use of their domesticated blue corn. Many other businesses have used blue corn or hybridized a blue-white corn and advertised it using Native American symbols and terms with no compensation to the indigenous people who developed the crop. When the principle is applied to medicinal plants, the potential income can be in the millions of dollars.

The environmental agreements of Rio are being modified and elaborated each year. The Rights of Indigenous People, which could clarify the problem of rights, is under consideration by the United Nations. There are also ongoing yearly or biyearly meetings that continue to call for a number of environmental regulations, such as the 1994 appeal for the end of the use of leaded gasoline.

A Critique from the High Technology Perspective

While there appears to be growing support for the shared technology perspective in the international arena, critics from the high technology perspective still abound. Some suggest that the shared technology view is simply too idealistic and perhaps a luxury that only the rich can afford. The countries of the world have never fully agreed to any goal of this breadth and it might be foolish to assume that they would now. In a way, shared technology advocates attempt to solve problems that do not exist. They believe these problems will occur, but there is no solid evidence to mandate expensive programs. Business, however, will invest money in the research and infrastructure necessary to develop worthwhile solutions to real problems, which will, in the long run, earn good profits. As problems arise, business will address them.

The economic needs of developing countries mandate increased energy utilization and they are unlikely to welcome barriers to their use of new technologies.

Likewise, the expense of ecological cleanups appears beyond the means of such countries. Finally, it is in just these states that the world is most likely to find relatively undisturbed ecosystems. The preservation of these areas falls disproportionately on the poorer nations. These countries have repeatedly argued that the industrialized nations that have become wealthy from the exploitation of their natural environments, as well as those in the developing world, now demand that they not do the same. In partial response to this, most international agreements include clauses that place the economic responsibility for ecological expenses worldwide largely in the hands of the industrialized nations. Advocates of high technology would argue that if these plans are implemented, the costs of doing business in these countries would increase. Employment for local people in poor countries would disappear if industries were forced to relocate because of economic pressures. Rather than help people, this would harm them.

APPROPRIATE TECHNOLOGY

Advocates of the appropriate technology perspective point to neocolonialism as a barrier to the successful ecological future of the planet. They believe that only those projects and techniques that fit both the cultural and physical setting of the people involved will work to serve the ecological purpose in the end. This is considered to be true in industrial and nonindustrial states alike. Projects should be locally devised and locally supported to be successful. Transplantation of projects from one place to another can only be done with the utmost care and with the full cooperation of the residents of the new site.

The idea of a global agreement or worldview on ecology challenges the diversity of cultural belief systems. Demands are made in UN documents for equitable treatment of men and women, and indigenous and migrant populations. Others assert the value of animals and plants as living organisms. All focus on the good of the globe as more important than local disputes. Many world cultures and religions inherently disagree with these basic assertions. Some cultures argue for the inherent superiority of men and the inferiority of nonhuman life as the plan of human creation. Women may be seen as protected by men, and animals and plants as created for human use. For many, to see things otherwise is heretical. For IGOSs and NGOs to demand action based on such heretical views is colonial paternalism at its worst, they would charge. The faith in education, in a way, supports this charge. Education means teaching people new ways of thinking and approaching problems. But if it is based on a Western technological paradigm, then it is likely to be viewed by those of different perspectives as a neocolonial form of education.

The focus of the appropriate technology perspective tends to be on small, low-energy designs; it rejects the wide use of high technology as a solution to environmental problems. In this sense, it differs radically from both of the other perspectives. Popular awareness of the appropriate technology perspective came with the 1973 publication of *Small Is Beautiful: Economics As If People Mattered*, by economist E. F. Schumacher. In this book, Schumacher argues that the goals of agriculture should be to perfect methods that are "biologically sound" and to "produce health, beauty, and permanence," and the goals of industry should be small-scale, nonviolent forms of technology "with a human face." (21). Peace and prosperity would thus go hand in hand. The progress of technology and industry is limited by the realities of the environment. The religion and goals of the people must also define the desirability of modern technology. According to Schumacher, new techniques that bring wealth in the Western economic sense may impoverish the culture and environment of other nations.

Proponents of appropriate technology will point to the majority of development cases around the world where industrial technology has imperiled the environment and the standard of living of local people. The results of some aspects of the green revolution highlight such problems. Smaller cases prove the point with equal clarity. In one well-documented case of inappropriate technology involving snowmobiles, Pertti Pelto (1973) describes the impact of this new form of transportation among the Sami of northeast Finland. On the surface, the snowmobile appeared to be perfectly suited for modernizing transportation in the Arctic north. With it, drivers could travel quickly over long distances that formerly had to be transversed using sleds and domesticated animals, and Sami herders could herd their reindeer with greater ease. But to own a snowmobile a Sami driver or herder had to have cash for both purchase and upkeep. Also, lack of technical skill often meant that broken machines were discarded rather than repaired. Pollution problems mounted in this fragile environment as a result of the gasoline and discarded machine parts. Inequality in this formerly cooperative culture grew between those who could initially support the new technology collecting larger herds and driving the poorer Sami into wage employment. Overall, the reindeer suffered as well. The new machines frightened the animals and interrupted their breeding cycle. After less than a decade with the new technology, Sami culture had changed and the people faced more problems than ever before. The nearly pristine northern ecosystem was compromised as well. The snowmobile, an apparently superior technology, was actually less appropriate for this situation than the simpler reindeer sled that preceded it.

The appropriate technology for a given situation may be a familiar traditional tool or it may be a new technology created out of easily accessible local resources. An example of the latter might be seen in the case of the Peruvian committee discussed in Chapter 4. The cooperative political structure and the farming techniques that have been developed fit the environmental and cultural needs of the village people.

India provides many other examples. The continued use of oxen-drawn plows for most work in village communities, which could economically afford individual tractors, demonstrates their understanding of suitable techniques. They rent tractors when such power is needed. Other, poorer Indian villagers have been successful with a newly innovated dung-burning stove. Wood for fuel has been depleted in many areas of India, so dung from the ever-present roaming cows is dried and used as fuel. Rather than encouraging oil or propane stoves, which would be too expensive and polluting for most families, a new appropriate technology has been developed by researchers. This new stove, inexpensively made of locally obtained clay, burns the available cow dung. It improves over the old open-fire techniques by making the fire more fuel efficient. These seemingly small advances in technology prove to be superior for the people who use them. Plows drawn by oxen and efficient dung-burning stoves allow people to live happier, more comfortable lives. In other words, they fit Schumacher's goal of technology "with a human face."

Critiques from the High Technology and Shared Technology Perspectives

While it is difficult for anyone to criticize the ideals of appropriate technology, advocates of both high technology and shared technology perspectives doubt the practical effectiveness of it in the face of the worldwide ecological crisis. Instead of solving problems for millions at a time, the solutions of appropriate technology involve only small local populations using rudimentary technology. Each solution must be reinvented for each community and each culture. Each community, further, must commit itself to ecological ideals for the regional cleanups to work. This is clearly not an efficient approach in economic terms.

Proponents of the shared technology perspective criticize the appropriate technology approach for its lack of interest in the world community. From the shared technology perspective, varied individual solutions work against the notion of concerted world cooperation. While local solutions can solve local problems, local solutions cannot solve the problems of the worldwide Commons.

Proponents of the high technology perspective note the lack of incentive for intensive research and development in the appropriate technology approach. There is little money to be made in the local technologies, and this means that the best research facilities would turn their interest to other, more profitable projects. Since this view, like the shared technology perspective, places its faith in the efficacy of modern industrial technology to save the environment, it concludes that appropriate technology cannot solve the important problems.

ECOLOGY PERSPECTIVES APPLIED TO THE RAINFORESTS OF THE BRAZILIAN AMAZON

Advocates of all the ecology perspectives discussed in this chapter have strong views about how to solve the environmental problems of the Brazilian Amazon while also improving the lives of Brazilians. Matrix 7.1 on page 138 summarizes some of their ideas.

Most states envy Brazil's store of natural resources. Symbols of luxury from emeralds to gold are abundant in this state. Likewise, the staples of a comfortable life—plants, animals, water, and timber—are available. From a global perspective, Brazil controls a tropical forest that helps stabilize the Earth's climate and atmosphere. The needs of the people of Brazil are in the hands of Brazilians. It appears, therefore, at least on the surface, to be the most fortunate of nations. It is ironic, then, that the ecological problems of Brazil, and especially of the Amazonian area, are among the most critical in the world. They possess so much but have much to lose.

Matrix 7.1
ECOLOGY PERSPECTIVES

	HIGH TECHNOLOGY	SHARED TECHNOLOGY	APPROPRIATE TECHNOLOGY
GOALS	Private enterprise (to protect interests and environment)	Equal distribution of technology	Egalitarian treatment Local control
KEY CONCEPTS	Progress	Sustainability Cooperation	Appropriate technology
STRATEGIES	Market system	International joint use	Individual solutions
TECHNOLOGY	Complex	Complex	Simplest for task
LOCUS OF POWER	Private enterprise	Governments	Local community
SEES CURRENT SYSTEM AS:	Good, but with too many constraints	Controlled by powerful states and businesses	Dominated by colonial forces

A View from the High Technology Perspective

Brazil is an area of untapped opportunity. Its abundance of resources means that there is a great deal of money to be made and that big business will invest heavily in the preservation of the environment that houses the resources. There admittedly has been a great deal of damage done to the Amazon, but it is the lure of wealth and the technological wizardry of modern technology that will reverse the damage and preserve the resources.

Almost 80 percent of the Brazilian population lives in cities, many of them in conditions of squalor. Advocates of high technology contend that with nearly 60 percent of the country forested, there must be areas of that forest where people can safely relocate and live more comfortably and productively. The rational way to accomplish this is to allow businesses to develop projects that create employment, which will lure workers. Some of these projects should be aimed at improving the infrastructure of the country. Despite the short-run problems, new dams need to be built to serve the energy-hungry cities and factories, and new roads must cut through the country to allow the movement of goods and the transportation of people. The technology to build these settlements, roads, and dams efficiently with minimal environmental effects exists and can be utilized as long as the companies are allowed to earn reasonable profits. Some of the Amazon must be sacrificed to benefit the whole of Brazil. New research and technology can manage ecological pressures that the rational limiting of the forest may create.

The problem of the dislocation of indigenous peoples and populations, like the rubber tappers, who have adapted to an antique way of life, should be limited. Modernization can be beneficial to these people. Western education can show them the advantages of modern life, and their children, given the opportunity, would surely choose the convenience of the new way of life. The tappers are recent immigrants to the forest who have chosen an economic system that is inefficient. They should be trained for more rational employment. For the present generation of Indians, the development of reservations or indigenous lands, as developed by the Brazilian government, will protect them from outsiders while clarifying the ownership of other lands. This should relieve the conflict with gold miners and others who have brought violence and death to these communities. Organized mining in ore-rich areas should also have this effect.

The Amazon is important to the future of Brazil. Exploration of the Amazon to learn the secrets of its plants and animals is economically important. It is unreasonable to assume that the Amazon forest will be unchanged regardless of environmentalists' wishes. The often mentioned point that there may be cures for diseases in the natural chemical makeup of plants unknown to the outside world is not a reason to keep business out of the forest, but good reason to collect those plants and test their potential as soon as possible. Local knowledge of these resources can be useful clues. As medicinal plants are located, their chemically efficacious properties can be reproduced in the laboratory, patented, and marketed. Already drugs have been developed in this way to fight glaucoma, depression, high blood pressure, inflammation, and other conditions (Reiss 1992:80). Millions around the world may be cured who had formerly suffered, and millions of dollars can be made in the effort.

Advocates claim that the future of the Amazon can safely be put in the hands of the Brazilian people as long as they are allowed to pursue a course of progress and prosperity. Many environmentalists mistakenly try to block this progress in the view that it will destroy the ecological system. What they need to recognize is that it is just this interest that will preserve the resources and replace the elements lost through new scientific inventions not yet considered.

A View from the Shared Technology Perspective

Brazil is a rich area that has allowed individual goals to override the general interest. It should recognize the needs of all the people of Brazil and ensure the prosperity of rich and poor, indigenous and nonindigenous. It must also recognize its obligation to the world and work with other nations to preserve the rainforest, which is an important part of the world's Commons. The problems are severe and modern technology can help, but they must be planned and applied in a cooperative manner.

The Brazilian Amazon is essential to the well-being of people throughout the world and its use and protection must be debated in the world arena. It is not only the atmosphere above Brazil that will change to threaten human life with the loss of rainforest, but also the atmosphere of the Earth as a whole. The sovereignty of Brazil must be respected, but the government of Brazil must, along with the governments of other nations, cooperate through NGOs and IGOs to ensure the health of the planet. Wealth and technology from other states must be made available to Brazil to help in the environmental effort.

The Rio Earth Summit of 1992 demonstrated a promising change in the government's approach to environmental issues. By inviting the world's leaders to Brazil to discuss environmental concerns, the country demonstrated an understanding of the problems and a recognition of the need for international cooperation to solve them. The need for sustainable development was embraced wholly by the signers of the Rio Declaration, including Brazil. Now that the country has dedicated itself to the concept, it remains to be seen how the practical applications will follow. Guarantees to protect indigenous rights on protected lands have been given but not strictly enforced. Funding for new dams has been requested from the World Bank without clear agreement from local residents or international ecological agencies, although it is evident that environmental problems are addressed in the planning documents. Tax incentives for short-term use of logged rainforest lands have ceased and the practice has become less attractive.

The rainforest must survive and the people of Brazil as a whole should benefit from the sustainable development of the land. The indigenous people must be assured of their lands and way of life because they have skills and knowledge that can be harnessed for further development. They should benefit from development along with other Brazilians. Others, like the tappers, who use the land in a sustainable manner, should also be consulted for their unique knowledge. Together with ecological scientists, they should develop new techniques to use the resources of the forest without destroying them. The poor of the cities must be taken into consideration as well. Opportunities for them to support their families in ecologically efficient ways should be sought out. When the people of Brazil understand the benefits they can reap by using new technologies to sustain their resources, little coercion will be necessary to enlist their cooperation. The technologies of people around the world who have faced similar problems will be made available to conquer those of Brazil.

The goals of the Brazilian government, as asserted in international documents, have changed dramatically to adopt the assumptions of the shared technology perspective. The influence of Brazilian environmental NGOs is growing with their alliances with international groups and the joining of individual NGOs into consortia. With support from these local and international NGOs and other states, there is hope that the environmental destruction, which resulted from the programs of previous governments, can be ended and reversed.

A View from the Appropriate Technology Perspective

Brazil is one of the worst cases of unrestricted high technology that destroy the physical environment and the lives of many different peoples. The original inhabitants, the indigenous people, have preserved the Amazonian forest, which is so critical to life on Earth, over the generations. Their lives can be improved with selected new technology, but the core of their lifestyle sustains them and the environment. Some new inhabitants, like the rubber tappers, have settled into an ecologically stable way of life as well. The expertise of these people should be used in association with successful technologies developed elsewhere that fit the Amazon.

Brazil is a large country with widely divergent physical environments and human cultures within its borders. Therefore, it is unreasonable to assume that generally applied technological solutions would solve problems in all parts of the country equally well. Diversity is the nature of Brazil and so must be its programs for change. Successful solutions to the many problems of the country must develop from the grassroots.

The problems of the indigenous people of the Amazon lie in the forest and should be solved following their ways of life. Subsistence techniques of horticulture and hunting long fed their families and, given enough secure land, as the government has repeatedly promised, still could. Locally made clothing and implements work well in the context of the area and do not tie people to a cash economy. These techniques do not cause permanent damage. There are Western goods that the Indians want. Metal implements make tools more durable and efficient, vaccinations make introduced diseases less deadly, and now telephones and airplanes allow their leaders to tell their story to outsiders. The appropriate technology perspective does not preclude the use of such modern tools but asserts that using some modern technology does not mean that one must use it all.

The rubber tappers demonstrate the combination of modern public relations with a low technological economy. The career and murder of Chico Mendez as a leader of these people, who attempted to preserve their way of life against the encroachment of big business, has become legendary among environmentalists. One of the important lessons of this heroic tale is that people are willing to fight, and even to die, in order to preserve the low technology, low polluting way of life that they value. A good life can be a simple life; industrial progress need not be the goal of all people. Resources and government support should encourage such environmentally safe ways of life.

While some technologies such as solar power seem broadly applicable, proponents of appropriate technology do not claim to have specific solutions that fit all situations. Individuals and local groups must be listened to and encouraged to take control over their own lives and land. There can be no one solution to the problems of Brazil. There must be many solutions to each problem. On the one hand, different people in similar physical settings may not accept the same methods of exploiting those settings. On the other, people of similar cultures many need different technologies to deal with their environmental problems. The inventiveness of people will be seen in each community and will not only solve its own environmental problems, but ultimately and jointly those of the globe as well.

TERMS AND CONCEPTS

Brundtland Commission
green revolution
sustainability

DISCUSSION QUESTIONS

1. Examine an environmental issue currently in the news. Do people disagree on what to do, if anything, about the problem? What assumptions and goals seem to underlie their differences?

2. The future of the Brazilian rainforest will ultimately affect people around the globe. How does the issue of state sovereignty conflict with the greater need of humanity in this case? Why is this a difficult issue?

3. Americans have long valued capitalism and much of the prosperity of the West can be traced to free enterprise. How do the goals of business conflict with those of global human and environmental health? How can these latter goals be good for business?

4. Choose a local environmental issue and apply to it the three perspectives discussed in this chapter. Which perspective most closely fits each of the following approaches to the issue: the government, business interest group, and your own approach?

5. The war on AIDS has been approached from all three ecology perspectives discussed here—the high technology, shared technology, and appropriate technology perspectives. How do advocates of each perspective approach the issue of AIDS? What are the strong points and weak points of each perspective on this matter?

RESEARCH PROJECTS

1. Choose an area of the world and review its most severe ecological problems. How has the government chosen to attack the problems? What obstacles does the government face?

2. Conduct some library and online research on the types of environmental issues currently being addressed by the United Nations. What types of problems are getting the most attention? Choose one or two of the issues and analyze their global impact.

3. Environmental groups have become politically important in some European states. Choose one of these states and describe the changes that have been brought about by environmentalists. How are these changes different than those found in countries with less powerful environmentalists?

4. Apply two of the ecology perspectives discussed in this chapter to the analysis of an environmental issue that occurs in both developed and developing nations. Describe how the issue is dealt with in two specific states, one from the industrialized world and the other from the developing world. Use the perspectives to explain the differences and similarities in the two states' approaches to the issue.

5. Review the United Nations commissions on environmental issues since the Brundtland report. What successes do they claim? Which environmental problems are not addressed at these meetings? Which perspectives are clearly reflected in their public statements? Are they worthwhile?

INTERNET RESOURCES

Amanaka'a Amazon Network: *http://www.amanakaa.org* This NGO's homepage offers links to numerous environmental sites relating to the Amazon and general environmental concerns.

Instituto Brasileiro de Geografia e Estatística (IBGE): *http://www.ibge.org/english/e-home.htm* This English section of a Brazilian site offers statistics and other information on the economy and ecology of Brazil as well as links to similar sites for other countries.

International Institute for Sustainable Development: *http://iisd.ca* This Canadian NGO's homepage provides archives of information about sustainable development projects and links to other sites of interest.

Rainforest Action Network: *http://www.rainforest-alliance.org* This energetic site provides children's programs, educational materials, political action opportunities, and links to related sites.

UN Environmental Program: *http.//www,unep.org* The UNEP's homepage offers updates on its programs as well as links to other sites.

8

Peace and War

At any given time somewhere in the world, violence is used by individuals, organized groups, and states as a means to achieve political ends. Whether the situation involves the taking of hostages, other terrorist incidents, mass killings, torture, or war, humans have proven adept at inflicting suffering in the name of a cause. The 1995 Oklahoma City bombing illustrates well the vulnerability of any society to politically inspired violence. Because they capture headlines, war and other violent acts seem an almost normal occurrence. In fact, they are not. Rarely do groups or states fight to achieve their objectives. Conflicts, from minor disputes to major clashes of interest, are dealt with peacefully virtually all the time whether they occur within countries or internationally. This chapter discusses several concepts that attempt to explain why groups or states sometimes react to unresolved conflicts violently while most of the time they do not.

The concepts also define degrees of both peace and war, which reflect the different relationships among the communities and countries in conflict. The term *war* is used to refer to a range of violent actions—from all-out, full-scale clashes of armies to smaller-scale incidents of terrorism. *Peace* can describe situations ranging from an uneasy or tense absence of war to a permanent peace wherein the participants consider the use of force unimaginable. Peace and war are not opposites; they merge with each other when force is threatened but not used. In such a situation, peace may be said to exist but only tenuously.

Earlier chapters have provided a general context for explaining why conflicts exist. At the end of the twentieth century, increasingly severe economic problems, exacerbated by destruction of the natural environment, can cause a society to split along its existing cultural and class lines or a state to act on long-smoldering grievances against another state. Political ideologies play a role as well by allowing the antagonists to perceive the causes of conflict as linked to higher principles, such as religious beliefs, ethnic or state nationalism, stability and order in defense of an existing political system, or general ideals like freedom from oppression.

Much of this chapter focuses on the circumstances in which communities or countries decide not to debate their opponents but to defeat them. Although abstract explanations represent real human suffering, the following account of the Segetalo family in Bosnia brings to life the toll violence extracts from its victims. The family's situation was reported by Chuck Sudetic in the *New York Times* on September 30, 1993.

> When war returned to this divided river city (in 1993), Asim Segetalo gave up expecting people to knock on his door before barging in. The 43-year-old metalworker's house . . . has become a detour for pedestrians trying to skirt sniper fire on a 30-yard stretch of a main shopping street. Each day, hundreds of people stream in the front door, through the kitchen he set up for his family on the house's well-shielded ground floor and exit through the back. Hundreds more pass in the opposite direction. Mr. Segetalo understands the necessity. A man who chose not to take the path through the Segetalos' kitchen was wounded by a sniper bullet on the main street today. Still, he said: "It's terrible to live with this crowd pouring through all day long. It's especially bad when we're sitting here eating dinner. Some people even ask us for food."
>
> The lives of Mr. Segetalo and the rest of Mostar's people are contorted in myriad ways by the battle for control of their city. . . . Now some 35,000 people, including thousands of refugees, are jammed into a pile of rubble that was once the houses and apartments on the east bank. They squeeze into basements with mattresses stretched out on the cement floors, drink water from a tanker truck brought in by the United Nations and feed themselves from supplies dropped by American cargo planes. . . . There has been no electricity here for three months. . . .
>
> "We've taken two direct hits since [being] attacked in May and seven others fell within 10 yards of the house," Mr. Segetalo said, bemoaning the repairs he will have to make to his 130-year-old family house once the war ends. His wife, Dzevahira, also complains about the crowds pouring through her kitchen, but she has turned the traffic into something of a business opportunity by offering haircuts to the passers-by. "I cut about 20 heads of hair each day, men and women," she said. . . . "Some people bring presents like cigarettes and soap in thanks," she said. "I do it for free for the people. But I want to open a beauty salon after the war, if I live through it."
>
> The Segetalo's 7-year-old daughter, Sabina, seems not to mind either the crowds or the grim kitchen-table talk of "ethnic cleansing" and neighbors who have died. Her 11-year-old brother, Sanel, died in a bombardment of a nearby town last year. "Look, here's a mortar shell," the little girl said, showing off the metal husk of an exploded shell. "It's a 105 millimeter. My father found it but I don't remember when." Without missing a beat, she showed off another prized possession. "Look, here's my turtle," Sabina said. "His name is Peti. I found him in the garden about a month ago." (Sudetic, 1993: A7.)

This family was caught in circumstances beyond its control. Wars can have deeply important but incompletely considered effects on individuals because explanations of the causes and results of wars focus on large-scale, long-term trends and decisions by political leaders. Most often society's elites determine major events. International relations specialists often begin an analysis of why political leaders choose peace or war by considering the nature of the *international system*, defined as the sum total of interactions among institutions beyond state borders, including IGOs, NGOs, and, primarily, states.

THE NATURE OF THE INTERNATIONAL SYSTEM

It often seems that people assume wars are more or less spontaneous. The phrase "war has broken out" implies a nondirective causation. Upon closer scrutiny, however, each use of violence "erupted" because decisions to do so were made by specific people for explicable reasons. Understanding why people decide to use war to get their way requires knowing how the international system works. International relations theorists identify the two most prominent, interrelated characteristics as state sovereignty and international anarchy. These two concepts apply to the behavior of states; however, when groups within states reject the authority of the government, they claim the attributes of sovereignty, at least as they see it. Some groups even declare independence from their former state, perhaps because, as explained in Chapter 1, the state remains the most powerful unit in the international system and groups want one of their own.

Sovereignty

Sovereignty means that states accept no political authority as superseding their own. This presumption, enshrined by centuries of hoary tradition, is considered by states as their chief characteristic in relating to each other. According to the principle, no international institution has the right to determine the laws and policies that apply to people within the borders of any sovereign state. Sovereignty has the effect, then, of designating government as the sole representative of the population of a state. At least since 1945, when states have used war to take over territory of another state, or change the governments or policies of other states, such violations of sovereignty have been denounced as aggression. To be effective, sovereignty must be mutually respected by all states.

Some people think that because international organizations have proliferated in number and influence since World War II, state sovereignty has been substantially eroded. A solid case can be made for this point of view, but the opposing opinion can also help explain world events; namely, that state sovereignty retains its validity. States have the vote when international governmental organizations pass resolutions and, even then, the resolutions do not apply within a state's borders until its government enacts legislation. Thus, states remain central in carrying out any internationally validated policy. Even "binding" resolutions are subject to interpretation and enforcement by each member government. Transnational corporations and other nonstate actors are growing in number and importance, but governments still set the rules for interactions across state borders. Governments also have military forces, unlike corporations and other organizations.

More than 190 sovereign states make up the current international system, 185 of them as members of the United Nations. In recognizing no political authority as superior to their own, they behave very differently from organizations within a domestic political system in one major way. Governments can threaten or use force in relating to each other, whereas businesses, unions, colleges, issue groups, and ethnic organizations cannot legitimately threaten violence, at least not in stable societies.

International Anarchy

Anarchy is perhaps more difficult to understand than sovereignty because it seems contrary to the practical experience of most people. Sovereignty conjures up thoughts of loyalty to the institutions of government, if not also to the government's present officials. Such patriotism is a common phenomenon. In thinking about anarchy, however, people who live in a stable state have a hard time imagining how force can seem a reasonable alternative in the absence of a highly structured social environment.

International relations theorists use the term *international anarchy* in explaining why force can be considered within the bounds of acceptable behavior in cases of extreme international conflict, but unacceptable in domestic political contexts. Defined as an absence of governance or political rule, anarchy applies to the international system of sovereign states. Each state acts as judge in its own cause because it recognizes no higher political authority. It can make a case for whatever policies and tactics it chooses, including war. Compared with what appears to be the certainty of centralized domestic institutions—courts, police, legislatures—international institutions appear to be weak. Yet in spite of the absence of an assured appeal to authority, states handle most of their disputes peacefully and even settle some now and then. Thus, anarchy as applied to the international system does *not* mean an absence of order. Whole networks of rules and relationships condition and limit the leaders of states in their choice of political as well as economic actions.

This refutes the commonsense connotation of anarchy as related to chaos, confusion, lawlessness, and disorder. To the contrary, states conform to recognizable patterns of behavior. Diplomatic immunity provides one case in point. For centuries, governments have mutually assured the physical safety of foreign ambassadors and other representatives. This is why most of the world's leaders were so shocked at the complicity of the revolutionary Iranian government in the 1979 seizure of the US embassy in Tehran, and the subsequent holding of its officials as hostage for over a year.

To take the point one step further, the regularity and confidence evident in some interstate relations even amounts to a sense of community complete with commonly accepted rules. People in countries that are members of the European Union, for example, cannot imagine a war among themselves. This situation presents a striking contrast with their history during the first half of the twentieth century. Decades of effective cooperation after World War II have eliminated force as a means of settling disputes among Western Europeans in the foreseeable future.

The development of this relatively permanent peace came after two all-out, world wars within only thirty years. World Wars I and II, in turn, produced history's greatest volume of slaughter and material devastation. The Second World War occurred as Nazism took nationalism to its illogical extreme. The Nazi brand of fascism eventually denied even the right of existence to its imagined enemies. Europe's Jewish minorities, as well as millions of other people, were killed, not as a means of winning a war, but because of a perverted principle. World War II's unimaginable destruction, plus the barbarity of the Holocaust, compelled Europeans to create new international institutions with the potential ability to affect state behavior. The institutions of the European Union (EU) have eroded the sovereignty of their members, and thus anarchy no longer provides the context for how EU member governments relate to each other. Yet for centuries the concept of anarchy did apply in Europe as it still does in much of the rest of the world today.

The concept of anarchy can apply within the borders of states where domestic order has disintegrated. Groups take on a semblance of sovereignty by renouncing the authority of the government, as in Lebanon in the 1970s and 1980s and in Bosnia in the 1990s. Thus, groups feel free to use violence just as states do when they fight. Such actions by groups greatly add to the complexity of international events. When domestic political systems destabilize, it virtually invites other states to intervene. An interventionist state can legitimize the seeming violation of the sovereignty of another state by labeling the leadership of one of the domestic groups as a potential government that has requested help.

Power Defined

Whatever the policy choice of groups within states, or of the states themselves, their relationship is determined by power. *Power* is the ability of persons, groups, organizations, and states to cause others to do what they want. Thus, power exists in relationships that enable those with greater power to achieve their desired results by affecting the behavior of others. Power is exercised most effectively when compliance is voluntary or when the presence of power in a relationship is not obvious. This occurs when those in leadership positions are aware of the needs and thoughts of others in the system and design strategies that make sense to them. Power is built up and exercised in three ways—through persuasion, economic inducements, and, rarely, physical force.

This definition of power counters the commonsense assumption that equates power with control and coercion. Such an overemphasis on power's negative connotation obscures the real way most decisions are made and leadership is exercised. Often people respond to the fact that much compliance is voluntary by trying to make a distinction between control and influence. Then they get into the problem of determining whether people are doing something somebody else wants them to because they agree or because they have no choice. Trying to draw such a fine line, which may be impossible in many real situations, is often not worth the effort. Therefore, power, as defined by most social scientists, includes a mix of both influence and control in many relationships.

This discussion about the potential coercive element in power brings up an important point. If exercised too overtly and with too much coercion, power can cause a negative reaction contrary to what those in power intended. Potential rebellions, whether overt or covert, can result in less power for the leaders. Thus, the concept of power has an annoying fluidity. Too much power can lead to less. Conversely, the appearance of less can mean more power exists. This analysis relates directly to the international system. History is replete with examples of states attempting to amass more and more power, as if it had no limit, only to go down in flames when their policy resulted in war. Other states finally thwarted the attempt at hegemonic aggression; Napoleon's France and Hitler's Germany are two examples.

The United States may be the world's remaining military superpower, but it needs to negotiate unless it wants to use a military solution for every issue. The United States must exercise political leadership and intelligently apply its clout with subtlety and sophistication in order to maintain its productive relationships with others in an interconnected world. The effectiveness of a government's foreign policy should not be measured by getting its way all the time with either equal or weaker states. The world's leading countries consider themselves relatively equal in power and such relationships are not easy to maintain. They require effort and ongoing consultations. While the powerful may be annoyed by having to bargain, convince, and negotiate with the less powerful, such power sharing is necessary in a peaceful context. Like domestic political systems, a stable international environment depends on most states in the system having a constructive role to play and getting something out of it for themselves. In an interdependent world, even the weak have some leverage.

Politics and Power

The process of decision making itself is called *politics*. The opposite of using force, politics means bargaining and negotiating. Those involved in making the decision have some level of power but usually they are not equals. Unfortunately, politics has a bad name for many people in the United States. It seems like common sense that power corrupts inevitably, and therefore the decision-making process of cutting deals somehow works against the interests of the "average person." People with this narrow view fail to realize that politics and power are exercised in many private and public relationships involving businesses, universities, and community organizations. Power applies not only to what happens in making government decisions; it is also inherent in all hierarchical organizations. It exists in interpersonal relationships as well, such as when one of person exercises more influence than the other in most decision-making situations.

In the international context, politics takes into account three elements of power: political relationships, economic wealth, and military forces. Whereas in domestic politics the role of physical force is minimal, international decision makers are aware of their level of military power and that of their counterparts in other governments. States are termed *small powers*, *regional powers*, or *great powers*—and, since World War II, the term *superpowers* has been added to the international system vocabulary.

Small powers, such as the Slovak Republic, can make decisions affecting their own affairs but have little influence elsewhere. Regional powers—India is an example—can have a direct effect on their neighbors and world region. Great powers extend their reach out of their region and some have worldwide clout. Japan's global economic influence and France's use of its military in central Africa serve as examples. A superpower can extend its political, economic, and military effectiveness around the world and sustain it for some time. A narrower definition of *superpower* that is sometimes used includes only those states with nuclear missile capability.

Russia may still qualify if nuclear weapon possession is the only criterion. Yet such weapons are irrelevant in almost every daily interaction with other states.

In choosing policies and tactics, government leaders do not only consider their relative level of international power. They must also take into account the interests of their country and the perceptions of its people, as well of those of other states. Therefore, the concepts of interest and perception are crucial in analyzing international events.

Interest and Power

Persons, groups, organizations, and states are said to have *interests* when they are able to use relationships or resources for their own benefit. As a practical matter internationally, the term *interests* relates to one or more of the three elements of power. States adopt positions and take actions that enhance their political, economic, and military capabilities. The problem arises in applying the concept to a specific situation. Most of the time, people disagree over exactly when their country's interest is at stake and when it is not.

In many international conflicts, no clear-cut interpretation of a country's interest is accepted by most of its people. The reason lies in the ambiguous nature of power itself. A state's reputation for power and its willingness to use it are just as important as any appraisal of exactly what capabilities the state may have. Such capabilities include the number, location, and battle-tested experience of troops; weapons and their sophistication; the level of economic resources that can be committed; and the political support of the population. These objective factors are only a part of the calculation a government's leaders make in deciding what action they can take. The probable use of these elements of power figure just as much into another state's reasoning. In other words, power is not just a condition, like the sum of currency and troops, for example. To influence decision making, states must be perceived as willing to apply the factors of power to a given situation. Here, interpretations, assumptions, and perceptions become important.

To illustrate, during a crisis somewhere in the world, often a knock-down, drag-out argument breaks out in the United States over whether its interests in the situation are strong enough to warrant taking action. Sending troops to Bosnia is a good example. All involved in the verbal joust solemnly claimed that their position reflected the true US interest. Supporters of sending US soldiers to monitor compliance with the peace agreement argued that the United States had an interest in the Balkans because if instability spread, Greece and Turkey could become directly involved. Since both are US allies as members of NATO, the United States would be dragged into an even more volatile situation than if this country had dealt with the problem in the first place. Opponents to committing American troops vehemently countered by asserting that the United States had no real economic or strategic interest in Bosnia. The problem was in Europe, so Europeans should handle it.

Perceptual Selectivity

Interest relates to the elements of power but, in applying it to a set of international events, policy makers filter it through their own *perceptions*. These attitudes and points of view are selective, by definition, and determined by cultural-historical, nationalistic, ideological, or religious preconceptions. The resulting values and beliefs cause what is called *perceptual selectivity;* that is, some information gets through to conscious thought, while other facts may be ignored or misinterpreted.

Humans often act on the basis of their expectations. Such actions prove effective when they fit the circumstances, defined partly by the expectations of others. When they do not, failure often results. To illustrate, although US leaders were convinced that the 1958 domestic violence in Lebanon was inspired by communism, it was subsequently revealed that their assumption was without any evidence or support. The landing by US marines helped shore up a minority government friendly to the United States but, within eight years, the country had dissolved into an ugly civil war. In a similar example of how perceptions can obscure reality, Kuwaiti and US officials in 1990 did not think Iraq would invade Kuwait. They interpreted Iraq's threatening troop movements as a bluff. Unfortunately, they were wrong, and it took the 1991 Gulf War led by US troops to force Iraq out of Kuwait.

A MODEL OF PEACE AND WAR

Analyses of international events made by the leaders of states have high-stakes consequences, particularly when they concern peace and war. Figure 8.1 offers a simplified model of international foreign policy making as it relates to security issues. The following pages discuss the three general choices states make to achieve their objectives. The explanation refers to states because they are the main international actors, but it can also apply to groups when they assume sovereignty and act like states.

As is depicted in Figure 8.1 on page 152, the relationships among several concepts are used by international relations theorists to explain peace and war. The figure's three prongs represent three different international political contexts and their related responses to conflict by states. The first refers to the use of force. The second policy choice also assumes a context of hostility, but in this case it leads to competition without violence. The third policy choice assumes that a sense of commonality or even community has developed; therefore, cooperative actions manage conflicts without the threat of violence.

The Strategies of War

A state or group that decides to use force has several choices regarding the various strategies of war. These choices reflect the state's or group's level of military power and are listed as five categories: show of force, terrorism, guerrilla war, conventional war, and nuclear war.

A *show of force* refers to the movement of a state's military forces into a conflict situation as an implied threat. Such an action is designed to cause the adversary to back down. Bluff is the appearance of intention rather than the initiation of actual fighting. A show of force only has a chance of success when the state making the threat has much more power in the situation than its adversary. An example of a show of force occurred in 1903, when President Theodore Roosevelt sent a warship to block Colombia's approach to Panama. A former province of Colombia, Panama

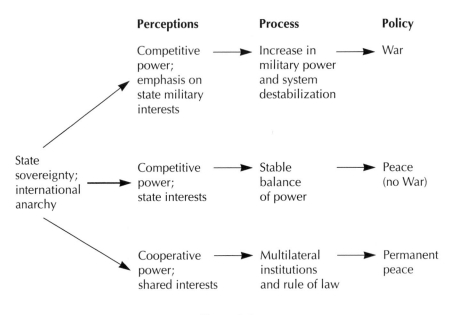

Figure 8.1
THREE INTERNATIONAL SYSTEM CONTEXTS

had declared its independence. The United States wanted to build a canal in Panama and the Colombian government had not accepted the US terms. An independent Panama, however, signed the treaty dictated by the United States. In this case, the United States used its political, economic, and military power to create a new state by violating Colombia's sovereignty.

Unlike a show of force, *terrorism* is a tactic of the weak. It uses specific acts of violence perpetrated by small numbers of people for the purpose of destabilizing an existing political system, or at least revealing it as oppressive, inept, and unworthy of support. Groups within states generally use terrorism when they have little power but want to make a big impression. Because they are few in number, terrorists employ clandestine, hit-and-run tactics, often against civilians. Targets are chosen to make the terrorists appear strong and to signify their grievances. They hide by blending into the general population. Although terrorist bombings, assassinations, robberies, and other attacks can be labeled as criminal and not acts of war, the terrorists usually consider themselves to be at war. What muddies these seemingly clear waters, however, is the fact that sometimes governments use clandestine operations against another state. Such government sponsored-terrorism uses the same tactics as group or individual terrorists.

Fighters of *guerrilla wars* often use small arms and hit-and-run tactics like terrorists, but they are in larger, more organized groups and can take on defended targets. They attack military outposts and ambush army patrols. Also like terrorism, guerrilla wars occur in domestic conflict situations, ironically called *civil wars* (civility hardly seems the objective). The term *guerrilla war* was first used during the Spanish Civil War in 1936. It combines the Spanish word for war, *guerro*, and *illa* which is a Spanish suffix meaning "little." Like terrorists, guerrilla fighters blend into the local population as their main defense. In some cases, though, they gain enough size and strength to establish strongholds within a specific territory. When they attract enough support, a full-scale civil war can ensue with the guerrillas setting up their own government functions. In these cases, the size of the military operation and the use of heavy military equipment can make the level of violence in a guerrilla war akin to that of a conventional war.

The word *war* to most people means *conventional war;* that is, the formally organized military forces of states, complete with uniforms, differentiated functions, command and control hierarchies, training, and a historical mission. Governments with sufficiently large economies invest in trained and fully equipped permanent military forces. Since industrialization has made possible mechanized armies and high-technology weapons, the scale of killing has greatly increased. The further technological and organizational sophistication of warfare in the twentieth century has so frightened the world's leading powers that they seem less likely to fight each other than at any previous time in recorded history.

As the most destructive conventional war of all time, perhaps it is perversely fitting that World War II ended with a weapon so powerful that it has been given a category all its own. *Nuclear war*, unlike the previous categories of force, is defined by the kind of weapon rather than the manner in which it is used. Nuclear, including atomic, weapons are produced from the release of molecular energy. They were developed by states with large-scale scientific and military establishments and, therefore, the requisite advanced technology and military capability. Currently, five states have officially acknowledged production and possession of nuclear weapons as well as the ability to deliver them to targets using various weapons systems: the United States, Russia, China, the United Kingdom, and France. Two states have tested energy-based weapons: India and Pakistan, and it was unclear as of June, 1998 whether they had delivery systems. Several others are strongly suspected of having or of being close to having such weapons: Israel and possibly Iran. Many people fear proliferation because the states with nuclear weapons may sell the technology and components to previously non-nuclear states.

The fact that the type of weapon provides the distinguishing characteristic of nuclear war has raised a hotly debated issue with important policy implications. Both military strategists and international relations theorists disagree over whether nuclear weapons can be treated as just another, although more devastatingly powerful, weapon system, or whether the difference is so great as to require completely new strategic thinking. A further issue is raised over whether such weapons can be used in warfare like any other weapon or whether they should only act as a deterrent to keep other states from using them. US policy makers accepted the former position when they dropped atom bombs on two Japanese cities in 1945, ending World War II. During the Cold War, however, US policy makers seemed to shift to the latter policy; the use of nuclear weapons was considered unthinkable except in retaliation for a direct nuclear attack.

Perhaps the US policy change occurred because the destructive capability of energy-based weapons greatly increased. A one megaton warhead is over eighty times greater than the bomb used on Hiroshima, and some ten-, twenty-, and thirty-megaton warheads were produced by the Soviet Union and the United States during the Cold War. In addition, the United States experienced severe adverse political fallout from being the only country to ever use an energy-based weapon in war. Commentators point out as well that US policy may have been influenced by the fact that when the atomic bomb was dropped, there was no threat that Japan could reply in kind. In contrast, the Soviet Union not only had what was called "the Bomb" but also delivery systems able to get it to the United States.

This section has summarized the various fighting strategies that states and groups use when engaged in armed combat. Before moving on to the two other policy choices depicted in Figure 8.1 (those designed to achieve peace), a caveat must be noted to the discussion thus far. It has tacitly accepted an underlying assumption that peace is preferred over war; however, wars have been used to change things for the better, as judged by the winners. Israelis, for example, would make the case that fighting was necessary in 1947 and 1948, to establish their country's existence. The US Revolutionary War may be cited as another example. However, World War II and the Holocaust directly produced the perceived need by Jewish people to create Israel as soon as possible. Also, perhaps the independence of the United States could have been achieved in the long run without war, as it was in Canada. Arguments over history can go on and on, but, the point remains that people will choose violent means to achieve what they perceive as a vital objective if they feel justified, think success is possible, and can see no other way. Other times, states or groups may decide not to use force when in conflict situations. One explanation for the different strategies is called balance of power.

Balance-of-Power Strategy

When governments or groups in conflict choose a balance-of-power strategy, the result is not war but peace, though peace may be temporary. In a *balance-of-power* system, states or groups choose not to use force because they consider the potential cost as too high. They may lose the war or experience so much destruction that their populations judge the deaths, suffering, and material sacrifices as not worth the foreign policy objective. In a balance of power, decision makers adopt the deterrence of an attack as their aim. To be successful, they rely on military power, but it doesn't necessarily have to be equal to that of potential enemies. Even small powers can pose a real threat to larger ones if they can fight a long-term guerrilla war and thereby split opinion in the attacking country. The Vietnam War is an obvious example.

In a balance-of-power situation, by definition, force is threatened but not used. Military power retains its importance, but it becomes one of several strategies rather than the only tool for achieving foreign policy objectives. It remains important to remind other states that a potentially hostile alternative exists to the peaceful strategies currently being employed. Peaceful strategies are derived from the other two types of power—economic power and political power.

Economic Power States can draw on several economic strategies, some providing positive incentives, others negative ones. All favor the powerful. Aid and the granting of favorable trade treatment can establish the basis for future positive relations. For example, granting most-favored nation trade status to China is an ongoing debate in the United States. Many Americans take exception to China's treatment of its political dissidents and would prefer punishment to business as usual. Others realize that not granting China the same access to US markets enjoyed by most other countries would only hurt importers and US consumers, while angering China's leaders and doing nothing to help those jailed for their criticisms of the Chinese government.

Governments employing negative economic strategies can cut off aid and reduce trade by setting a quota, or eliminate trade by carrying out an embargo. States take such actions individually, or collectively in the form of *economic sanctions* voted by the United Nations. Sanctions are punishment for actions deemed in violation of international norms. In Iraq, for instance, economic sanctions applied after its 1990 invasion of Kuwait continued for years, given Iraq's harsh treatment of its rebellious ethnic groups. Sanctions also are designed to encourage states to change their policies. Cutting off trade and financial flows, admittedly long-run strategies, only have a chance of success when carried out by virtually all the target country's trading partners. However, Cuba provides an example of how economic sanctions can fail.

After Cuba's 1979 revolution and subsequent seizure of foreign-owned property, the Organization of American States voted to impose economic sanctions against Cuba. In addition, the United States eliminated its Cuban sugar quota, a trade policy that had assured a high level of Cuban sugar imports. This action virtually eliminated the US market for Cuban sugar, the country's one major cash crop. In response, the Soviet Union became Cuba's main trading partner. The economic embargo has had no visible effect on Cuban political policies to this day. In contrast, evidence exists that years of economic sanctions had an influence on South Africa's ruling white minority in its decision to hand over the government to elected representatives of the black majority. These examples show that most states in the international community, and all great powers, must cooperate for economic sanctions to be effective.

Political Power States also can use political power to influence other states. Announcing policy positions and providing information are strategies designed to have a desired impact whether communicated formally, through diplomatic channels, or informally, using public media. Like those based on economic or military power, sometimes political strategies work while at other times they do not. Take, for example, propaganda. Defined as an attempt to influence through emotional appeals, *propaganda* can be either true or false but its negative connotations prevail in the public mind. Its strategies include public statements by government officials, articles planted in the print media, informational fliers, and films, among others. Their purpose is to affect the opinions of other government leaders or the general population in the same or other countries.

The problem with propaganda as a political strategy is the danger that the targeted groups might react differently than policy makers intend or expect. Iraq provides a case in point. During the months of waiting to see what would happen after his invasion of Kuwait, Saddam Hussein evidently wanted to send a message portraying himself as a reasonable, decent human being. He invited worldwide television coverage of his meeting with a few Europeans his government was holding in Iraq. Unfortunately for the benevolent image he wanted to project, the world saw malevolence as the Iraqi president awkwardly attempted to put his arm around a young British boy whose face reflected confusion and fear. As with economic strategies, the powerful have an disproportionate chance of success; however, the clever use of public media can allow a weaker state to make its case to the world. President Castro of Cuba, for example, seems adept in meeting with prominent figures from other countries, allowing tourism to prosper and encouraging educational contacts.

Diplomacy, another political strategy that is often overlooked but that can prove potent at times, includes all the communications between two or more governments or IGOs. The most commonly understood form of diplomacy, *negotiation* takes place when officials talk to each other directly or through an intermediary. Indirect communications have come to be considered a form of diplomacy as well. Called *signaling* or *tacit negotiations*, this process involves officials saying or doing something with the intent of sending a message to another government without telling it directly. Stating a shift in position can signal a willingness to break an impasse and negotiate a peaceful resolution to a dispute. Devising an offer to accompany a threat enhances the chances of reaching an agreement. The Cuban Missile Crisis of 1962 provides a much studied example. Reconnaissance photographs taken by a US spy plane showed that the Soviet Union was deploying missiles with nuclear warheads in Cuba. The United States demanded their removal and signaled how seriously it considered the crisis by mobilizing its forces and blockading Cuba. The Soviet Union faced a hard choice: back down or risk a war with the United States. The confrontation was resolved peacefully when the United States promised not to invade Cuba in exchange for the Soviet Union's removal of the missiles and their warheads.

Revisionist and Status Quo States   Some balance-of-power relationships are volatile, while others more stable. The difference depends on the existence of a minimum of states with revisionist foreign policies and a maximum of status quo states. States are labeled *revisionist* when they aim to change their existing level of military power by accumulating more troops and weapons. Sometimes they do this because they have decided a war may be needed to get what they want (such as a piece of a neighboring state's territory), or to stop a perceived enemy from becoming a major influence in a third country. Other times, revisionist states aim for a preponderance of power and use fear and bluff in forcing adversaries to give in. In contrast, *status quo states* are satisfied with their existing level of power. But they may feel threatened by a revisionist state's power buildup. Such a reaction is prudent in an anarchic situation. If a revisionist state continues its aggressive policy, other states will add to their arsenals, producing in turn higher levels of fear, tension, and overall instability. A degenerating cycle sets in as destabilizing relationships result in less predictable behavior and more unknowns, thus increasing distrust, fear, and misperception. The greater the destabilization, the more the military buildup.

The Middle East is a regional power system noted for its great instability. In the decades since World War II, at least ten wars, innumerable terrorist incidents, periodic domestic demonstrations and rebellions, and several high-profile assassinations have taken place in the Middle East. Much of this violence can be explained by the fact that the region is filled with revisionists. Iraq has never accepted its present boundaries, drawn by the British after World War I. Neither has Syria, whose most recent colonizer, France, took control of the area by force after World War I. In Israel, a major segment of its population, as represented in the Lekud ("unity") Party, thinks the West Bank and parts of Jordan should belong to the Jewish people rather than to the Arabs who live there. Iran and Libya retain revolutionary ideologies with expansionist overtones. Palestinians may be the ultimate revisionists because they are demanding part of the land they see as their historical heritage so they can have a state, and this is the same territory many Israelis perceive as theirs. This leaves few status quo states in the Middle East: Egypt, Jordan, the oil-rich gulf sheikdoms such as Qatar and Saudi Arabia, and Turkey.

Northeast Asia has been a relatively stable region since the Korean War ended with a cease-fire in 1953. Violent incidents have occurred there but they have not led to war. North Korea carried out several terrorist attacks on South Korean officials, most notably the 1983 assassination in Burma of four South Korean cabinet ministers and other officials. North Korea also seized the US Navy's reconnaissance ship *Pueblo* in 1968, but then released its crew months later. In spite of these and other provocations, a threat of war did not develop. Every state in the region had a status quo foreign policy, though for different reasons. Japan's trading economy meant it needed peace to prosper. It built the world's third-largest navy but did not threaten other states in the region. The United States and, until its dissolution, the Soviet Union, shared an interest in keeping the sea lanes open. They also had more pressing international issues in other parts of the world. Thus, as supporters and suppliers of the respective Koreas, they used their influence to keep their clients from destabilizing policies. Also, avoiding war was in South Korea's interest as it concentrated on economic development. China was involved internally with economic development mixed with political conflicts, most notably the 1966–1976 Cultural Revolution.

In the late 1990s, however, China's military buildup has drawn the attention of states worldwide. The key question being considered is whether China's policy change has resulted from its understandable quest to become a great power, or if China has become revisionist and will use its modernized army and new navy to threaten other states in the region. The spectacular growth of China's economy makes it plausible that its military forces are designed to facilitate bargaining more effectively like other great powers. Yet the same military power could be used to coerce its neighbors into regional agreements favorable to China. Either way, other states with interests in the region may decide they need to strengthen their own military capabilities.

Maintaining an effective balance of power requires understandable policies that are clearly communicated to both friend and foe. Some ambiguity may prove useful as a tactic in a specific situation, but general intentions must be seen as peaceful. Particularly with adversaries, decision making must be flexible with a willingness to negotiate. Unknowns heighten anxiety and create a context fostering suspicions that military power exists not for defense but for offense. In a viable balance of power, states can remain adversarial but do not fight each other. Some international relations analysts consider such a situation, however tenuous, as the best hope for peace. Others, however, think a stable balance of power can evolve into a more permanent kind of peace, as it has in Western Europe. As the third set of policy choices in Figure 8.1, a rule of law is both an indicator and implementor of permanent peace.

International Rule of Law

A *rule of law* evolves when states follow commonly accepted rules of behavior and orderly processes for peacefully working out conflicting interests. There are two ways behavioral standards become established. First, they develop traditionally as norms because they are commonly practiced over time, as in the case of human rights standards. Resolutions of the UN General Assembly are taken as evidence of customary law if they are passed over and over again by virtually all the world's states. Resolutions condemning colonialism are an example of such a consensus. Second, rules are formulated by states acting together through treaties. Security Council resolutions fall into this category because their authority is derived from the UN Charter, which is, in effect, a treaty. Thus, peaceful patterns of state interaction are legitimized formally and by common practice. They become reinforced by increasing networks of peaceful, problem-solving interactions whether the issues are economic or security related.

The number of international organizations has continued to grow since World War II. States and groups have become woven together through these institutions because they are deemed necessary for dealing with the whole range of human interactions. IGOs have become important in diplomacy for all states—small, regional, and great powers. The United Nations, World Bank, and other IGOs (such as the Organization of African Unity), provide effective representation for small powers that are at a disadvantage when interacting with larger ones bilaterally, one-on-one. They gain at least some leverage within a multilateral context because they assert common positions and vote with other less powerful states. Such blocs can have an effect on the development of international institutions.

The Role of the State   The increase in negotiating power of a single state by linking with others in international institutions is one of the reasons newly independent states join the United Nations as one of their first acts. This legitimization of their newly acquired sovereignty is ironic because, in a sense, becoming a functioning part of the world's organizational networks erodes independent action on some level. Membership in international institutions carries with it acceptance of international rules of behavior. Yet, to illustrate another political ambiguity in international relations, sovereignty remains the dominant international norm because, first, states are the voters in IGOs, and second, they can choose to abide by or disregard international standards. International law needs the states themselves for implementation. Those to whom the law applies are also its enforcers. Only the barest beginnings of an international police force or system of courts exists in the international system.

The *World Court* , headquartered in The Hague, Netherlands, only has jurisdiction in cases where states are both parties. Individuals have no standing to sue. Established in 1946, the World Court consists of fifteen judges from different countries elected to nine-year terms by both the UN General Assembly and the Security Council. Private citizens, groups, or businesses cannot bring a grievance against their own or another state in the World Court. States have refused to obey World Court rulings. The United States, for example, was sued by Nicaragua in 1984 for placing mines in that country's main harbor. After losing the case, the United States announced that it did not have to comply with court's decision. An example of success occurred in the 1992 settlement of a border dispute between El Salvador and Honduras, when both countries accepted the World Court's ruling.

By far, the most cases involving international law are brought to courts within countries because treaties often give states the right to carry out their provisions. For example, the Law of the Sea treaty (discussed in Chapter 6) authorizes each signatory with a shoreline to pass its own legislation implementing control of its twelve-mile limit, continental shelf, and two-hundred-mile economic zones, which are key sections of the treaty. *United States v. Ray* (1976) illustrates the point. Ray had attempted to construct a casino on stilts fourteen miles off the Florida coast, two miles outside the twelve-mile limit. Unfortunately for him, the stilts rested on the continental shelf over which the US government has exclusive right of control according to the Law of the Sea treaty and US legislation. Ray lost the case. Reliance on state court systems to enforce treaties is further reinforced by the fact that states cannot be sued in the courts of other states. Thus, legal action against treaty violations occurs within each state or, more often, in negotiations between state governments.

World policing also is carried out by states. The UN Security Council can impose economic sanctions on a specific state and authorize election observers or peacekeeping missions. The first such mission was sent to Cyprus in 1956; by 1996, peacekeeping forces were still in Cyprus, as well as in Lebanon, Cambodia, Haiti, and Bosnia. All material and personnel for peacekeeping missions are paid for and provided by specific states. Actual wars have been fought under UN authorization. The Korean War in 1950, and the Gulf War in 1991, are the two "police actions" that implemented Security Council resolutions. Both were under US command as the war-fighting coalition's organizer, most powerful state, and contributor of the most troops. In fighting those two wars the international community had responded to the purest form of international aggression; that is, territorial invasion aimed at taking over the victim and eliminating its sovereignty.

This last point illustrates the fact that since it was introduced, international law has been in the interest of the great powers. The first two issues, from the seventeenth century, included the need for protecting commercial shipping from seizure during peace, and the treatment of noncombatants and prisoners during war. Both were in the interest of countries with the most trade and wars, but they also benefited smaller powers. Establishing rules sets principles of behavior that any state can use in making a diplomatic case. Because it legitimizes a universal consensus, international law can establish a moral imperative as well as accomplishing the more mundane task of regulating commonplace interactions across borders. In spite of well-publicized violations of international standards in extreme cases, mostly involving human rights, the vast majority of international rules govern ordinary transactions and are followed most of the time. States honor passports, issue visas, deliver mail, and enforce contracts. All the world's daily interactions are regulated by international law and compliance is the norm.

Even concerning their political and security interests, states would have to invent the United Nations and its specialized agencies and formulate international rules if they did not exist. They offer states, particularly the great powers, the cover of legitimacy that bilateral negotiations do not. Rules governing state interaction and authorized by international institutions give structure to cooperation and reflect a general consensus. Such institutions also provide for participation by all interested parties. Thus, international law and organizations parallel domestic law because powerful people in a society pass the laws that they too should obey.

International relations theorists substantially disagree about the degree of commonality between domestic law and international law. Clearly, differences exist because of the lack of international police and courts and the reliance on voluntary compliance. Some analysts emphasize the differences by pointing out that military force remains a constant element in the usual power equation between and among states. The subjects of the law also enforce it and those with the stronger militaries will have a greater influence in making decisions. This distinction between international and domestic rules had led to calling the former *norms* and the latter *law*.

Other international relations analysts reply that distinctions between domestic and international law are matters of degree, not substance. The neat line between the two becomes blurred when law is understood as commonly accepted and sanctioned behavior. Since international norms are followed most of the time, their effect on behavior could be interpreted as similar to that of domestic laws. Thousands of people and millions of transactions pass across state boundaries every day. They are regulated and regularized by systems of rules that, for the most part, are taken for granted. As in domestic political systems, international codes of conduct condition behavioral choices by ruling out some actions and ruling in others. They affect what states actually do.

In contrast, laws are often ignored in domestic political systems. In extreme cases, if enough laws are violated by enough people, a domestic system can take on characteristics of the international system, in which people or groups become the judges of their own behavior. The last months of President Mobutu's regime in Zaire provides a case in point, as does Lebanon during its civil war. Government only exists when it can govern; that is, when most of the people under its authority accept and obey its laws as a matter of course. If coercion has to be applied to make people obey, a political system is in long-term jeopardy. Distinctions between domestic and international political systems are more ambiguous than many people assume. In many daily routine interactions, international law parallels domestic law in its high level of compliance. In neither is force eliminated but becomes almost invisible when a rule of law exists.

The European Union provides an example of a set of international institutions that, on occasion, actually cause states to do what they otherwise would not. For example, the European Union sued in the European Court of Justice seeking to compel Greece to end its policy denying landlocked Macedonia use of a Greek port for exporting its products. This lawsuit was a significant factor in Greece's decision to drop its trade embargo of Macedonia. There are many other examples of EU member states enforcing rules with which they disagree and rejecting policies inconsistent with agreed-upon rules. In other words, EU members accept constraints on their own behavior imposed by international institutions. They have yielded sovereignty to the extent that individuals can sue them in the European Court of Human Rights. The process of community creation is far less developed in universal governmental organizations such as the United Nations. Yet the UN maintains a forum for negotiations. In the process it reinforces precedents for differentiating acceptable from unacceptable state behavior.

At the end of the twentieth century, world problems are less and less bound by state borders. Thus, international institutions grow in numbers and international law increases in importance. Expanding populations and communication and transportation systems have necessitated regularized processes for human interaction beyond state boundaries. The ethnic, economic, and environmental issues explained in earlier chapters have produced violent responses, but they also have led to positive, multinational coping strategies. The mobility and mixing of diverse peoples, economic interdependence and poverty, and threats to human ecosystems have brought out both the worst and best of human behavior. The issue of peace and war illustrates, perhaps better than most, the evolution of international rules of behavior, because it involves high-risk policy making by definition.

The Evolution of Human Rights   International law concerning war and peace has long been focused and filtered by the concept *just war.* Debated for centuries by philosophers, theologians, political leaders, and writers, a consensus has developed that a war is "just" when the combatant fights in self-defense and accepts limits on its actions, such as preventing the slaughter of civilians and prisoners of war. A problem of interpretation exists because virtually every group or state using violence claims self-defense in blaming its enemy for causing the conflict. Also, when the tactics of war result in "collateral damage" (the US military term for civilian deaths in the Vietnam War), states shrug and say such unfortunate events are a by-product of war.

In the latter half of the twentieth century, the just war issue has become part of a more broad concern with *human rights,* particularly the treatment by governments of their own citizens. After World War II, the first War Crimes Tribunal tried and punished Nazi leaders for "crimes against humanity" in their planned, systematic annihilation of ten million Jews, Gypsies, and others designated as "undesirable." A

1948 international agreement codified international law by specifying *genocide*—the attempt to exterminate members of a specific cultural group—as a crime against humanity. Most of the world's states and, with the ratification of the United States in 1992, all the major powers have signed and ratified the Convention on the Prevention and Punishment for the Crime of Genocide.

Another statement on human rights was adopted by the UN General Assembly in 1948. Called the *Universal Declaration of Human Rights*, the document specifies fundamental freedoms, including religious and political rights, a ban on torture, and the right to economic well-being. The broad range further expands human rights norms by covering abusive actions of governments and groups in peace as well as war. Scholars disagree as to whether the Universal Declaration of Human Rights should be considered international law. Most think the General Assembly does not have the authority to legislate international law. Since 1948, eight additional human rights treaties have been negotiated and signed (for example, the Convention Against Torture and Other Cruel, Inhuman, or Degrading Treatment or Punishment), but they have not been ratified by enough signatory states to go into effect. A case can be made that human rights are basic principles of law, and thus violations could be punished; however, in every case but genocide this represents a controversial position. As with other major issues facing the world at the end of the twentieth century, international nongovernmental organizations monitor compliance by gathering information and pointing out problems. Amnesty International and Human Rights Watch are the two most prominent international human rights IGOs.

A grand debate among international relations specialists exists over how far international institutions and law have advanced in their development. The arguments for and against are compelling, as Chapter 9 will illustrate. There is a general acknowledgment of the importance of IGOs and of the European Union's supranational authority in specific areas of state interaction. Yet the argument attempts to assess the extent to which these factors substantially affect the policies and actions of governments: Has the international system undergone such a transformation as to make the concepts of anarchy and state sovereignty outdated and irrelevant? Suffice it to say that as international institutions continue to take shape, their role in sovereign state conflicts becomes increasingly more significant.

Whatever their long-term viability, the concepts of international rule of law, sovereignty, anarchy, and balance of power are still needed to analyze issues of war and peace . In the following case study, we apply these concepts to help explain the war in Bosnia—a recent and appalling example of mass violence. In Bosnia, certain ethnic groups recognized no authority higher than their own and they therefore had no loyalty to the "state," as it was formally recognized by other states. Bosnia's experience illustrates state disintegration. Some analysts believe this phenomenon can lead to similar conflicts elsewhere, though it is hoped the savage violence and extensive suffering in Bosnia will not be repeated.

THE WAR IN BOSNIA:
THREE PEOPLES IN SEARCH OF A STATE

In 1991, two member republics of the state of Yugoslavia, Slovenia and Croatia, declared their independence. A year later, Bosnia-Herzegovina, another Yugoslav republic, announced its state sovereignty. Within a couple of weeks, leaders of the Serb minority within Bosnia declared their own Serb Republic of Bosnia-Herzegovina, and the war in Bosnia began. The fighting lasted until a 1995 agreement was reached in Dayton, Ohio, brokered by the United States. The disintegration of Yugoslavia was accompanied by large-scale brutality reminiscent of World War II. The number of deaths in Bosnia has been estimated at about 200,000, and more than a million people of the prewar population of 4.3 million were displaced.

The war in Bosnia was characterized by casual cruelty, systematic, ruthless torture, rape, murder of children and adults, and enternment camps. These tactics were designed to create "ethnically pure" areas by either killing people or forcing them from the homes where their families in many cases had lived for centuries. With the intentional slaughter of innocents, the war in Bosnia has matched other examples of pitiless bestiality in the twentieth century. Called "ethnic cleansing" by the news media and "genocide" by the United Nations, the violence in Bosnia ensued in one form or another until the Dayton Accords established a cease-fire, the separation of warring factions by European and US troops, and various political measures designed to foster peaceful interaction. The question remains, however, whether in the long term the antagonists will accept the status quo or resume fighting after outside forces are withdrawn.

A Tangle of Participants

In the years before the 1990s, Yugoslavia, and particularly Bosnia, had been extolled as an example of how a cooperative and sophisticated multiethnic society could emerge from a history of mutual antagonisms. The 1982 Winter Olympics in Sarajevo, Bosnia's capital, had showcased the vibrant lifestyle created by the interaction of various cultures. A developing economy encouraged the flourishing of art and architecture, music and entertainment, and literature and media from several cultures. A true multicultural lifestyle was part of daily life in Bosnia, and in the 1980s approximately 30 percent of marriages in urban areas were reported as "mixed" (Malcolm 1996:222). But a decade later the war in Bosnia destroyed what had been a flourishing multiculturalism. Symbols of its diverse heritage—churches, mosques, libraries, and other historically important structures—were demolished by artillery bombardment. Multicultural personal relationships were also destroyed by individual acts of fiendish cruelty.

The war in Bosnia thus raises compelling questions: Why did the war explode so quickly? How did it degenerate into such depths of depravity? The answers to these and other questions are complex, but most explanations begin with an assessment of the perceptions and interests of the various participating groups, states, and international governmental organizations. Sorting out the participants takes some effort given their large numbers and the complex, changing nature of their relations.

The participants included the three major ethnic groups within Bosnia—Muslims, Serbs, and Croats. In addition, several outside governments are vital to explaining the war's causes, particularly the governments of Croatia and Serbia. (Serbia, as the main part of what is left of Yugoslavia, has kept the formal name of Yugoslavia because it includes not only Serbia but also three other smaller sections of the former Yugoslav state.) Further, news reports of the Bosnian war add to this list of participants several states that played a secondary but important role in the flow of events: the United States, the United Kingdom, France, Germany, and Russia. Finally, international governmental organizations played their parts, specifically the United Nations (UN), the North Atlantic Treaty Organization (NATO), and the European Union (EU). To help simplify this complex assortment of groups, states, and organizations, the following discussion categorizes the various participants into three levels of involvement: (1) groups within Bosnia, (2) states within the Balkan region, and (3) other states and IGOs in the larger international system.

Groups Within Bosnia   Bosnia's three ethnic groups provide the context for the conflict. Before the war, the breakdown of these groups was generally about 44 percent Muslims, 31 percent Serbs, and 17 percent Croats. Of the five countries carved out of the former Yugoslavia, only Bosnia had no majority ethnic group. Most towns, and all cities, had mixed populations.

To an outsider, the similarities among the three ethnic groups seemed obvious, but as the situation in Bosnia disintegrated in the early 1990s, the differences became more important. Before the breakup of Yugoslavia, all three groups spoke a language is called Serbo-Croatian. Now the language differences are emphasized so that they are treated as two separate languages. For centuries, written Croat used the Latin alphabet of Western Europe, whereas the Serbs used the Cyrillic script of Russia. Other language differences such as in vocabulary have become central as the two groups continue to distance themselves historically and culturally. Religion reinforces the linguistic distinctions—Croats generally identify with Catholicism and Serbs with the Eastern Orthodox version of Christianity. Muslims are descendants of those who converted to Islam when the Balkans were ruled by the Ottoman Turks. The entire region was part of the Ottoman Empire for over three centuries.

Nationalistic perceptions based on linguistic and religious distinctions are reinforced by each group's notion about its place in history. As is often noted, Bosnia lies right on the fault line where three great civilizations meet: Western Europe, Eastern Orthodox Europe, and Islamic Asia. As a result, the most ardent nationalists among the Croats and Serbs see themselves as outposts defending the rest of their civilization against enemies. Symbolized by their defeat in the 1389 Battle of Kosovo, Serbian nationalists portray their role as a bulwark against Islamic barbarism poised to invade the Christian world. They believe themselves to be the true Christians firmly holding out in the epic struggle, as compared with the weaker Catholics. Dominance in the region, therefore, is seen as the well-earned historical right of the Serbs.

Croatian nationalists, in contrast, perceive their role as upholding enlightened and economically progressive Europe as it stands against the forces of the East, be they Orthodox or Islamic. Muslims see themselves as synthesizers of the best Eastern and Western traditions as well as preservers of their own Islamic distinctiveness. Whereas before the war Muslim nationalists took pride in Bosnia's multinational and multireligious character, during the war many began instead to extol their Islamic identity, particularly its opposition to oppression.

The differences among Serbs, Croats, and Muslims had existed for centuries, during which time the groups lived side by side in peace and shared a common history. As in any multicultural society, Yugoslavia's ethnic groups evidenced "both coexistence and conflict, tolerance and prejudice, suspicion and friendship" (Bringa 1995:6) Since the war, however, only a few accounts have included points illustrating the capacity of the country's people to interact positively. One example cites the fact that, in the 1980s, more than three million of Yugoslavia's population of twenty-two million people were in ethnically mixed marriages or a product of them (Woodward 1995:36). Although religion distinquished Bosnia's three major ethnic groups, there is evidence that as late as the 1980s it was not important to a majority of the republic's people; a 1985 survey put the proportion of religious believers at 17 percent (Malcolm 1996:222).

Contrary to the impression left by news coverage of the war, reinforced by the comments of many analysts and US political leaders, simmering ethnic hatreds did not spontaneously combust to create a violent conflagration. Nor was the war inevitable. To the contrary, it took years of menacingly nationalistic propaganda for polarized politics to become the norm. As we will see in the next section, specific events caused those with aggressively hateful nationalisms to dominate political decision making within the various Yugoslav republics.

The Balkan States   Many analysts see the breakup of Yugoslavia as foreshadowed by the death of its leader, Marshal Tito, in 1980. Tito, who had ruled the country since 1943, stood for a multiethnic Yugoslavia under the leadership of the Communist Party. The one-party rule was designed to foster a set of ideals that superseded narrow ethnic nationalism. After the leader's death, those with ambition were without the historic and countrywide basis of Tito's appeal. Aspiring leaders in Serbia, Croatia, and Bosnia, thus needed to build their own base, enabling them to unite large numbers of people under their leadership.

In Serbia, leader Slobodan Milosevic used the Serbian Communist Party as a means for building support and promoting followers. But he shifted the party's emphasis from equality and multiculturalism to an extreme form of Serbian nationalism. As a result, in the late 1980s and early 1990s, Serbs' paranoia about the designs of their presumed enemies—particularly Croats and Muslims—grew considerably, and in response to this threat Milosevic proposed the old nationalistic idea of a "Greater Serbia." This state dominated by Serbs could be Yugoslavia itself or a geographically larger Serbia. After Milosevic became Serbia's party leader in 1987 and president in 1989, he used his party connections to displace the leadership in three of Yugoslavia's other constituent units, replacing them with people of his own choosing. This meant that by 1989, four of the eight parts of the country were under his control, two republics and the two formerly autonomous regions. Severe economic problems assisted him in undermining other political leaders. Austerity measures that had been adopted in the mid-1980s to fight inflation and make foreign debt payments served to worsen an already shrinking economy and arouse a yearning for the strong, decisive, self-assured leadership Milosevic promised.

In 1990, Milosevic's plans to achieve Serb dominance within Yugoslavia crashed with the disintegration of the communist party. This cut off his means for manipulating events in other republics. It also unleashed the strident nationalists in each of the republics not controlled by Serbia; namely, Slovenia, Croatia, Bosnia, and Macedonia. Using an exaggerated rhetoric, the new nationalist parties reinforced the fears of the other ethnic groups.

The role of Serbia's President Milosevic in contributing to war highlights the importance of leadership in appealing either to a society's moderates or its extremists. By using the government-controlled media to foster hypernationalism and putting overwrought nationalists in decision-making positions, Milosevic gained political power over his opponents. The logic of his nationalist ideology included the goal of enlarging Serbia, either through Serb control over Yugoslavia, or failing that, an enlarged and more ethnically homogenous Serbia. Thus, the case can be made that the resulting wars in Croatia and Bosnia did not originate as civil wars produced by a spontaneous outpouring of Serbian nationalism with atrocities as an unfortunate by-product. Instead, a deliberate policy of expansion used war and atrocities as the means for achieving a "Greater Serbia."

With the Communist Party's collapse, Franjo Tudjman's newly formed political party won the 1990 election in Croatia. With Croatian nationalism as its ideology, Tudjman's party proceeded to pass a law creating an autonomous Croatia. In contrast to sovereignty, *autonomy* means the ability to establish and enforce laws covering most governmental functions except foreign policy and defense. The centuries-old Croatian flag was thus flown and its red-and-white shield evoked memories of the fascist Croatia created by the Nazis during World War II. Croatian's new currency, the kuna, also harkened back to the Croatia of the second world war. The military of this earlier Croatian state had slaughtered some say hundreds of thousands of Serbs as well as others before being overthrown by Tito's forces in the 1940s.

Stirred by these memories and their own nationalism, Serbs in Croatia reacted against Tudjman's new government. In an area of Croatia where they were a substantial majority, Serbs organized their own militia, held a local referendum, formed their own parliament, and declared autonomy. Their clashes with Croatian police resulted in several deaths. These Serbs then asked local units of the Yugoslav army for help. With an officer corps dominated by Serbs, and implementing Milosevic's policy, the army acted to assist the Serbs in Croatia with arms, equipment, and trained troops.

In 1991, Croatia declared its independence from Yugoslavia. Serbian paramilitary forces, supported by the Yugoslav army, fought a war against Croatia. By the time the Croatian forces became organized, about 30 percent of Croatia was controlled by Serbs. The fighting stalemated early in 1992, but its atrocities and ethnic cleansing had foreshadowed the much longer war soon to be fought in Bosnia.

The violence in Croatia took on a logic of its own. The individual acts of cruelty carried out by Serbian paramilitary units created vested interests. More and more people got caught up in the degenerating, downward spiral of mutual retribution and ever-more violence. Hatreds were reinforced and perceptions hardened. The atrocities made real their victims' worst fears. Such actions became justification for similar acts of revenge by Croats and, later in Bosnia, by Muslims. In this context, the exaggerated claims of excessive nationalists seemed correct. The more violence ensued, the more reasonable those claims appeared. The strident nationalists were looked to for leadership, particularly those to whom violence came easily. People surfaced as needed protectors who in peacetime would be considered suspect. Ideologues took over and for them there were no innocents.

The declarations of independence by Croatia and Slovenia put Bosnia in an untenable position. It was clear that war would result from Bosnian independence. Yet with a government and ruling party predominately Muslim, Bosnia could not remain within Yugoslavia, now controlled by Milosevic's ultranationalist Serbia. There was no hope of redressing grievances through the bargaining and compromise of politics. Caught with no viable option, Bosnia held a referendum on independence in 1992. The ballot read, "Are you in favor of a sovereign and independent Bosnia-Herzegovina, a state of equal citizens and nations of Muslims, Serbs, Croats and others who live in it?" (Malcolm 1996:231). Since the Bosnian Serbs in areas dominated by their nationalists boycotted the vote, the results were almost unanimous in favor of independence. As in Croatia, Bosnia's new party leader, elected by a majority in 1990, also became the country's president. Thus, Alija Izetbegovic became the only head of state in a former Yugoslav republic who had not been a leader in the now-defunct Communist Party.

The reaction of the Serbian nationalists in Bosnia to the declared independence of a Bosnian state was predictable given the parallel events in Croatia. Their own parliament announced the existence of a "Bosnian Serb Republic." A few months later, the Bosnian Croat Party, with the same name as that of Tudjman's party in Croatia, declared a "Croatian Community of Herceg-Bosnia." The Muslim-majority government in Bosnia responded to the Serbs' and Croats' actions by claiming to represent the whole of Bosnia. This situation resulted in over three years of war, with each group claiming different reasons for it. The Serbs called the war in Bosnia a civil war they had to fight for their own survival against Muslim oppression and extremism. The government of Bosnia saw the struggle as needed for Muslim survival against the regionwide attempt by Serbia to unite Serbs in the Balkans and achieve regional hegemony. The Croats perceived self-defense as their motive in responding to threats by the other two groups to take them over and, more than likely, force them out of Bosnia. Given their superior firepower, the Serbs controlled about 70 percent of what had been the Bosnia-Herzegovina republic by 1993.

As for the ordinary people in Bosnia, many villagers resisted becoming part of the war. Unfortunately, some joined in when the fighting finally came in the guise of a military unit of outsiders attacking to drive out local people from a different ethnic group. In general, however, many expressed the sentiment, "We always lived together and got along well; what is happening now has been created by something stronger than us" (Bringa 1995:4).

Belligerents in the war used several strategies. In committing atrocities, members of the Serbian paramilitary units acted like terrorists. As the war wore on, some Croats and Muslims also committed torture, rape, and murder. Their strategy fit the commonly accepted definition of *terrorism* in several ways. In Bosnia, violence was used to terrorize people into abandoning their homes, thus clearing the area for repopulation by the dominant ethnic group. Other fighting strategies were also used in the war. In areas where conventional war tactics were unavailable, the warring factions used guerrilla hit-and-run attacks. As front lines firmed up, however, conventional assaults against enemy positions were attempted.

International Actors   States in the European Union, particularly the United Kingdom, France, and Germany as great powers, attempted to decide on a policy to stop the war or at least mitigate its effects. They were horrified by the scale of violence not seen in Europe since the Second World War. They also feared it would cause more states in the region to become involved. The United States, Russia, the United Nations, and NATO shared the aim of the Western Europeans, but it took years for all these secondary actors to overcome their differences of interest and perceptions and to agree on a plan for peace. In addition, although they were well intentioned, some of their actions exacerbated an already disastrous situation.

As the situation in Yugoslavia became chronically unstable in the late 1980s, Germany took the lead among the European states in setting a policy. One of its most significant actions was announcing that it would recognize the independence of Slovenia and Croatia before consulting with other members of the European Union. Some analysts point out that this act forced the issue and extinguished whatever faint hope existed of negotiating a compromise. They also note that Germany traditionally had included the Balkans in its area of influence and was particularly interested in expanding political and economic ties with Slovenia and Croatia. Germany explained its unilateral policy by saying that decisiveness in recognizing the two new states had a chance of forestalling a Serbian use of force. Unfortunately for German policy, the opposite occurred.

Russia also had a longstanding interest in the Balkans as a supporter of Serbia. Serbia had gained its independence in 1830, when Russia fought a war against Ottoman Turkey. Serbia and Russia also shared a cultural affinity through their common alphabet and Orthodox Christianity. Russia has traditionally perceived itself as the protector of the Serbs. Like Germany in Croatia, Russia sought to build friendly political relations and economic interests in Serbia. Strong nationalistic Russian sentiment emphasizing its Slavic heritage explained why some Russians were reported to be fighting for the Serbs during the war in Bosnia.

Support for their potential client states caused Germany and Russia to have a different view of events in Bosnia from the United Kingdom and France. The latter two states had shown no clear interest until the conflict had degenerated into ethnic cleansing, become a European embarrassment, and threatened to draw in the Balkans' larger states. Then the United Kingdom and France coordinated policy through the European Union and United Nations. Both contributed thousands of troops to the UN peacekeeping forces.

If Britain and France could be accused of a slow reaction to the problem in volatile Bosnia, the United States realized the need for intervention even later. President Bush's administration considered the breakup of Yugoslavia and its violent aftermath as a European problem. US policy makers thought little could be done by outsiders if local people were determined to use violence in responding to deeply felt grievances. Anyone caught in the middle would fail no matter how well intentioned. The US approach changed little during the early years of Clinton's presidency. He articulated a US policy of working in concert with European allies; that is, the Europeans were expected to take the lead in setting a common strategy. Clearly, during the early stages of the war, US government leaders had decided that their country had no significant economic or political interests in the Balkans. They later changed this policy assumption.

From 1993 to 1995, the United States squabbled with its allies but took no unilateral action. However, the United States advocated a firmer approach toward the Serbs after they had stopped UN peacekeeping troops from delivering food and medical supplies. It also recommended using of NATO air power to take out the Serb artillery that was shelling Sarajevo or to force the Serbs to withdraw. The United Kingdom and France opposed military actions because they had lightly armed troops on the ground with the UN forces. Their soldiers were at the questionable mercy of the combatants, particularly the Serbs who promised retaliation if NATO attacked them. The United States, which had no soldiers among the UN peacekeepers delivering humanitarian aid, felt free to threaten Serbs with NATO air strikes. Perhaps more than the European states, the United States sympathized with Muslims as the group that had suffered the most atrocities. This position coincided with US interests in maintaining good relations with the oil producing Arab states, which wanted the United States to alleviate the plight of Muslims in Bosnia.

As indicated in the foregoing discussion, international governmental organizations had become involved in the Bosnian war. The institutions of the European Union, the United Nations, and NATO provided the negotiating networks for devising common policies and actions aimed at ending Bosnia's agony. Peace proposals, peacekeeping troops delivering food and medicines, and possible NATO air strikes all contributed to the mix of options and actions. One particular decision by the UN Security Council has taken on long-term significance. In 1993, the Security Council established an International War Crimes Tribunal for investigating, indicting, and prosecuting individuals who had violated human rights in the former Yugoslavia. By 1997, according to a *Washington Post* article, a total of seventy-eight suspects had been indicted, mostly Serbs. Nine were in custody, not including the two-highest ranking Bosnian Serbs: Radovan Karadizic, the former president of the Bosnian Serb Republic, and Ratko Mladic, the republic's former army commander (Drozdiak 1997: A14).

The Dayton Accord

Since the United States stood back during the first years of the war in Bosnia, the first attempt to negotiate a settlement was sponsored by the United Nations and the European Union. At this time in history, whenever possible the world's great powers work through an international governmental organization, in most cases the United Nations. Thus, their policies are legitimized by international institutions and standards of behavior. Yet even the most powerful states in the international community cannot directly control the events in and the policies of sovereign states, or even local groups that choose to act as if they possess sovereignty. The first peace plan failed in 1993, due to its rejection by Bosnian Serbs. A second peace agreement was proposed in 1994, by the five great powers formalized as a *Contact Group*—the United Kingdom, France, Russia, Germany, and the United States. The Serbs also refused to accept this peace plan, because it did not cede to them all the territory they had taken during the war.

By rejecting the peace agreements, Bosnian Serbs parted company with their main outside supporter, President Milosevic of Serbia, who had recommended acceptance of both agreements. He recognized that in spite of the fact the Serbs would have to reduce the Bosnian territory they controlled from about 70 percent of Bosnia to nearly to 50 percent, their claim would be legitimized by the international community. Milosevic was not without his own interest in ending the war because of the economic sanctions imposed on his country by the UN Security Council for aiding Bosnian Serbs. The sanctions, which had produced a severe recession in Serbia, would not be lifted until an agreement was successfully negotiated.

The situation changed quickly in the summer of 1995, when Serbian forces were sent in pell-mell retreat from western Bosnia by the Croatian and Bosniak armies (the Muslim-dominated Bosnian government had begun calling its people "Bosniaks"). During this time, the United States asserted itself by becoming the leading outside mediator. This change in US policy came in reaction to two key events. The first was the February 1995 shelling of a crowded market in Sarajevo resulting in sixty-eight deaths, a record number for one such incident up to that date. Although no determination was made as to whether the source of the mortar round came from a Serbian or Bosniak government-controlled area, the carnage captured news headlines worldwide and was blamed on the Serbs.

The second key event occurred in July 1995, when Serbs overran Srebrenica and Zepa, two of the six "safe areas" in Bosnia, protected by UN peacekeeping troops and sheltering thousands of Muslim refugees. In Srebrenica alone, over sixty thousand people were surrounded by Serbian forces and barely living on drops from US cargo planes and intermittent truck columns. When the Serbian attack came, the few hundred Dutch peacekeepers could do nothing, not only because of their small numbers and light arms, but also because they had orders to fire only if directly fired upon. They were also ordered not to respond to attacks on the Muslims under their "protection." After consolidating their control, the Serbs separated women and young children from the male population, as they had time and again in the early phases of the war. Many of the men were never seen again. Dutch soldiers reported that hundreds of bodies littered the routes trucks had taken to carry away the men and older boys. It was estimated that five thousand to seven thousand males were killed in cold blood.

With US urging, NATO responded with two weeks of air strikes against the Serb's ammunition and weapons supplies. This action, plus the successful assault by Croatian and Bosniak forces, left the Serbs in disarray. Milosevic gained the upper hand and he took on the authority to negotiate on behalf of the Serbs in Bosnia. The other parties to the peace talks also fell into line. Croatia's President Tudjman had been quoted off and on as wanting permanent control of western Bosnia. In the areas populated by Croats and taken over by his army, the telephones were being connected to the exchange in Croatia's capital and cars began to appear with Croatian license plates. Yet Tudjman's new military strength was built and supported by German and US aid, and his government needed international loans, so he was subject to great power pressure to negotiate. President Izetbetgovic of Bosnia was even more dependent on outside assistance and had supported the previous two agreements. Thus, the stage was set for the presidents of Bosnia, Serbia (Yugoslavia), and Croatia to accept the US invitation to meet at the Wheeler Air Force base in Dayton, Ohio, and negotiate a peace agreement.

The resulting Dayton Accord ended the fighting and established a framework designed to achieve long-term peaceful interaction among the former combatants. The agreement's key provisions included territorial adjustments, with Serbs accepting about 51 percent of Bosnia as their Republika Serbska, leaving the rest to be administered by the Bosniak-Croat Federation, a paper union since 1994. The armies of the three factions would be separated by an international peacekeeping force of sixty thousand under NATO's command, not the UN's, and it included twenty thousand US troops. The framework for a unified Bosnia took the form of a constitution creating a common legislature, a court, a central bank, and a multi-member presidency. The three factions would retain their own legislatures, presidents, local officials, and army. The provision on war criminals indicted by the War Crimes Tribunal stipulated that they could not hold elected office. The three presidents pledged cooperation in holding those indicted accountable, but the agreement included no explicit provision for arresting them.

None of the three presidents considered the Dayton Accord in his interest. All had to give up something they held dear. Bosniaks received the form of a unified Bosnia but not its substance. Serbs gave up important territory but got to keep one key corridor, ensuring a connection between the western and eastern sections of their republic. Croats retained their own forces and government but had to remain in federation with the Bosniaks.

The Dayton Accord includes a provision to arm and train Bosniak forces. This implies that establishing a balance of power among the factions within Bosnia is necessary to achieve peace in the short run. If the Bosniak army becomes a credible threat, the forces of the Republika Serbska, as well as of Croatia, may be deterred from attacking when the international forces withdraw. Those supporting the Dayton agreement explain that a strong Bosniak army is consistent with the overall objective of forging a framework for peaceful interaction.

Yet opponents of the arm-and-train provision point out the inherent contradiction between wanting to encourage the gradual building of trust among the factions while strengthening the war-making capability of one of them. Some Bosniak leaders have stated their view that the Republic of Serbska is an illegitimate reward for aggression and must be reunited with the rest of the country. Therefore, the Bosniak government might be tempted to win back its perceived lost territory by fighting if it thinks the Bosniak army has enough military power to win a war. In that eventuality, the strengthening of Bosniak forces as a means of achieving peace would backfire.

In response to the type and scale of violence, outside intervention was required to attempt implementation of international standards through the War Crimes Tribunal. Most observers consider the Tribunal central to the reconciliation process in Bosnia, which is why it is included as a provision in the Dayton Accord. Most of those indicted are Serbs, including the former Bosnian Serb president and the army commander during the war. Their continued strong following among Bosnian Serbs has protected them from arrest and prosecution, which remains an ongoing source of tension among Bosniaks. Yet implementation of the Dayton agreement depends on Serb as well as Bosniak and Croat cooperation. Therefore, minimal action has been taken to arrest indicted Serbs. The peace agreement's inherent contradictions cannot be avoided, but they are often cited as a stumbling block to achieving a meaningful peace. This situation illustrates the paradox of the international system: since there is no international authority, sovereign governments are not only the subjects of international law but also its enforcers.

The intervention of the great powers was also needed for conflict management in the form of the Dayton Accord. The outside powers hope the agreement will establish political structures and peaceful interaction processes to bring about permanent peace among the three groups. Yet a military protection force, with soldiers from all the interested great powers plus other states, is still needed three years later to police the tenuous peace. This fact highlights the need for a constructive show of force as an element in implementing international agreements. Force also played a role in arriving at the Dayton agreement in the first place. Not until

NATO planes attacked Serbian positions and weapons supply centers, followed by Croatian and Bosniak military successes, did Bosnia's Serbs accept an agreement. This exemplifies the fact that in some cases of violent conflict, force provides a necessary support for the imposition of international norms. Paradoxically it seems, in an anarchic context judiciously applied force can create conditions needed for negotiations.

Analysis

The war in Bosnia illustrates all three of the policy reactions depicted in Figure 8.1, on page 152. First, its belligerents used a variety of war strategies. Second, following the Dayton Accord, the United States aimed to establish a balance of power as the basis for future peaceful interaction. Third, outside powers first attempted to impose a rule of law by implementing UN resolutions and human rights standards and then negotiating an agreement. The Bosnia case study also provides lessons about pressing international issues that will continue into the twenty-first century. One issue involves the potential for instability in multiethnic states and the important role of ethnic group leaders in increasing or decreasing the tension. Another point highlights the self-perpetuating nature of violence, particularly in response to terrorism. The war in Bosnia also illustrates the conditions needed for successful intervention by outside mediators, even powerful ones.

At the turn of the twentieth century, the existence of multiple ethnicities within the same state has become one of the most significant political issues the world faces. Fortunately, there is no reason to consider the war in Bosnia as the wave of the future because many examples exist of how to deal peacefully with ethnic conflict. For countries that cannot hold together, the division of Czechoslovakia into the Czech Republic and Slovakia shows that breaking into separate sovereign states can be accomplished without violence. Most countries, however, are continuing to devise political structures and strategies for accommodating ethnic based interests and perceptions. The case study on Nunavut in Canada (in Chapter 2) explains a planned transfer of most government functions to a new, local ethnic authority. While this model remains exceptional, all multiethnic states face the ongoing challenge of managing their existing political systems, not only to protect but also to promote their different and sometimes clashing ethnic interests.

International relations analysts disagree on the potential impact on the international system of more states dividing into sovereign ministates. Some predict that more wars would likely result. Others disagree, pointing out that the new states would need peaceful and cooperative interaction to ensure their economic viability. Still others contend that events in Bosnia may frighten groups in other countries from agitating for their own sovereignty. All commentators agree, however, that the further disintegration of states into more ethnically pure ones would have a major effect in their world regions. As Chapter 9 will demonstrate, analysis based on alternative perspectives helps in assessing the reasons for war and possible peace in Bosnia. Applying these perspectives to peace and war in general highlights the various approaches for reducing the number of wars and their level of violence.

TERMS AND CONCEPTS

autonomy

balance of power

conventional war

diplomacy

economic sanctions

genocide

great powers

guerrilla war

human rights

interests

international anarchy

international rule of law

just war

negotiation

nuclear war

peace

perceptions

perceptual selectivity

politics

power

propaganda

regional powers

revisionist states

show of force

small powers

sovereignty

status quo states

superpowers

tacit negotiations (signaling)

terrorism

Universal Declaration of Human Rights

war

World Court

DISCUSSION QUESTIONS

1. Give examples of states that fit into each of the four power classifications: small powers, regional powers, great powers, and superpowers. On what basis did you make your determinations?

2. What is the difference between state politics and international politics?

3. In your opinion, why do groups or states sometimes choose violent means to achieve their objectives? Which of the following three categories best summarizes your answer: characteristics of human nature, certain kinds of states, or the international system itself?

4. Do you think international law affects state behavior? Why or why not?

5. What factors account for the cease-fire in Bosnia? Which concept do you think best applies—a balance of power or the actions of international organizations? Explain your answer.

RESEARCH PROJECTS

1. Read news accounts of the events that led to the Gulf War (August 1990–February 1991). How do the following concepts explain what took place: interests, levels of power, international law, economic tactics, propaganda, and diplomacy?

2. Conduct some research on a civil war in recent history (for example, in El Salvador in the 1980s). Analyze the case by determining the factors that caused the war as well as those that played a role in the peace process. Compare your analysis with the case study of the war in Bosnia in this chapter.

3. For one international issue, such as human rights, list the NGOs that deal with the issue. Then describe what they are doing to address or resolve the issue.

4. Choose a world region, such as southern Africa, and find some basic information about the states located within that region. Use what you find to interpret the states' interests in relation to each other.

5. Read news accounts about a foreign policy issue, such as sending troops to Bosnia, noting in particular how members of the US Congress reacted to the issue. What different perceptions do their reactions reflect?

INTERNET RESOURCES

Foreign and Commonwealth Office, UK: *http://www.fco.gov.uk/reference/briefs/yugo_ chronology.html* The chronology of events in the former Yugoslavia (from January 1990 to November 1995) found on this site is among the most inclusive and useful.

US Department of State: *http://www.milnet.com/milnet/state/1996/year.htm* The State Department's reports on terrorism are included on this site.

World News Index: *http.//www.stack.nl/~haroldkl* This is one of the best inclusive link sites to news articles in papers from around the world.

9

Perspectives on Peace and War

Until these war criminals are delivered to justice in The Hague, we will not have the basis in this country for free elections with democratic principles and therefore we will continue to have a country that is divided.
—*Muhamed Sacirbey, Bosnian foreign minister (quoted in Sciolina 1995a)*

A sovereign state, recognized by the world community, is under attack from forces encouraged and supplied by another power. This is not a civil war but a war of aggression. . . . A well-armed Muslim-Croatian alliance would confront the Serbs with a quite new and unwelcome challenge. It might even prompt the Serbs to settle.
—*Margaret Thatcher, former British prime minister (1994)*

War has been considered one of the four scourges of humankind for centuries, joining disease, starvation, and death. It seems as though these four horsemen of the apocalypse have galloped around the world nonstop throughout the twentieth century. Their human agents have been active particularly in war, the calamity directly caused by people themselves. Except for extreme nationalists who see war as necessary in eliminating enemies, people view peace as a longed-for normalcy. The three perspectives presented in this chapter each diagnose why wars occur, and what it will take to diminish or maybe even eliminate them.

When people think about peace and war, they often make either conscious or unconscious assumptions about what institutions deserve their primary loyalty and, therefore, should be the means for interacting internationally. The dominant perspective sees the world as primarily made up of states held together and legitimized by the patriotism of their citizens. Another perspective has persisted for centuries and been reinforced and revitalized by the veritable explosion of international institutions in recent decades. It emphasizes the similarities all humans share and views states as historical artifacts, perhaps now artificial and outdated. A third perspective focuses on what may be termed *nationhood* instead of statehood. As the often neglected but ever-present primary source of identity, cultural groups should determine the form their international interaction should take whether in states, international organizations, or their own newly developing interactive processes.

STATE SOVEREIGNTY

Clearly the prevailing perspective holds states as the main means of international interaction. As the most prominent and powerful actors in the international system, states benefit from centuries of legitimacy enshrined in international law and enlivened by patriotic emotion. They have fought wars, but achieved peace as well. At this time, war is far from probable and may be not even possible among the world's most powerful states. Thus, people with a state-centered perspective consider themselves vindicated since a case can be made that states have proven capable of managing conflict in an increasingly complex world.

The state sovereignty perspective is not only based on the state's functional role as the most effective unit for setting the rules for international economics and politics. People ardently loyal to their country also view it as the embodiment of the best of their own history and group values. They consider their state as more than the sum of its parts, as not simply everybody living within its borders under the authority of a common government. A patriotic feeling of identity has power in its appeal to the sense of loyalty and self-sacrifice in people. With the decline and even demise of other ideologies, particularly those of the left, nationalism has become the dominant ideology firmly in place at the beginning of the twenty-first century. Whereas other ideologies, such as communism, are not specific to a group of people, nationalism offers a time-honored, often uncontested idea of a person's location in the world and place in its flow of history.

People with the state-centered perspective realize that anomalies exist in the international system, including multinational corporations, international governmental organizations, and nongovernmental organizations. Yet states make the rules by which the international system is run and, as armed actors, they are the only enforcers of the rules. International relations theorists call the state perspective *realism* in its recognition that states have the power and that security is their main interest.

Some advocates of the state sovereignty perspective would go further in asserting that states remain the world's central actors not only because they are powerful, but also because their legitimacy derives from patriotism, the emotional loyalty of their population. Therefore, they alone can speak for the world's people. Competing loyalties within a state are viewed as a problem. As the greatest threat at the present time, ethnic nationalisms at their worst cause wars within states. In fact, this kind of war is flourishing even while wars among states are diminishing. Even when it does not lead to attempts to dismember an existing state, ethnic nationalism can undermine a country's ability to act internationally in maintaining a balance of power.

For most people with the state sovereignty perspective, a balance of power remains the way to peace. International governmental institutions can be useful vehicles for enhancing the foreign policy interests of states. Thus, they play a constructive role in achieving stability as they facilitate a balance of power. International governmental organizations, however, must not become a means for undermining the power and authority of states. If IGO leaders act independently from the policies of member states, it becomes harder for states to maintain an effective balance of power.

Deterrence

To achieve a balance of power, states adopt a deterrence strategy because military force remains an option if economic and political tactics prove ineffective. *Deterrence* means states must pose a credible military threat to enemies and potential enemies. If a state seems weak, it could invite attack. An adversary may calculate that using economic, or political strategies will take too long, prove ineffective, or end in an unwanted compromise. In this situation, the temptation exists to use force. To deter such a decision, states must have not just military power alone but also the reputation for a willingness to use it. This leads to a balance-of-power paradox. To be credible, military force has to be seen as potentially effective. Using it now and then is the surest way to demonstrate military potency. Thus, policy makers sometimes argue that to forestall a large war, a small one may be necessary. *Balance of power* is defined as an absence of war but, according to its own rules, it can be used to justify military actions.

Policy makers must deal with another paradox in establishing deterrence. They are presented with what international relations theorists call a *security dilemma*. Governments have to decide how much military power is enough to deter potential aggressors. If they increase their force capability too much, it will threaten other states in the region that, in turn, may well build up their own military forces. The result is the same or less security than existed originally. Any expansion in military forces can be seen as an aggressive act by a potential enemy. In a context of distrust and conflicting interests, it can produce an arms race and destabilize the existing balance of power. Instability emphasizes mutual fears and hostile perceptions, which become reinforced by a cycle of actions and reactions. People who forestall such a cycle are called *statesmen,* they perform the difficult task of putting military power at the service of political power and achieve foreign policy aims without using force. This task is easier for a great power than for a small one.

The nuclear arms race between the United States and the Soviet Union during the Cold War provides an example of deterrence and, some would say, a security dilemma. Both states built weapons during the 1950s and early 1960s, employing a policy called *mutually assured destruction (MAD).* Each superpower planned to deter an attack by the other nuclear superpower by building more weapons with bigger payloads. Therefore, it could launch a devastating second strike even after it had taken a first strike. Later in the Cold War, another policy was adopted by both sides. Called *nuclear utilization theory (NUT)*, it assumed a nuclear war may be winnable if it was limited to smaller nuclear weapons allowing some of the population to survive. Therefore, each superpower sought to deter the other by producing a wide range of weapons. Then they would not have to rely only on a massive, all-out retaliatory strike. With first the MAD and then the NUT strategies dictating policy, the nuclear arms race reached the point of producing over forty thousand warheads. The question could well be asked whether they produced more or less security for the cold warriors. People with a state sovereignty perspective, however, would point out that this security dilemma question is irrelevant: The fact that no nuclear war occurred means deterrence must have worked.

WORLD ORDER

The world order perspective sees states as the problem, not the answer to minimizing war and maximizing peace. Unfettered state sovereignty and international anarchy have allowed the most destructive human tendencies to dominate too often. People with a world order perspective hold a wide variety of basic principles, some of them contradicting others (which will be explained on the following pages). Yet all *world order* advocates emphasize the development of international law and institutions as the means to achieve the conditions for peace. The proliferation of nongovernmental organizations, in particular, is inherently beneficial since people interact with each other beyond state boundaries without the filter of state power. Yet whether IGOs or NGOs, the world is more and more tied together through growing networks of human interaction. Called *complex* or *functional interdependence*, increasing numbers of people find themselves working with others in decision-making processes across international borders. Businesses, for example, with subsidiaries in other countries must interact with governments, other corporations, workers organizations, and often NGOs, such as environmental groups. In some areas, such as oil production, international cartels have been organized and must be added to the decision-making mix of contacts and considerations. Whether marketing a product, investigating human rights abuses, or accomplishing a myriad of other tasks, millions of people engage with each other beyond state borders as a way of life.

World order advocates recognize that at this time in human history, the potential use of military force is still a threat. Although the number of international organizations, multinational businesses, and personal contacts among people continue to increase exponentially, they have not removed war as an option. Thus, the world order perspective has a strategy for managing threats to the peace. Called *collective security*, this concept describes a situation when the United Nations, or a regional security IGO, identifies a rogue state or group bent on aggression. Resolutions are passed promising a group response, in the form of economic sanctions or military actions or both, if the aggressor state continues its use of force. The Korean and Gulf wars can be interpreted as examples.

There are at least four variations of the world order perspective. As highlighted in the following explanation, they may be referred to as *one world, functional interdependence, US leadership*, and *world government*. While people advocating any one of these four agree to the strengthening of international law and organizations, they have different reasons for doing so.

One World   The first set of assumptions leading to the world order perspective sees the world as one in its essentials. It recognizes that all the world's people share a common humanity as well as economic needs and dependence on the natural environment. It considers building a sense of community based on social justice as the only path to true, permanent peace. Differences among people, their languages, behavioral characteristics, and identities are not inherent. They have to be taught. As people come to realize that they are held together by increasing global interdependence, more and more will learn that their similarities are more basic and important than their differences. The true realists are those who understand how interwoven human life on the planet has become.

The need to develop a sense of community by learning to cooperate can arise from idealism but also from interest. Interdependence produces conflicts as well as the need for cooperation. Communities do not end tensions among the different interests and perceptions of their members; they provide incentives for managing them. Advocates of this interpretation of world order accept the idea that international organizations will develop processes like the pluralist political systems in Europe and the United States. They also define human rights as belonging to individuals and not culture groups. Establishing processes for dealing with and solving common problems produces trust. It is in everyone's interest to interact and negotiate disagreements peacefully. In learning how to make decisions together, one-world advocates see themselves as appealing to the best in human nature not by ignoring the worst, but by coping with it.

Functional Interdependence   Those identifying functional interdependence as the most effective way to achieve an orderly world illustrate their approach by pointing to the ongoing integration of European states. Based on a set of ideas articulated in the 1940s and 1950s, European integration was envisioned as a way to make war obsolete for two reasons: (1) economies would become so tied together that a state could not produce war-fighting material on its own, and (2) shared economic vested interests would require social and political cooperation because of the need for common policies. The integration process was to proceed incrementally beginning with specific, technical, economic activities. The European Coal and Steel Community was the first step, chosen because its products were so essential to a modern industrial economy. Encouraged by free trade policies, the European Common Market followed the European Coal and Steel Community as the integration process continued in other economic sectors. The density of contacts created by the Common Market had spillover effects by revealing a need for cooperative social and political policies. To illustrate, member states encouraged the movement of workers by adopting similar social benefits so that workers would move from one country to another as needed and not be influenced by better unemployment compensation programs. The name of the organization changed to the *European Community* when a common legislature was instituted. The latest step planned will produce an integrated banking system and currency, to be called the *euro*. This stage in the integrating process was initiated in 1991, with the Maastricht Treaty. The name of the organization then became the *European Union*.

US Leadership   Some analysts, as well as US foreign policy makers, define *world order* as requiring US hegemony. As the remaining superpower, it falls to the United States to mediate many of the world's conflicts and, failing this, to fulfill a police function. Yet this asserting of the central role of one state, with its own interests and perceptions, is not what many advocates of the world order perspective generally have in mind. They are uncomfortable with US dominance. Theoretically, the development of cooperative decision making can occur among participants with varying levels of power, maybe even with one having more power than the others; however, rule making and enforcement must be a group effort.

World Government   Sometimes the world order concept is taken to mean world government. It seems the logical antidote to state sovereignty and international anarchy, and the nascent institutions already exist in the United Nations. To many with a world order perspective, however, the idea of a world government misses the point. Multilateral decision making in response to mutually experienced, global problems can and does take many forms. Answers are needed now and cannot depend on instituting a world government. Besides, if such an institution behaves like current governments, it may not be an improvement over the present multi-institutional international complexity.

As demonstrated by this discussion, the world order perspective includes a wide variety of viewpoints since, unlike the state sovereignty and ethnic autonomy perspectives, it does not have one kind of institution as its focus. One of the most important differences among world order adherents is their varying attitudes toward the state. Some think that loyalty to country is compatible with their advocacy of international cooperation because states as well as private groups, businesses, and international organizations need to work together on global problems. Yet loyalty to a state cannot be blind. Governments make mistakes concerning global issues that can prove destructive to their own people in the long run. In cases of mistaken policies, criticism becomes a public duty. This reasoning implies that true patriots take an enlightened, long-term view of their state's interests and see them as intertwined with those of other countries.

Those with a one-world interpretation of world order consider nationalism, whether state or ethnic, as a major problem. It can become a central cause of war. Permanent peace is possible, at least in the long run, but only if nationalist identities diminish and stop inhibiting cooperation among peoples of varying countries and ethnicities. At their worst, states, or groups acting like states, insist on absolute loyalty and justify killing people for nationalistic reasons. Increasingly outmoded, indeed irrelevant in this global age, states developed long ago in a different age. The institution of the state spread at the expense of other political forms of organization and, like empires in their time, must now face decline and demise.

A Critique from the State Sovereignty Perspective

Those with the state sovereignty perspective prefer to call the world order perspective idealistic. Actually, this is the kindest of their possible repertory of responses. Downright dangerous would be another. One-world advocates, to choose an example, want to make the world better, more peaceful and just, while ignoring the fact that states remain the only real means of taking action. What they should be doing is participating in the policy-making process of their own governments to develop effective solutions to global problems. Ardent state nationalists would go further in criticizing world order thinking. They consider it as undermining loyalty to country. This constitutes a threat because, if such disloyalty spreads far enough, states will not be able to fulfill their essential role as protectors of the livelihoods and lives of their citizens.

ETHNIC AUTONOMY

A growing number of commentators, academics, and members of ethnic groups are realizing that cultural groups provide the primary identity for human beings. The loyalty this engenders can challenge the loyalty required by centralized states. A state's government expects, indeed demands, the ultimate loyalty of every person within its jurisdiction. This creates a major source of tension, particularly when many people do not consider their state legitimate in demanding their loyalty. Coercion and violence can result.

Those with an ethnic autonomy perspective think that the structure of the international system should allow ethnic representation in addition to states, corporations, voluntary NGOs, and IGOs. Because the ethnic autonomy perspective is relatively recent, its institutionalization is still taking shape. Only the barest beginnings have emerged indicating how cultural groups will organize themselves internationally. International conventions of representatives from many of the world's cultural groups have established that cultural rights—not individual rights—are the basis for their representation. The UN Commission on Human Rights has a Sub-Commission on Prevention of Discrimination and Protection of Minorities. Among other statements, it is formulating a declaration of the rights of indigenous peoples, which includes as Article 3, "Indigenous peoples have the right of self-determination. By virtue of that right they freely determine their political status and freely pursue their economic, social and cultural development." While the charter is only one of many political activities various cultural groups are using to assert their own identity, it shows that at least indigenous peoples see themselves as part of the international community. They seek to establish international norms representing their own interests and perceptions. In the process, they are appealing to existing international organizations to foster and legitimize cultural rights.

The Nunavut case study in Chapter 2 provides an example of a state that will allow a cultural group to govern itself. The case study describes Canada's granting local autonomy to the Inuit living in part of its Northwest Territories. The experiment has been called *semisovereignty* because the new territory will be able to make decisions about all government functions except Canada's foreign policy and defense. The uniqueness of this Canadian initiative reinforces the ambivalence about the role of the state felt by those with an ethnic autonomy perspective. Generally, the governments of states have acted as enemies in their insistence on subordinating group interests to what they have termed the "national interest." At their best, states have granted only individual rights that, by implication, require people to subordinate their cultural identities. No state has a government truly representative of all its cultural groups.

Ethnicities more powerful than indigenous peoples are demanding greater participation in governmental decision making within existing states. Others are fighting for states of their own. The breakup of the Soviet Union provides a compelling precedent. Virtually every country in the world is experiencing some form of increased political pressure from its underrepresented groups; examples include French-speaking people in Canada, Scots in the United Kingdom, Tibetans in China, Kashmiri Muslims in India, Latinos in the United States, and Muslims in Norway. More demanding nationalists in some ethnic groups are using violence to achieve their own state; such as Kurds in Turkey, Basques in Spain, Chechins in Russia, Tamils in Sri Lanka, Hutus in Burundi, and Abkhazis in Georgia. Lists could go on and on of examples in both categories of ethnic group assertiveness; that is, those wanting sovereignty, and those wanting more power within existing states. The issue of conflicting loyalties between state patriotism and ethnic nationalism will preoccupy world leaders over the long term. Cultural identities do not go away. They remain basic to how individuals learn what it means to be human. For states to remain viable, they will have to establish more effective political processes for accommodating the interests of their less powerful ethnic groups. If they cannot, then various forms of autonomy will be invented or more parts of the world will fragment into ministates.

Critiques from the State Sovereignty and World Order Perspectives

People with the state sovereignty perspective find worrisome the potential for state fragmentation. They think the creation of more ministates driven by their own nationalistic animosities toward their neighbors bodes ill for peace. The world needs more stabilizing influences, not fewer. The future is frightening if every cultural group were to try establishing its own sovereignty or even semisovereignty. Cultural groups should make use of the political processes within states to achieve their aims. Established state politics allow the leaders of groups to bargain and adjust government policies in their interest.

Advocates of the world order perspective differ over whether ethnic groups will act in ways compatible with international law and institutions. Such groups have used international institutions as a means to present their grievances and recommend action. In so doing, they have expanded the number of NGOs and thus created institutional expressions of their interests and perceptions. There is a danger, however, because some ethnic groups choose not to develop peaceful ways to articulate their grievances. As the Bosnia case study in Chapter 8 illustrates, unless an international rule of law is strengthened, groups can use violent strategies and cause extensive human suffering. World wars may not loom as an immediate threat, yet people in various parts of the world continue to find reasons to fight each other. Wars are smaller in scale but just as lethal to the people involved. Thus, war remains a major world problem.

PEACE AND WAR PERSPECTIVES APPLIED TO THE WAR IN BOSNIA

Matrix 9.1 summarizes the main points made in this chapter. As noted in Chapter 8, the war in Bosnia has enough complexity to require analysis using the widest range of concepts, including those explaining war, balance of power, and international rule of law strategies. It also has the scale of human suffering and inhuman brutality to capture headlines and, perhaps, frighten people in other countries. Events in the former Yugoslavia may either forestall or foreshadow the breakup of other states. Bosnia's horrors show what can happen if propaganda acts like kerosene poured on inflammatory nationalist passions. Leaders of both ethnic groups and governments must act wisely with flexible politics. Yet the different perspectives people possess on peace and war issues cause them to propose opposing recommendations on what specific actions and policies will produce peace.

This chapter's three perspectives provide different reasons for the war in Bosnia and recommend alternative actions to forestall other conflicts from turning violent. They disagree over which institutions are the problem and which the answer. In maintaining state sovereignty as the answer, the first perspective accepts the prevailing view of the world as primarily a collection of states that hold the key to solving the problems facing humankind, including the use of violence. The second and third perspectives view states as contributing to the problem of war. They demand major institutional changes in how the world's people are presently organized. The world order perspective points out the growth in number and authority of international organizations as sources for standards of international behavior. The ethnic autonomy perspective views cultural identities as the focus of primary loyalty for many of the world's people. Political institutions must, therefore, reflect ethnic group interest.

A View from the State Sovereignty Perspective

The breakup of Yugoslavia proved the key factor causing the war in Bosnia. Historically, states developed as a means of reducing the kind of chaos Bosnians experienced. Respecting and working within existing states may not solve every interethnic wrong, but it is an improvement on the violence unleashed in Bosnia.

Patriotism, by definition, subordinates ethnic nationalisms to larger interests and perceptions. Instead of reinforcing narrowly based responses to problems, loyalty to country requires developing the negotiating skills of bargaining and compromise. When this process broke down in the former Yugoslavia, stability eroded and uncompromising, extreme nationalists were unleashed to accomplish their ruthless task. As one of the first to fan the nationalistic flames, Milosevic sought to use them in expanding his own and the Serbs' power. In spite of professing his desire to hold Yugoslavia together, by encouraging and legitimizing nationalist sentiments, he knowingly replaced Yugoslav patriotism with Serbian nationalism.

Matrix 9.1
PEACE AND WAR PERSPECTIVES

	STATE SOVEREIGNTY	WORLD ORDER	ETHNIC AUTONOMY
GOALS	Peace, often temporary	Peace; force not an option	Peace Ethnic justice
KEY CONCEPTS	International anarchy	International rule of law	Ethnic rights
STRATEGIES	Balance of power	Strengthen international institutions	Decentralize power
MAJOR PROBLEMS OF EXISTING SYSTEM	Etnic threats to state stability Aggressor states	State actions based on narrow interest and perceptions	Domination by state governments
SEES CURRENT INTERNATIONAL POLICAL SYSTEM AS:	Too limiting of state power, at least potentially	Too state centered	Too state centered
ROLE OF FORCE	Deterence	Collective security	Dangerous in most situations, given the power of governments

The logic of the state sovereignty perspective could also fault German haste to recognize the independence of Slovenia and Croatia. This virtually forced the same decision on Bosnia. In so doing, it negated the already feeble efforts to negotiate autonomy for member republics within Yugoslavia. While the rest of the great powers were hesitating in a search for a negotiated response, Germany acted unilaterally. Its action highlights the importance of the fourth characteristic of a state as defined in Chapter 1—namely, the recognition of other states.

Having said this, however, once the world's great powers had recognized the sovereignty of the new states, they should have intervened in their defense against Serbian aggression, at least by providing them with economic and military aid. Bosnia would then have had some chance of standing up to the Serbs' onslaught. Croatia eventually was strengthened and played a role in thwarting expansionist Serbian ambitions. Yet Bosnia was not. This interpretation of the state sovereignty perspective is exemplified by the Margaret Thatcher quote at the beginning of this chapter. The great powers must assume their roles and responsibilities as defenders of stability and opponents of aggression.

Advocates of a state sovereignty perspective have difficulty with the Dayton Accord, even though they realize it may well have represented the only achievable agreement at the time. They doubt that it will work in the long run because its provisions reinforce Bosnia's deficiencies in all four of the basic factors defining a state; that is, its territory, government, patriotism, and recognition by other states. Bosnia's claim to the territory it had when a member republic in the former Yugoslavia remains only on paper. By at least tacitly accepting partition, the Dayton Accord ratifies the lack of loyalty to Bosnia by Serbs and Croats living within its old borders. The fact that each of the three ethnic groups has its own governing institutions makes the central government of Bosnia a hollow shell. Finally, some states in the international arena, mainly Russia and Greece, at least tacitly recognize the validity of the Serb Republic within Bosnia.

State sovereignty analysts could take a pragmatic approach and accept the inevitability of partition as the only workable political solution in the foreseeable future. They might advocate assistance to the Bosniaks so they can defend themselves and, in the long run, perhaps either form their own state or negotiate out of strength with at least some Croats in beginning to piece together a new Bosnian state.

A View from the World Order Perspective

The depths of depravity reached during the war in Bosnia provide yet one more historical example of sovereign states' ineptitude when confronting ruthless aggressors. By putting their own narrow self-interest first, they cannot take effective, early action. Only international institutions, capable of setting and enforcing world standards of behavior will provide a viable, permanent solution.

Whether state patriotism or ethnic nationalism, virulent exclusionary ideologies have similar effects. In all cases they act as an enemy to orderly, peaceful interaction, the kind needed for cooperative problem solving. Since pressing issues cross international borders, and certainly transcend ethnic differences, building a sense of community is not only a nice idea but a practical necessity. Healthy, constructive interaction is not only needed for economic growth and development, but also to liberate the possibilities for ennobling creativity. World order advocates understand that to make the international community more than just a figure of speech, a commonly agreed-to, legitimized rule of law must be established as a prerequisite.

Few benefit from violence and brutality. In the case of the war in Bosnia, ordinary people in all three groups underwent ethnic cleansing. In the summer of 1995, when Croatian and Bosniak forces invaded formerly Serbian held parts of Bosnia, it was estimated that about 150,000 Serbs were forced out of their homes. This augments the 200,000 or so people killed after the breakup of Yugoslavia, and the over a million made homeless in Bosnia alone. These figures take on even greater significance in light of the fact that before the war, Bosnia had a population of about 4.3 million. In some wars, the winners are hard to find.

World order analysts find plenty of blame to go around in explaining the causes of the war in Bosnia. They would point out that there was little to make hyperbolic nationalists think their actions would be opposed. This not only encouraged them but also strengthened their internal position while undermining the moderates. Yet the fact that intervention by the international community via the United

Nations and the European Union came late and was lame misses the point. Since IGOs can only do what their leading member states will support, they cannot be considered independent actors. The world's great powers remain the problem. Clearly, international organizations need more authority if they are expected to take timely and effective action. The extreme suffering caused by the war in Bosnia lends credibility to those advocating implementation of the UN Charter's Article 47. This article authorizes establishing a Military Staff Committee. If the Security Council took this action, and provided the committee with a permanent peacekeeping force, the potential would exist for early reactions to human rights violations.

If the Bosnian calamity will have any positive lasting legacy, it will be through the precedent of the War Crimes Tribunal. The international community will at least in a moral sense redress the carnage if it successfully prosecutes those indicted for crimes against humanity. If, however, the indicated go unpunished, the international rule of law will receive a very real setback, one that in the short term may prove irreparable. The international covenant on genocide has been ratified by enough countries to go into force. It provides the Tribunal's unassailable legal basis. If even clearly stated, commonly accepted and enforceable legal standards are not upheld by a prosecutor's office and court set up by the Security Council, then those wanting to flout universal norms of conduct will take heart. In Bosnia, if justice via the law proves ephemeral, those wronged may well think that war is their only option. All groups in Bosnia have reasons for revenge. Thus, without justice providing at least a ray of hope for reconciliation, those advocating retribution will be strengthened.

A View from the Ethnic Autonomy Perspective

Milosevic's actions imposing Serbian domination on other ethnicities in Yugoslavia provide the key to understanding how the war in Bosnia happened. Respect for other cultural groups is essential in today's technologically linked yet culturally diverse world. As ethnic conflicts develop, communication must be open and power must be shared. Sometimes this means designing new and autonomous political structures.

Hatred is not inevitable or natural. It must be taught and nourished. Tolerance and mutual respect can become accepted norms. Recognizing the contributions cultures make to the larger society enhances everyone's life. When the clash of interests and perceptions proves too deeply rooted to be solved by existing political processes, various creative relationships can be invented. The war in Bosnia offers a stark illustration of what can happen when ethnic autonomy is not calmly and respectfully negotiated. Mutual destruction and long-term bitterness will preclude working together for years at least.

Developed gradually over time, peaceful interaction and even trust can become ways of life. Substantial evidence for this process can be found in Bosnia before the war. According to an anthropological study carried out in the late 1980s, Croats and Muslims lived side by side in peace and some had established friendships. Proud of their multiethnic society, the 1982 Olympic Games had provided a forum for many Bosnians to celebrate their various cultural heritages with the whole world looking on. A small but noteworthy number of Bosnia's population, 5.5 percent, had identified themselves as Yugoslav before the war (Bringa 1995:26) and, by the late 1980s, about 30 percent of Bosnia's marriages in cities and towns were between people of different ethnicities (Malcolm 1996:222).

Those with an ethnic autonomy perspective point out that the international state system provided the context, rationale, and means for Bosnia's ethnic groups to fight a genocidal war. Leaders appealed to negative nationalism by inflaming resentments and fears. Serbia's Milosevic initiated the process by using his control of the major media to broadcast misleadingly selective information, and even downright falsehoods, about how Croats, Muslims, Slovenes, and others were treating Serbs. The more nationalistic among these groups responded in kind and voices pleading tolerance and compromise were drowned out. Each group came to believe that being ruled by people of a different ethnicity was dangerous and that only its own sovereignty made sense. Serbia's army aided Serbs' paramilitary units responsible for ethnic cleansing. Other states provided military aid to Croatia and Bosnia, whose forces engaged in their own violent population removal plans. The concept of the state and its sovereignty lies at the core of the mess.

This chapter's three perspectives differ over the causes of the war in Bosnia and recommend alternative actions to forestall other conflicts from turning violent. State sovereignty advocates blame excessive ethnic nationalism, and the resulting breakup of the Yugoslav state, for the war. This process unleashed strident nationalists and legitimized massive deaths and destruction. State sovereignty analyses see strengthening states as the long-term remedy for such wars. Many states have proven their ability to provide institutions through which ethnicities can constructively work out their differences. Political stability is a necessary condition for peaceful interaction.

The world order and ethnic autonomy perspectives both recognize the need for stability but think that states are the problem, not the answer. In the case of the war in Bosnia, the lure of statehood, with its centralized governmental power, heightened real and imagined fears and allowed demagogues to seize control. Proponents of world order and ethnic autonomy propose major institutional changes in how the world's peoples are presently organized, yet differ significantly over which institutions should be enhanced in order to diminish the power of states. The world order perspective points out the need for strengthening the organizations in the international community and their ability to impose universal standards of behavior on states. In contrast, ethnic autonomy analysts believe that people are demanding more decision-making power over their daily lives. They want local, decentralized institutions in order to have an effect on the global trends that impact them. Because cultures provide people with their primary identities, ethnicities should be the basis for new forms of political representation.

TERMS AND CONCEPTS

collective security	functional interdependence
deterrence	security dilemma
European Union (EU)	world order

DISCUSSION QUESTIONS

1. Which perspective discussed in this chapter do you think best explains the reasons for the war in Bosnia? Which perspective best explains the reasons for the peace in Bosnia?

2. What do the world order and ethnic autonomy perspectives have in common? The state sovereignty and ethnic autonomy perspectives? What do all three have in common?

3. Choose a security issue facing the world community today, such as the proliferation of weapons of mass destruction, or a violent conflict in the Sudan, Kashmir, East Timor, or some other location. How would each of the three perspectives explain its cause? What would each suggest be done about the problem?

4. In your opinion, what are the common assumptions about why wars occur? What do the people you know think about it? Which perspective or perspectives do they reflect the most?

5. What role should the United States play in the international system to achieve peace? Which perspective (or perspectives) does your view reflect?

RESEARCH PROJECTS

1. Read or listen to the analyses of several political leaders regarding an issue of war and peace. What perspectives do their comments reflect?

2. Write a short list of questions about the causes of war from the point of view of each perspective. Pose the questions to five or more people and record their answers. What perspectives do their responses seem to reflect?

3. Research the position of a country on a current violent conflict in the world. What perspective does its position reflect?

4. Read a general overview about the history of relations between the United States and Central America, including Mexico, in the twentieth century. What perspective seems to apply?

5. Read about the development of the European Union since its beginning as the European Common Market in the 1950s. What factors account for its success? How do the three perspectives apply?

INTERNET RESOURCES

Amnesty International: *http://www.amnesty.org/index.html* The homepage of this foremost international human rights NGO includes information about its history and current activities, as well as links to other human rights organizations' sites.

Out There News: *http://www.megastories.com/bosnia/index.htm* Complete with pictures and maps, this site also offers an interactive policy choices section as well as brief histories of the three major ethnic groups.

University of Western Australia: *http://www.law.ecel.uwa.edu.au/inlaw* One of the most useful linkage sites available, it offers a wide variety of sources of the texts of treaties and conventions.

10

A Postcript

This book has challenged you to look at the world using your own perspectives as well as understanding those of others. It has offered a context and categories for thinking about issues rather than asserting that there is one right way to interpret world events. The goal has been to weave concepts and perspectives from several disciplines and contrasting value systems into an explanatory tapestry. You will have found some perspectives and data more satisfying than others, more compatible with your own prior knowledge and assumptions. This book has not attempted to change your perspective, but to challenge you to understand why you have particular reactions. Effective education requires that thinkers can clarify their own perspectives as well as those of others. They not only know that they agree and disagree with specific people and policies, but they know why they do so.

This book presents a holistic approach to learning about, and acting on, the world's problems. Cultural, economic, ecological, and political events and trends interrelate, thereby affecting human behavior. Information about all four is necessary for adequately assessing the reasons for the deep and durable issues facing the world today. No topic is uniquely ecological or political without also having economic and cultural aspects. The academic distinctions are just that. It is foolish, and perhaps, dangerous in the modern world to present simple answers to complex questions.

Applying perspectives implies that values are inherent in understanding international issues. Each evaluation of why problems exist and what should be done about them presumes events have an underlying meaning. Making judgments assumes some human behavior is more moral, virtuous, or effective than other behavioral choices. If people were unaware that their points of view on issues were surface manifestations of deeply held values, they may be surprised that discussions with those committed to another perspective could become heated. People's perspectives emerge from the mixing and matching of religious, philosophical, political, and socially acquired ideas of their culture, with the idiosyncrasies of their own lives. Even within the same culture, differences in perspectives can be quite wide because gender, class, education, religion, and other factors lead to different life experiences.

Knowing what stated or unstated perspectives are being applied to a given issue provides an insight vitally important for understanding a situation. A one-dimensional, simplistic analysis of the human condition in the modern world brings a false sense of clarity. One's own values can be taken as universally prevalent and profound and others are then rejected as wrong. Sorting out and thoughtfully reflecting on various perspectives can be difficult, but doing so results in a more realistic assessment of what actions may work. Dealing with problems in the modern world invariably involves working with others who may have different perspectives. Some things can be compromised, and some not, but it is vital to know which is which.

You may have discerned a pattern as the various perspectives were explained. It may have seemed that some from different chapters overlapped, were mutually reinforcing, and even coalesced into a single world view, sometimes called a *paradigm*. The world view most commonly held by world leaders in the late 1990s is a synthesis of state primacy, liberal economics, high technology, and state sovereignty. An alternative paradigm could combine global unity, dependency, shared technology, and world order. These assume the world functions as a whole, whereas the first set of perspectives focus on the state. A third world view sees human interests, commitments, and ability to affect problems as localized. A synthesis recognizes parallels among cultural pluralism, participatory development, appropriate technology, and ethnic autonomy.

You may have discovered your own positive and negative reactions to various perspectives do not neatly fit these three patterns. Mixing and matching perspectives can also provide a coherent view of the world. Pundits in the United States have argued that the American voting public tends to be socially progressive and economically conservative. If a country's population can thrive with such apparently conflicted ideas, certainly individuals can synthesize varying perspectives. Cultural pluralism is not incompatible with liberal economics, for example, and state sovereignty can fit well with dependency. By selecting perspectives as they analyze world events and trends, people can construct their own world views.

Intermingling perspectives relevant to the same general global issue can also provide useful explanations. In fact, such inventive thinking might be the key to fresh solutions. Achieving a synthesis of seemingly conflicting ideas may lead to the resolution or management of specific world problems. People who disagree, but know why, can work through a common response. Unfortunately, often a problem has to become ominous or result in a horrible loss of life before people with differing perspectives feel the need to search for a solution together. Before then, emotional responses may make solutions more difficult.

The interrelatedness of issues and perspectives finds a parallel in the connection between the daily lives of individuals and worldwide trends. Consumer decisions, for example, or behavior toward people of different ethnicities, have larger effects whether or not individuals are aware of them. Actions do not happen in individualistic isolation. Trends are the cumulative effects of many specific events, just as the reverse is also true—that particular happenings result from ongoing trends. Cause and effect become blurred. Ignorance of interconnections fosters a fictitious, artificial illusion. Ignoring reality does not change it.

Making sense of complex international issues becomes more difficult in an age of transition. A case can be made that at least since the 1960s, rapid change has been a constant. Major realignments of power and technological advances occur over decades instead of centuries. The pace has picked up in the rise and decline of dominant states, in observed changes in the natural environment, and in technological innovations and their application. An age of transition calls for a wide variety of differing perspectives to use in responding to events.

The challenge to readers is clear: You will be the citizens and leaders of the increasingly global world. As members of democracies, you must wisely use both your knowledge and perspectives to form your country's domestic and international policies. A well-considered voting public is the hope of democratic systems. Educated people form the leadership ranks of business, the professions, and government. As leaders, their opinions and actions influence others and create policy. The challenge is to approach the issues of the world knowing not only what you believe, but why you believe it.

Glossary

acculturation: the modification of a culture by the adapting of traits from another culture.

acid rain: sulfur dioxide in smoke chemically reacts with the water in the atmosphere to create sulfuric acid (H_2SO_4), which is maintained in the clouds and falls to earth in rain.

agriculturalism: a subsistence strategy based on the exploitation of domesticated plants. The social organization of most simple agricultural societies is the tribe.

alternative perspectives: sets of interpretive ideas that determine how individuals analyze issues.

apartheid: a recently ended practice in South Africa in which the numerical majority in the state—the original inhabitants—were legally defined as inferior and had all aspects of their lives severely circumscribed.

assimilation: the adaptation of a new culture that replaces the customs and beliefs of a previous one.

autonomy: the ability to establish and enforce laws covering most governmental functions except foreign policy and defense.

balance of payments: an annual summary of all a state's international economic transactions.

balance of power: an interaction system of states, or groups, who choose not to use force because they consider the potential cost as too high.

basic needs strategy: an approach designed to enable a preponderant percentage of the population to have life's essentials; that is, adequate shelter, food, clothes, and medical care.

bilateral international interactions: two states that deal with each other on a one-to-one basis.

bipolarity: an international system with two dominant states.

Brundtland Commission: the UN-established World Commission on Environment and Development that investigated the state of the world's environment and proposed solutions in its 1987 document, "Our Common Future."

capital: the finances and facilities needed to produce wealth. There are three types of capital: (1) infrastructure, or physical capital, which includes factories, roads, farms, railroads, communication systems and machinery; (2) financial capital, including monetary investments such as bank deposits and interest, earnings from trade, and currency; and (3) human capital, including an educated, healthy, skilled population and able leadership, which are needed for self-sustaining economic development.

carbon dioxide: CO_2, is a colorless, odorless, gas that is a natural part of the atmosphere, used by plants as a necessary part of their respiration.

carrying capacity: the number of people who can be supported indefinitely in a given environment with a given technology and culture.

cash crops/primary commodities: products grown or mined and sold in their unprocessed condition, such as tea leaves, cotton balls, coffee beans, and bauxite ore.

class: a category of social hierarchy that groups people based on culturally defined differences in wealth, power, or general abilities.

clines: the frequencies of particular genetic traits, such as blood type, in different parts of the world.

collective security: a strategy used by IGO members in which they act together militarily in response to an aggressor state.

the Commons: those areas of the world that are publicly owned and open for general use, such as oceans and public parks.

comparative advantage: the production of a good or service at a lower cost than the competition's.

conventional war: when states battle each other using their formally organized military forces.

cultural relativity: the concept that the actions of people within each culture should be evaluated according to the rules of that culture.

culture (human and specific): patterns of behavior and belief learned by individuals as members of society. Human culture is the basic adaptation device all people share. Specific cultures are those systems of belief and behavioral rules that members of a particular society share.

culture areas: analytic categories of geographic regions based on the similarity of ethnic groups within them.

deforestation: the rapid destruction of forests, especially tropical forests, which leads to atmospheric and soil degradation.

demographic transition: a process by which a society with a high birthrate and high death rate becomes more characteristic of economically developed societies by transitioning to low birth- and low death rates.

dependency: the unequal relationship between the industrialized and developing worlds resulting from their economic interactions.

desertification: an increase in areas of extremely arid land.

deterrence: a situation in which states present a credible military threat to their potential enemy.

developing countries/world: states that have primarily agricultural-based economies and low wealth production, as reflected in macroeconomic data.

development: an economic process that enables an increasing number of people to produce enough wealth to support an acceptable quality of life.

diplomacy: direct negotiations between two or more governments or international governmental organizations.

dual economy: a characteristic of many developing countries, in which the majority of the population lives in poverty along side a small, dominant elite that lives the consumer lifestyle more typical of industrial societies.

economic growth strategy: an approach designed to produce enough earnings to invest in machines, to purchase the fossil fuels to run them, to educate people to fix them, and to ensure the constant flow of new technology to update them; also called, *industrialism.*

economic sanctions: actions designed to encourage states to change their policies by cutting off trade and financial flows.

economies of scale: the economic principle that a product's per-unit cost will decrease when a company manufactures more of it because plant, personnel, and other overhead costs will remain about the same.

ecosystems: the complex interconnections of plants, animals, and physical and chemical factors that make up natural environments.

ethnic group: a category of people who share a set of cultural traits. The term is often used to refer to minority groups in large, heterogeneous nations.

ethnocentrism: the judging of another culture according to the standards of one's own culture. See also *tolerance.*

ethnocide: the total destruction of a culture.

European Union (EU): formerly called the European Community, the EU is the regional international governmental organization furthest along in developing of a functional plan of integration for its member states; the plan will include an integrated banking system and a common European currency called the *euro,* for example.

external changes: new ideas, skills, inventions, or other influences that enter a society as a result of its interactions with another society.

foreign aid: the financial capital provided by state governments and international governmental organizations to other states, usually in the form of a loan to a developing country.

foreign exchange: earnings from exports.

foreign exchange rate: the worth of a state's currency in relation to that of another state's currency.

free trade: a government policy aimed at eliminating all restrictions on imports and exports.

functional interdependence: the theory that the economic integration of states will deter or eliminate war.

gathering and hunting: a subsistence strategy that emphasizes the gathering of undomesticated plants and the hunting of undomesticated animals. The social organization associated with this strategy is egalitarian bands.

gender: a cultural definition of the different capabilities and roles of men, women, and sometimes other perceived sexual categories.

General Assembly: an institution of the United Nations that serves as a forum for debating and voting on resolutions dealing with world issues; each member state has one vote.

generalized reciprocity: a form of economic exchange wherein people living in bands share with one another without the expectation of equal or immediate return.

genocide: an attempt to exterminate a specific cultural group, which was designated as a crime against humanity in the 1948 international treaty.

global warming: a small, but regular and significant, increase in the temperature of the Earth.

great powers: states whose policies can directly affect events outside of their world region.

greenhouse gases: atmospheric gases, including CO_2, methane, ozone, and chlorofluorocarbons (CFCs) that decrease the energy lost into space and increase the warmth of the Earth's atmosphere.

green revolution: a development approach that focused on the transfer of high-technology farming techniques, including new seeds and chemical fertilizers, to developing countries of the world.

gross national product (GNP): the total monetary value of all goods and services produced by an economy in a given year, including international transactions. (See also *per capita gross national product (GNP)*.

guerrilla war: the use of hit-and-run tactics by organized groups who oppose a political system and who often blend into the local population as their main defense.

hard/convertible currencies: those state currencies used in international markets because corporations and other governments accept them.

holism: the idea that all traits of a culture influence all others and, consequently, any change in one cultural trait will affect the whole culture.

human rights: the just and fair treatment by governments of their own citizens.

ideologies: a set of interrelated ideas that people use to give meaning to events.

import substitution: an economic development strategy designed to produce domestically at least some of the products imported from the industrial world.

indigenous peoples (First Nations)*:* the original people of an area who have lost political control over their ancestral lands and do not fully recognize the moral authority of the state government to dominate them.

industrialism: a subsistence strategy that changes the productive focus of the state system to the manufacturing sector. See also *economic growth strategy*.

interests: the relationships and resources that persons, groups, organizations, and states can use to their benefit and to enhance their power.

internal changes: new cultural elements introduced or invented by people within a society that is undergoing change.

international anarchy: the absence of a common political rule in the international system. It is the primary characteristic of the current international system, according to international relations theory.

international governmental organization (IGO): an international organization with states as members, such as the *United Nations* and *European Union*. See also *nongovernmental organization. (NGO)*.

International Monetary Fund (IMF): an international governmental organization that provides loans to member states to stabilize their currency.

international rule of law: the commonly accepted rules of behavior and orderly processes that states follow for peacefully working out conflicting interests.

international system: the organizations and processes that people and states use to interact across state borders.

invention: a new idea or technique, that is constructed from the mass of collected knowledge and adopted as valuable by members of the society.

involuntary changes: a form of external change wherein members of a weak society are forced to adapt some traits of a more powerful society.

just war: military action that is taken in self-defense and that abides by accepted rules of warfare, such as preventing the slaughter of civilians and prisoners of war.

labor-intensive technologies: the use of simple tools powered by wind, water, sunshine, and muscles, in contrast with capital-intensive technologies that rely on complex machinery powered by fossil fuels.

Law of the Sea: the UN-sponsored treaty of 1984, which established general rules for conduct in the oceans.

legitimacy: the acceptance by citizens and other states that a government is justified and its laws should be obeyed.

malnutrition: a medical condition caused by insufficient caloric intake and a poor diet.

most-favored nation status: an agreement between two states to lower their tariffs with each other to match the lowest that each charges any trading partner on a specific product category.

multilateral international interactions: states' negotiations and actions within the framework of international governmental organizations.

multinational corporations (MNCs): private businesses with subsidiaries or operations in two or more countries. See also *private investment.*

multipolarity: an international system with several states as centers of power.

national identity: the primary affiliation of a group of people who see themselves unified as forming a unique culture.

nationalism: an individual's feeling of identity with an ethnic group based on several shared characteristics, such as language, history, and religion.

negotiation: communications among state officials, performed directly through face to face discussion or indirectly through a designated intermediary.

neoimperialism/neocolonialism: often used as a synonym for *dependency,* the unequal relationship between industrial states (the colonizers), and developing states (their ex-colonies).

new epidemics: contagious diseases, including AIDS, that have spread widely in recent years.

New International Economic Order (NIEO): the series of UN resolutions made in the 1970s that was favorable to the developing world but never went into effect.

nongovernmental organization (NGO): an international organization with individuals or private groups as members, such as the World Council of Churches and the Red Cross. See also *international governmental organization (IGO).*

nuclear war: the use of weapons produced by the splitting apart, or fission, of uranium or plutonium atoms (atomic weapons) or by the fusion of atoms made possible by the heat generated in a fission explosion (hydrogen or thermonuclear weapons).

pastoralism: a subsistence strategy based on the use of domesticated animals. The social organization of most pastoralists is the tribe.

paternalism: literally "acting as a father," or more broadly, taking a superior position over others and trying to control their actions.

patriotism: the placing of one's primary identity and loyalty in the state.

peace: when conflicts are handled without the use of violence.

per capita gross national product (GNP): a statistic derived by dividing a state's GNP by its total population. See also *gross national product (GNP).*

perceptions: those attitudes and points of view resulting from one's particular cultural, historical, philosophical, ideological, or religious preconceptions. See also *perceptual selectivity.*

perceptual selectivity: the process of ignoring or misinterpreting information because of one's preconceptions. See also *perceptions.*

politics: a decision-making process characterized by negotiation and bargaining.

power: a quality possessed by a person, group, organization, or state that is used in relationships with others to influence their actions.

primitive states: a social system based on a centralized political organization. The economic system is elaborated to include complex economic specialization and market exchange built on an agricultural base.

private investment: the financial and physical capital provided by *multinational corporations (MNCs)* in the states in which they operate.

productivity: an economic calculation that measures the output of goods and services in relation to the number of work hours used to produce them.

propaganda: emotional appeals that attempt to affect the opinions of others in some specific way and that often use the mass communications media as a means to doing so.

protectionism: a government policy using tariffs and other regulations to restrict imports and thus keep out foreign competition.

race (biological): a subspecies designation of animals. The only surviving human race is *Homo sapiens sapiens.*

race (social): a culturally defined classification of people into categories that are based on perceived physical differences.

racism: the judging of groups or individuals based on culturally defined understandings of biological differences.

regional powers: states whose policies can directly affect neighboring states.

revisionist states: those seeking more power, usually by adopting a policy that will increase their military forces. See also *status quo states.*

Security Council: an institution of the United Nations that the UN Charter has given the important role of responding to issues of peace and war.

security dilemma: a policy problem faced by a state that wants to build up its military strength. If the increase in military forces is perceived as a threat by other states, and they in turn increase their forces, the result can be the same or less security than existed previously.

sex: physical categories among animals based on differences in reproductive biology.

sexism: the judging of groups or individuals based on culturally defined understandings of the differences among men, women, and any other perceived gender category. See also *gender.*

show of force: occurs when a state deploys its military forces as an implied threat.

small powers: states whose policies affect their own people but have very little impact on other states.

social cohesion: when people in a society share a common identity, value system, and commitment to an established political system and thus have achieved stable economic and political decision-making processes.

sovereignty: the key characteristic of states in the international system, meaning they accept no authority as superseding their own.

state: a complex political structure that may include citizens from a variety of nations. Considered the most powerful institution in the international system, states have four characteristics; territory, a central government, a loyal population, and the recognition by other states.

status: a social position defined by a particular culture. In some cases status is ascribed, or determined by birth, whereas in others it is achieved, or earned by an individual's actions or accomplishments.

status quo states: those satisfied with their existing level of power. See also *revisionist states*

subjugation: the control of people in a weaker culture by those from a stronger culture.

subsistence: in economics terms, an agricultural-based lifestyle wherein people produce enough to live on and very little more.

superpowers: states whose policies directly affect events in most areas of the world simultaneously.

sustainability: the idea that development projects should be designed for long-term success.

syncretism: the mixing of cultural ideas from different sources to create a new reality.

tacit negotiations (signaling): sending a message to another government without telling it directly or using an intermediary.

technical assistance: specialists from outside a country brought in usually to work on a specific development project for a short period of time.

terrorism: a military tactic using violent incidents perpetrated by small numbers of people for the purpose of calling into question or destabilizing an existing political system.

tolerance: the acceptance of cultural differences without ethnocentric judgment. See also *ethnocentrism.*

United Nations: an international governmental organization whose members include almost all of the world's states.

United Nations Environment Program (UNEP): a UN agency that monitors the world's environment.

Universal Declaration of Human Rights: adopted by the UN General Assembly in 1948, the document designates individual freedoms for all humans, including the right to economic well-being, and religious and political freedoms.

voluntary changes: a form of external change wherein members of a society choose to adapt innovations from another area of the world. See also *external changes.*

war: politically motivated violent acts ranging from clashes of armies to specific incidents of terrorism.

World Bank: an international governmental organization that provides loans to member states for specific development projects.

World Court: a tribunal with jurisdiction only in cases involving states.

World Health Organization (WHO): an international governmental organization that is mandated to promote health throughout the world.

world order: a means for achieving peace through the development of international laws and institutions.

World Trade Organization (WTO): the successor to the General Agreement on Tariffs and Trade (GATT), this international governmental organization works to foster free trade.

References Cited

Alder, Jonathan, Peter Cazamias, and David Monnack. 1995. "Benchmarks: The Ecological and Economic Trends That Are Shaping the Natural Environment and Human." In *The True State of the Planet*, ed. Ronald Bailey. pp. 393–453. New York: Free Press.

Allen, John L. 1994. *Student Atlas of World Politics*. Guilford, CT: The Dushkin Publishing Group.

Amstutz, Mark R. 1995. *International Conflict and Cooperation*. Madison: Brown and Benchmark.

Anderson, Ian, and Rachel Nowak. 1997. "Australia's Giant Lab," *New Scientist,* 153, (February 22): 34-37.

Baer, Werner, 1995. *The Brazilian Economy: Growth and Development*. 4th Ed. Westport, CT: Praeger.

Balaam, David, and Michael Veseth. 1996. *Introduction to International Political Economy*. Englewood Cliffs, NJ: Prentice Hall.

Balikci, Asen. 1984. "Netsilik. " In *Handbook of North American Indians*. Vol. 5: *Arctic,* ed. David Damas, pp. 415-430. Washington, DC : Smithsonian Institution.

Bodley, John H. 1996. *Anthropology and Contemporary Human Problems*. 3rd ed. Mountain View, CA: Mayfield.

Bringa, Tone. 1995. *Being Muslim the Bosnian Way: Identity and Community in a Central Bosnian Village*. Princeton, NJ: Princeton University Press.

Brown, Lester. 1981. *Building a Sustainable Society*. New York: W. W. Norton.

Brown, Wilson, and Jan Hogedorn. 1994. *International Economics: Theory and Context*. Reading, MA: Addison-Wesley.

Buckley, Richard. 1992. *Amazonia: An Ecological Crisis: Understanding Global Issues,* The Running, Cheltenham, England: European Schoolbooks Publishing Limited.

Carroll, Raymond. 1996. "Water: A Dangerous Endangered Resource?" In *Great Decisions,* ed. pp. 42-51. New York: Foreign Policy Association.

Commission for the Creation of the Yanomami Park. 1989. "The Threatened Yanomami." *Cultural Survival Quarterly,* 13: 45-46.

Cushman, John H., Jr. 1996. "Report Says Global Warming Poses Threat to Public Health." *New York Times,* July 8: A2.

Denslow, Julie Sloan. 1988. "The Tropical Rain-Forest Setting." In *People of the Tropical Rain Forest,* ed. Julie S. Denslow and Christine Padoch, pp. 25-36. Berkeley: University of California Press.

Dickason, Olive P. 1992. *Canada's First Nations.* Norman: University of Oklahoma Press.

Dostert, Pierre Etienne. 1996. *Latin America, 1996.* Harpers Ferry, WV: Stryker-Post Publications.

Drozdiak, William. 1997. "German Court Convicts Bosnian Serb of War Crimes." *Washington Post,* September 27, 1997: A14.

Dumas, David. 1984. "Central Eskimo: Introduction." In *Handbook of North American Indians.* Vol. 5: *Arctic,* ed. David Damas, pp. 391-396. Washington, DC: Smithsonian Institution.

Earle, Sylvia A. 1995. *Sea Change.* New York: Fawcett Columbine.

Facts on File. 1993. "Global Environment: News in Brief." *Facts on File World News Digest,* 153 July 22: 539.

Franke, Richard W. 1974. "Miracle Seeds and Shattered Dreams in Java." *Natural History,* LXXXIII (Jan.): 10-12f.

Franke, Richard, and Barbara Chasm. 1994. *Kerala: Radical Reform as Development in an Indian State.* Oakland, CA: Institute for Food and Development Policy.

Goodwin, Paul, Jr., ed. 1996. "Chile: Country Report." In *Latin America,* ed., pp. 71–74. Guilford, CT: Dushkin/Brown and Benchmark.

Graburn, N. H., and M. Lee. 1990. "The Arctic Culture Area." In *Native North Americans: An Ethnohistorical Approach,* ed. D. Boxberger, pp. 23–64. Dubuque, IA: Kendall/Hunt.

Grmek, Mirko D. 1990. *History of AIDS.* Princeton, NJ: Princeton University Press.

Hardin, Garrett. 1968. "The Tragedy of the Commons." *Science,* 162 (Dec. 13): 1243–48.

Harrison, Paul. 1984. *Inside the Third World.* New York: Penguin.

Hileman, Bette. 1995. "Climate Observations Substantiate Global Warming Models." *Chemical and Engineering News* (Nov. 27): 18–23.

Historical Tables, Budget of the United States Government, Fiscal Year 1997, http:///www.access.gpo.gov/index.hlml

Karlen, Arno. 1995. *Man and Microbes.* New York: Simon & Schuster.

Klein, Laura, and Lillian A. Ackerman. 1995. *Native American Women and Power.* Norman: University of Oklahoma Press.

Malcolm, Noel. 1996. *Bosnia: A Short History.* New York: New York University Press.

Mattera, Philip, 1992. *World Class Business: A Guide to the 100 Most Powerful Global Corporations.* New York: Henry Holt & Company, Inc.

McElroy, Ann. 1976. "The Negotiation of Sex-Role Identity in Eastern Arctic Culture Change." *Western Canadian Journal of Anthropology,* 6: 184–200.

McElroy, Ann, and Patricia K. Townsend. 1996. *Medical Anthropology in Ecological Perspective.* Boulder, CO: Westview Press.

Moran, Emilio F. 1988. "Following the Amazonian Highways." In *People of the Tropical Rain Forest*, ed. Julie S. Denslow and Christine Padoch, pp. 155–162. Berkeley: University of California Press.

Nanda, Serena. 1990. *Neither Man nor Woman: The Hijras of India*. Belmont, CA: Wadsworth.

Nunavut Implementation Commission. 1995. *Footprints in New Snow,* Report 1, Mar. 31.

Odum, Eugene P. 1993. *Ecology and Out Endangered Life-Support Systems*, 2nd ed. Sunderland, MA: Sinauer Associates.

Paisano, Edna. 1997. *The American Indian, Eskimo, and Aleut Population*. Washington, DC: US Census Bureau. http://www.census.gov/population/www/pop-profile/amerind.html

Pelly, David F. 1993. "Dawn of Nunavut." *Canadian Geographic*, 113: 20-31.

Pelto, Pertti J. 1973. *The Snowmobile Revolution: Technology and Social Change in the Arctic*. Menlo Park, CA: Cummings.

Prance, Ghillean T. 1990. "Rainforested Regions of Latin America." In *Lessons of the Rainforest*, ed. Suzanne Head and Robert Heinzman, pp. 53–65. San Francisco: Sierra Club Books.

Purich, Donald. 1992. *The Inuit and Their Land: The Story of Nunavut*. Toronto: J. Lorimer.

Reiss, Bob. 1992. *The Road to Extreme*. New York: Summit Books.

Rourke, John. 1993. *International Politics on the World Stage*. Guildford, CT: Dushkin.

Schmink, Marianne. 1988. "Big Business in the Amazon." In *People of the Tropical Rain Forest,* ed. Julie S. Denslow and Christine Padoch, pp. 163-171. Berkeley: University of California Press.

Schumacher, E. F. 1973. *Small Is Beautiful: Economics As If People Mattered*. New York: Harper & Row.

Sciolina, Elaine. 1995a. "Enemies in Bosnia Devise Structure for a Government." *New York Times*, Sept. 27: 1, 8.

———. 1995b. "Bosnia Talks Snag on Fate of Two Serbs." *New York Times*, Nov. 17: 3.

Sponsel, Leslie. 1994. "The Yanomami Holocaust Continues." In *Who Pays the Price?,* ed. Barbara Rose Johnston, pp. 37-46. Washington, DC: Island Press.

Stern, Paul C., Oran R. Young, and Daniel Druckman, eds. 1992. *Global Environmental Change*. Washington, DC: National Academy Press.

Stone, Roger D. 1985. *Dreams of Amazonia*. New York: Viking.

Sudetic, Chuck. 1993. "In Mostar's Muslim Area, 35,000 Endure in Rubble." *New York Times*, Sept. 30: A7.

Tannenbaum, Edward. 1965. *European Civilizations Since the Middle Ages*. New York: John Wiley.

Thatcher, Margaret. 1994. "Stop the Serbs. Now. For Good." *New York Times,* May 4: 23.

Tylor, Edward. 1871. *Primitive Cultures*. London: John Murray.

United Nations. 1994. *International Trade and Statistics Yearbook*. New York: United Nations.

———. 1995a. *World Statistics Pocketbook*. New York: United Nations.

———. 1995b. *The World's Women, 1995: Trends and Statistics*. New York: United Nations.

————. 1996. *Human Development Report, 1994, 1996*. New York: Oxford University Press.

Vallee, Frank G., Derek G. Smith, and Joseph D. Cooper. 1984. "Contemporary Canadian Inuit." In *Handbook of North American Indians*. Vol. 5: *Arctic,* ed. David Damas, pp. 662-75. Washington, DC: Smithsonian Institution.

Vandenbeld, John. 1988. *Nature of Australia: A Portrait of the Island Continent.* New York: Facts on File.

Wade, Betsy. 1997. "Warding off Malaria." *New York Times*, Apr. 20: sec. 4, pp. 4–5, 28.

Wenzel, George. 1995. "Ningiqtuq: Resource Sharing and Generalized Reciprocity in Clyde River, Nunavut." *Arctic Anthropology,* 32(2): 43.

Williams, Walter. 1986. *The Spirit and the Flesh*. Boston: Beacon Press.

Woodward, Susan. 1995. *Balkan Tragedy: Chaos and Dissolution After the Cold War*. Washington, DC: Brookings Institution.

World Bank. 1979, 1994, 1995, 1997. *World Development Report.* New York: Oxford University Press.

Index